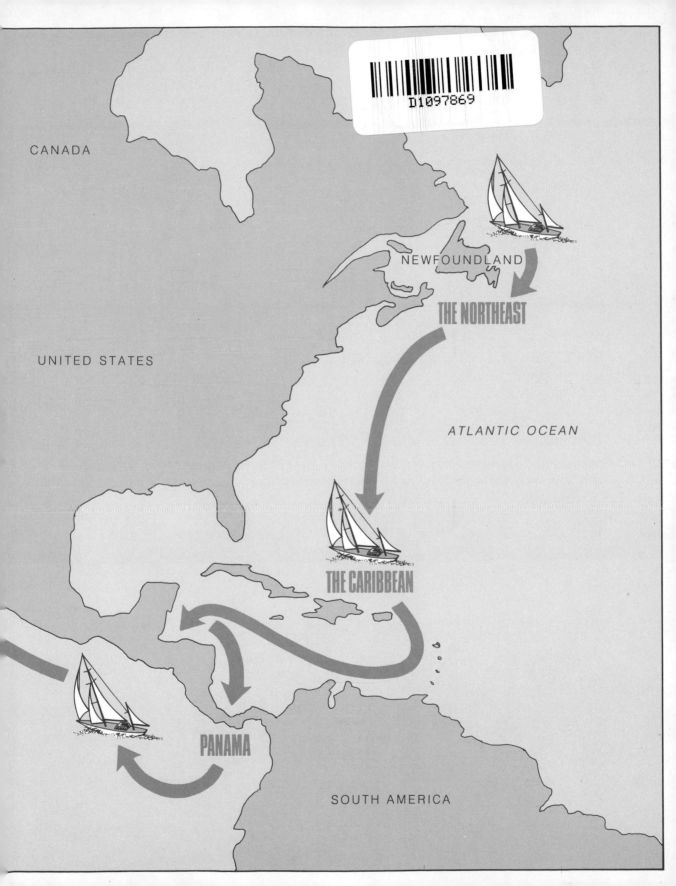

CANADA

NEWFOUNDLAND

THE NORTHEAST

UNITED STATES

ATLANTIC OCEAN

THE CARIBBEAN

PANAMA

SOUTH AMERICA

D1097869

WINDIGO
NEWFOUNDLAND TO ALASKA

WINDIGO
NEWFOUNDLAND TO ALASKA
SANDY WELD

HEARST MARINE BOOKS

New York

 HEARST BOOKS

Library of Congress Cataloging in Publication Data

Weld, Sandy.
  Windigo, Newfoundland to Alaska.

  1. Windigo (ship)   2. Sailing—North America.
I. Title.
GV822.W48W44 1982   797.1'4   82-11988
ISBN 0-87851-219-5

Hearst Marine Books
224 West 57 Street, New York, N.Y. 10019

Book design by Janet Czarnetzki with Mary Ann Joulwan

THIS BOOK IS DEDICATED
TO THOSE WHO SAILED ON
WINDIGO,
THUS MAKING THE ADVENTURE POSSIBLE

Contents

Windigo's Background

In the spring of 1956 Hal Haskell of Wilmington, Delaware, christened his beautiful blue yawl *Venturer*. She was a new Sparkman & Stephens-designed Henry Hinckley–built 73-foot ocean-racer built to campaign against all the top 1930s boats.

Venturer's competitors were famous—*Bolero, Baruna, Cotton Blossom, Escapade,* and *Windigo* among them—and they had been winning for ten and twenty years. *Venturer* herself soon became known along the East Coast. She sailed spectacularly. In her first year she broke the old Bermuda Race record established by *Highland Light* in 1932 and was beaten in that race only by *Bolero*. Henry Hinckley would later call her "the best wooden boat ever built."

In 1960 *Venturer* was first to finish that year's Bermuda Race, a feat she repeated two years later under new ownership and now named *Northern Light*. Her name was changed again in 1963, to *Audacious*, and new owner Baldwin M. Baldwin moved her west to California just in time for the 1963 Transpac. She finished second, behind only *Ticonderoga*. The boat was now painted white and became the darling of southern California, competing in races to Mexico and in the Big Boat Series in San Francisco Bay, as well as in major local events. She finished fourth in both the 1965 and 1967 Transpac Races, winning Class A on corrected time in 1967.

In 1968 she headed east again, to Oyster Bay, New York. She was now called *Windigo* by her new owner Walter Gubelmann. The earlier *Windigo*, a 71-foot Sparkman and Stephens yawl, had been campaigned vigorously and successfully by Mr. Gubelmann for twenty years. The new *Windigo* sailed in the Bermuda Race in 1968, 1970, and 1972 and in local events out of Oyster Bay, and acquitted herself well. Her main boom was shortened in the 1960s when racing came under the IOR rating rule, which favored smaller mainsails far more than did the CCA rule.

I bought *Windigo* in November 1973, and, liking the name, kept it. In her nine years with me she has proven herself the most stalwart and beautiful of cruising vessels.

SANDY WELD
Weston, Massachusetts, 1982

"At dawn a young boy rowed his small skiff out to watch us leave. His dreams at that moment must have been similar to each of ours at one time or another, of sailing off on a beautiful ship to see the world. *Windigo* was well past him before he seemingly let go of those dreams, and raised his arm in a farewell wave."

Isle aux Morts Harbor,
Newfoundland
1974

PART ONE
THE NORTHEAST

CANADA

Gulf of St. Lawrence

NEWFOUNDLAND

St. George's Bay

Bird Rock

Grande Entrée

Magdalen Is.

Cabot Strait

Isle aux Morts Harbor

Port aux Basques

Cap aux Meules

Prince Edward I.

Pleasant Bay

Cape Breton I.

Bras d'Or Lakes

Quebec

St. John's

NOVA SCOTIA

MAINE USA

Halifax

Sable I.

Trinity Bay

Conception Bay

Avalon Peninsula

St. Mary's Bay

Merasheen I.

Placentia Bay

ATLANTIC OCEAN

Boston

1 *Underway*

As a boy, one of my dreams was to join world sailor Irving Johnson for one of the cruises on board his lovely brigantine *Yankee*. But I was still in school when he made his last voyage on her in the late 1950s. My desire to see some of the world by boat persisted. Ocean racing finally gave me the chance to do this, when I joined family friends abroad after finishing my time in the U.S. Army in Germany. The races were fine times, introducing me to England's south coast, the coasts of France, parts of Italy, Holland, Denmark, and Australia, and parts of our own northeast coast. This was, as I had hoped, a great way to see places and meet people.

The racing was always on other people's boats; I never had one of my own until I bought *Windigo* in 1973. I still remember how she looked when I first saw her, stored in a huge shed in Oyster Bay, New York. Standing on the dirt floor beneath her overhanging stern I had to crane my head all the way back to get a view of her lines. Her deep full-length keel was painted red and looked as smooth as when she was first built. I climbed an extension ladder to reach her deck, and had to duck under the building's ceiling supports to walk along it. I had a good feeling about her instinctively.

In my nine years with her, *Windigo* has shown her self ideally suited for long-distance cruising, with excellent and beautiful performance under sail. I meant to take three years to cruise both coasts of North and Central America. But three years became six, and still there was more to see and not nearly enough time for it all.

This book deals with the people and places we did visit between 1974 and 1979, from Nova Scotia and Newfoundland in the Northeast, to the Caribbean through the Panama Canal to the Pacific and up along Mexico's west coast, and finally north to Alaska. I have touched upon both the high and the low points of the venture.

I have not dwelled upon mechanical breakdowns, but a voyage like ours is a dramatic experience for someone who relies on his sails to get him places, with the engine purely an auxiliary. I sailed *Windigo* up to many a dock, when the engine wouldn't start, and generally the local mechanic could be at hand for repairs. But at sea or along a remote coast we were on our own. I had my share of mechanical troubles—like replacing the fresh water pump while drifting off a

During the nine years author Sandy Weld has owned the yawl Windigo *he has pursued his dream of long-distance cruising.*

barren Mexican shore in the middle of the night, and pulling the head off the engine to dry the piston cavities and injectors after salt water backtracked through the exhaust system while we were running before a storm. The engine is also more than mere propulsion—it charges *Windigo's* batteries, which in turn are the source of power for all her lights and for her refrigerator compressor and freezer, vital parts all.

I found it immensely satisfying to cope successfully with problems like those, with all the unexpected things that happen aboard a boat. I loved the challenge of getting boat and crew safely to the next anchorage, of constantly flirting with the unrelenting forces of wind and water, of knowing unequivocally that we are all no more than specks on the world's surface. I came to treasure the sense of discovery in entering a harbor for the first time, and the satisfaction of figuring at sundown what sails would work best for the all-night so they would not need to be changed until daylight. In making these discoveries, these decisions, often with nothing more than a look at the sky to help me, I'd get tense weighing the probabilities, and snap at someone's unknowing question or comment. I surely learned much about quick thinking and steadfastness during middle-of-the-night dangers, about delight in new things or commonplace things, about people, about myself.

I enjoy finding new anchorages and meeting the people there, but the areas I seek out seem to be in conflict with this. I should in theory stay in southern California or Long Island Sound where people and boats abound. But no, it is the quiet anchorages along nearly deserted coasts, with only wild birds and animals ashore and the occasional fishing boat for company, that offer the strongest attraction to me. It is Canada's east and west coasts, southeast Alaska, Mexico's west coast, Panama, and certain parts of the Caribbean that I have found especially enjoyable, each in its own way. This book is about these places, and the first of them all was Nova Scotia, far north of *Windigo's* new home waters around Cape Cod, Massachusetts.

I'm still not sure which really came first, the voyage I had dreamed of for so long or the boat that took me on it. But, one November afternoon in 1973 I found myself the proud and nervous owner of the graceful seventy-three-foot wooden yawl *Windigo*.

She was the first sailboat I'd owned, and at seventy-three feet the largest I'd ever been on, much less been responsible for. Had I taken on more than I could handle? I had done plenty of racing in Cape Cod and other East Coast waters, and plenty more abroad. But could I cope not only with sailing *Windigo*, but with the logistics of such a long cruise? My vague plans for a voyage now had to be put into reality.

I remember all the preparations. *Windigo* spent the winter right where she was when I bought her, in Jakobson's shipyard in Oyster Bay, on Long Island Sound, while I was busy getting ready. I certainly wasn't going to sail her alone, but I also didn't want the same crew for the whole trip. So I decided to sign on two permanent crew members who would know the ropes, and different groups to join *Windigo* for short stretches. For the groups I looked for people of different ages, from high school students on up, to keep changing the tempo and atmosphere on board. With one or two ads in *Yachting* Magazine and lots of conversations with friends, I found the crew for the first summer. They were mostly from the U.S. Northeast, with two from Ohio as it turned out. Some had agreed to meet us in Cape Cod for the trip north, and the rest to join us at specified harbors later.

Windigo was launched the day before I arrived at Jakobson's, in late April. The next day, a Saturday, a special yard crew came in to step the masts. I was eager to watch them lift the huge mainmast, with all its rigging attached, then swing it out and over to lower it inch by inch through the hole in the deck, to sit squarely on the mast step below in the main cabin. I wasn't a bit concerned, for the yard had hauled and stepped this spar plenty of times in the past.

I slept on board and was up and waiting when the yard crew arrived at 7:30 A.M. I couldn't believe it, however, when the crew boss asked me to start *Windigo's* engine and bring her around to the dock beside the crane. I hadn't the slightest idea how to start the engine. Neither did any of them. We pulled her around with lines instead. All went smoothly, and by noon the masts were in place and secured and the yard crew off for the weekend.

Steve, a high school senior from Boston, joined me for this period of commissioning. Our work for the weekend had just begun. We were busy sorting out equipment and deciding where to stow it. Most of it was restowed three or four times during the next week as we found better ways. I also learned how to start the engine, along with many of the other electrical and mechanical systems on board.

Everything had to be stowed by the next weekend, for a crew of local sailors was coming aboard for a sail, my first on *Windigo*. Some of the crew had raced on her before and were a tremendous help in showing me how the lines were led and in general how things had been done. As we backed out of the dock I tried to maintain a composed exterior, knowing full well I'd lost control over my insides, which were doing the jitterbug out of step with my pounding heart. How would she sail? How would she handle? The next hour would tell a lot about what I was in for during the next several years.

Off Oyster Bay's Seawanhaka Corinthian Yacht Club the mainsail went up. The wind out on Long Island Sound was a steady twenty-five to thirty knots, from the northwest. I decided to set the number three genoa, to take a look at the sail I anticipated we would use a lot in the future. *Windigo* was a cruising boat now, usually sailed without the large crew to handle the large racing headsails. Once clear of the harbor the number three was hoisted, and as it went up my reaction was of disappointment. The sail was awfully small, but when it was sheeted in and filled as we fell off to a close reach, I was glad it was no larger. *Windigo* heeled and gained speed, the sails drawing well, the sheets bar tight. The forces were incredible.

I'm told a smile spread across my face from ear to ear and a twinkle of delight danced in my eyes, as I stood behind the wheel that first day. Our speed steadied at nine-and-a-half knots. Water churned into white foam, curling from under the lee bow, while spray occasionally came up over the windward rail. In gusts the lee rail dipped under, sending water rushing along the deck. *Windigo* was steady as a rock, heeled well over, driving through the seas caused by the strong wind. What an unbelievable feeling of power.

Smaller boats close by us were taking green water over their windward rails and in general having a hard time in these conditions. *Windigo's* stern wave rolled smoothly off the quarter, leaving little disturbance in our wake. She reacted just like the forty-foot racing boats I was used to—admittedly in a far grander manner, which would take me time to adjust to, but she sailed as a sailboat should.

I relaxed and thoroughly enjoyed that first sail. It was a rare day for spring on Long Island Sound—sky bright blue with an occasional puffy white cloud hurrying by high overhead, the air crystal clear, sunlight sparkling over the deep blue-green water bespeckled with whitecaps. Everyone was caught up in the moment, with no thought for the biting cold wind.

Then came a time of decision. One incentive used to line up the day's crew had been the promise of sailing to City Island to see the launching of the potential America's Cup Defender, the new twelve-meter *Courageous*. Nearing the boats gathered waiting off the yard, we rounded up into the wind and dropped the genoa. I noticed a hesitancy in the crew about taking the sail down. It turned out I wasn't the only one who would rather keep on sailing than see a twelve-meter being launched. Without delay we turned back down the Sound and reset the genoa. What a day. What a boat. *Windigo* was obviously at ease in the kind of waters I wanted to explore, as long as I didn't do something foolish to jeopardize our safety. It was now up to me.

"But exactly how high are the power cables?" I kept asking the lock supervisor. We had just tied alongside the lock in the St. Peters Canal, the southern entrance to Nova Scotia's Bras d'Or Lakes, after a beautiful late-afternoon spinnaker sail down the province's northeast coast. It was two months since that beautiful first sail off Oyster Bay. We had sailed up from the Cape in seven days with a crew of ten—*Windigo* can sleep ten comfortably—and several crew changes were to take place in Newfoundland and Nova Scotia harbors. We were underway at last.

My chart showed a hundred feet of authorized clearance under two sets of power cables that across the channel I hoped to use, to get into the Lakes. But how accurate was this? Part of my concern was that I didn't really know to the inch how high *Windigo's* mast was. I knew it was about ninety feet, but with our antenna extending above the mast, and just a little sag in the power cables over the years, the difference could have narrowed to an electrifying closeness.

The lock supervisor wasn't sure himself and called the power company. No one there could help because it was Saturday evening. The supervisor then called the home of the man in charge of building the towers and stringing the cables, who confirmed the clearance shown on the chart.

During the wait for the lock I decided I should know exactly how high *Windigo's* mast really is. A line was pulled up to the masthead on the spinnaker halyard, then pulled tight and marked where it entered the water: eighty-seven feet. This was all reassuring news. Hidden almost completely by towering spruce trees on each side of the Canal was the first set of cables. We passed easily underneath them and approached the swing bridge at the inner end of the Canal, where cars were stopped. The passengers waved and wished us luck as we passed.

We were now in the Bras d'Or Lakes. The southern portion of the Lakes is low, wooded river country, with numerous islands and water arms, some deep and others blocked by shallows and sand bars. A well-marked channel winds through it toward the open Lakes about five miles away.

The second set of cables appeared suddenly as we rounded a bend in the channel. The cables' sag between the two supporting towers is lowest right over mid-channel, so we stayed safely over to one side. It's not easy to judge heights like these from on deck, but as we approached, our situation certainly did not look good.

The wind was off the starboard quarter, pushing us gently toward the cables. *Windigo's* reverse, as with most sailboats, is not very effective. So I took the precaution of dropping an anchor over the stern, paying out anchor line as we approached the cables. I could now stop our forward momentum very positively by securing the anchor line. I also sent two crew members ashore to climb the bank under the cables, where the best view of the relative heights would be. Even with them waving us on I wasn't at all sure we would clear the cables until we were finally beneath them.

We did clear them. It was still impossible to guess the margin but it must have been at least thirty-five feet. The stern anchor was not needed, but it was certainly a comfort to have.

Proceeding, we enjoyed the deep evening colors as the sun sank behind the hills, and anchored behind the narrow sand spit in Cape George Harbor, in the Bras D'or Lakes. We had the little harbor all to ourselves, along with thousands of mosquitos that fortunately disappeared with darkness.

What a day. What a week. I recalled our seven-day sail from Cape Cod to the Lakes. We were just getting to know *Windigo*.

As I tried to get the anchor up alone in Cape George Harbor the next morning, I woke up Rick, a friend taking time off after college who had agreed to be my right-hand man on board for the year. He had been sleeping on the foredeck, for no reason other than the beautiful night, and was quickly alert. With his help the anchor came up, the sails were set, and we headed out before a light southerly. Below, the rest of the crew woke up more slowly.

After breakfast the spinnaker went up and we drifted along under a cloudless sky. The midmorning sun warmed us to the point of thinking of a swim. And why not; the promotional literature I had read spoke of warm summer swimming in the Lakes. *Windigo's* speed was less than a knot and the dinghy was towing astern, so I could easily climb into it and get back on board. Over I went. The water was far from mid-summer temperature. I got out in a great hurry! Half of *Windigo's* crew braved the water too and, after the first shock, enjoyed it.

2 *George's First Sail*

Many place names aptly describe what they name, like Muddy Hole, Wreck Cove, Three Rock Cove, Otter Bay, Bay of Islands, and Seal Bay, all of them in Newfoundland and all true to the promise of their names. Thus I assumed that southwest Newfoundland's Port au Port Bay would be a harbor with good anchorage and the town of Port au Port large enough to have at least limited supplies for us. I was thus surprised as we ghosted along the Bay's eastern shore late one afternoon, for we saw no signs of a town or even of docks or fishing boats.

Our only chart of these waters was a small-scale one, which showed little detail. About all it indicated was that Port au Port Bay had plenty of water and no obstructions or shallows within it. We could see a few homes dotting the hillside beside us, but even in the corner of the Bay where the chart showed the town to be, we saw no cluster of buildings, and no trace of the town at all. In the two coves just west of where the town should have been there were no boats, not even a dory pulled up on the beach.

I was becoming concerned. It was getting late and we needed an anchorage soon. We circled the two coves and I chose the larger of the two, just wide enough to swing in, but not deep enough for us to get very far inside. Fortunately the weather was settled, with a light wind blowing off the beach. We'd be fine as long as the weather held.

At anchor I checked the Newfoundland Cruising Guide again. I should have realized there was no development here, for its information on Port au Port was scanty. About all the "town" ever was, I gathered later, was a garage and a general store.

The Guide itself, incidentally, had already proved helpful along Newfoundland's south coast. I had been interested to discover that the guides to Nova Scotia and Newfoundland had begun thirty years ago, when editor/sailor Charles Bartlett lamented the lack of a guide, and was asked by the Cruising Club of America's Boston Station to take on the task. He did so, with co-sponsorship by the Royal Nova Scotia Yacht Squadron and the C.C.A.

Today, after Charles Bartlett's careful guidance over the years, the Nova Scotia Guide has well over a hundred location descriptions and about as many contributors. And, the Newfoundland Guide has even more locations described by fifty contributors. Copies are hard to find, but I managed to track one down through friends. Without these books I certainly wouldn't have tried taking *Windigo* into certain anchorages that turned out to be terrific, nor would I even have known about many more.

In the morning I rowed ashore in search of the town of Port au Port, wanting ice and a few provisions. I pulled the dinghy up on the rocky beach and scrambled up the embankment to the road. Three men stood beside a pickup truck, watching me and looking out at *Windigo*. They were all about my age, friendly, and dressed like us in shirts and jeans. I asked them about ice. They discussed this for several minutes, finally deciding the only likely place was the fish plant. But it would be closed today.

George, the owner of the truck, offered me a ride up the hill to the town of Port au Port, which consisted of one garage, owned by George, and a small general store, owned by his parents. At the garage George made several telephone calls on my behalf. Into his truck we piled, driving through the bigger town of Stephenville and onto the old U.S. Air base, whose buildings have been taken over by industry. I have no idea what kind of plant we went to, but someone was there and they had ice. I worked in the storeroom on the second floor, shoveling broken ice down a chute to a chopping machine. George and the man from the plant filled plastic bags with chopped ice. I wasn't allowed to pay for it, or for George's time or even the gas used.

Instead I invited George and his wife on board for lunch. George had been born in Port au Port and was someone I came to enjoy talking to very much. He had spent his life right here on the water in Newfoundland, but the boats he knew were the workboats, which are all power vessels by now, so he had never had the chance to do any sailing. The happy outcome of all this was that I asked George to join us for the eighty-mile sail to Port aux Basques next day. He looked at his wife and smiled. "Too bad you have to work tomorrow," he said, "but my garage is closed." All was agreed upon and off they went. George was due back that night at 10:00.

Shortly before 6:00 P.M. we heard someone calling to us from the beach. It was George. I was afraid he had changed his mind. One of the crew rowed in and brought him back. It seems he couldn't wait for 10:00 so had closed the station early and came straight along.

With George on board early and several hours of daylight still left, I decided to get underway immediately. We spent the night off an island at the entrance to Port au Port Bay, to shorten tomorrow's trip by nearly fifteen miles.

Groans came from all corners of the boat next morning as I rousted everyone out with the sun. It was cold and damp on deck, but promised to be a nice day with a moderate southwest wind. Underway, we were heeling but the water was smooth. It was a good time to get breakfast over with before the leg to Port aux Basques, when we would be hard on the wind.

Leaving me on deck to steer, the rest went below for pancakes, hot maple syrup, and coffee at *Windigo's* unique gimbaled table. Somebody's ingenuity had moved the pivot point from the table's center line to the hinges on which the table's sides swing up and down. The center of the table thus remains fixed, parallel to the deck as the boat heels, but lead weights low under the table's top keep the sides parallel to the horizon. It is on these two outer sections of the table that it is "safe" to place plates and glasses.

George sat at the end of the table so as to get a good look at this unique table in action. The two angles of the table top, with the cabin tipped on its side, didn't coincide with the balancing mechanism of George's inner ear. He quickly left his breakfast uneaten and joined me on deck. The stable horizon and fresh air were not enough. George spent most of the morning hanging over the rail. By the end of the day and after one more incident that happened later, he was fine.

Breakfast meanwhile had its other casualties. Someone placed the hot maple syrup pitcher on the middle section of the table, thinking that since it wasn't moving, or didn't appear to be moving as the sides of the table were, it was the safest place to put this hot, sticky liquid. Before the syrup could be rescued it slid down the sloping center and upended in front of a crew member's plate. She reacted instinctively to elude the hot syrup. Placing her hands on the edge of the gimbeled table she pushed down. Everything from hot syrup and coffee to pancakes and orange juice landed on those sitting to leeward, and on the settee cushions. Much of the stuff then seeped under the settee and all over the canned food stored there. Up on deck I heard the cry and the crash as everything went, and knew instinctively what must have happened. There was no point going below and reading the riot act. I heard Rick say "don't tell Sandy until we get this place cleaned up."

By late morning we had recovered from breakfast and were sailing hard on the wind with full mainsail and number three genoa. But the mainsail wasn't set well. The after third of the sail sagged off to leeward—not the way a racing boat's main should set. Moving the main sheet traveler didn't help. The sheet itself needed trimming. Rick and another crew member winched the sheet in a little. The sail looked better, but was still not right. In it came some more; still better. About one minute later a seam ripped from leach to two-thirds of the way along the boom—about twenty feet of stitching let go like a flash.

Down came the sail. We continued under genoa and mizzen until I got over my surprise. I'd never seen a sail rip. Now, after six years of cruising with *Windigo*, I have seen a mainsail go from leach to mast, genoa from leach to luff, and a spinnaker go from head to foot long both luffs. We were not in trouble this time, though, for the parted seam was below the reef points. We tied in a reef and reset the sail, and got on with our long sail to Port aux Basques.

It was now that George's memorable incident took place. He had gathered his remaining energy to leave the rail and get below, seeking warmth in his bunk. To his dismay he wasn't over the seasickness yet so now he sought out the head. Once there he decided not to leave. With a pillow under his head right beside the toilet bowl he lay down for some rest, his upper body on the head sole, the rest of him stuck out the door and across the passageway.

George semi-awoke quite soon, when cold water splashed on his face, and he wondered how anyone would be sadistic enough to do this to him in his present condition. But no one else was below. He dried his face with a towel and lay down again. Moments later another cupful of cold water hit him squarely in the face. This time he awoke fully. The culprit was the head itself, overflowing with icy sea water let in unwittingly by George himself, rocking back and forth as *Windigo* hit the biggest waves, pushing down the foot pedal to open the sea cock. The fellow gamely emptied the bowl and retired to his bunk till evening. I wondered how George could even think of more sailing after that, but he joined us for other sails with no trouble at all.

Windigo rounded the southwestern corner of Newfoundland well after dark. The night was clear and the navigation lights off Port aux Basques guided us in. We entered cautiously, trying to untangle the lights on the buoys and breakwaters from those of the busy ship terminal directly behind them. Virtually all freight and passenger traffic that doesn't fly into Newfoundland enters through Port aux Basques. It is the terminus for the narrow-gauge Canadian National Railroad that runs to St. John's, as well as for the newly completed cross-island highway. During the summer some ten passenger and rail ferries arrive and depart at all times of the day and night, in very limited space.

We got in at last, and seeing no place to anchor safe from the ferries coming and going, retreated to tie up at a fish pier that we had seen on the way in. It was shortly after 1:00 A.M. The harbor had a busy night, full of ferry whistles. We had a good sleep nevertheless.

3 *"Plenty of Water" Harbor*

Repairs began on the ripped mainsail the next morning. The two edges of the torn seam were tied on top of each other, with the original stitch holes carefully aligned so they could be reused. Small pencil marks every few inches along both edges of the seam helped us check that the holes stayed aligned as sewing progressed. Quite a task with the sail still on the boom.

A team of two started sewing from each end of the tear. They had sailor's palms and pliers for pushing and pulling the needle through the stiff old cloth. Progress was slow but the sail was ready for use again by mid-afternoon. How long our handiwork would last I had no way of knowing, but I hoped it would hold until we got home to equipment large enough to do a professional job. Our stitching, in fact, lasted for the rest of the sail's life. Twelve months later the whole sail fell apart from cloth deterioration, simply from old age.

From Port aux Basques my plan was to spend several days on Newfoundland's south coast, where we had already cruised several weeks earlier. I fondly remembered places like Isle aux Morts, where we anchored behind the big island northwest of town. The cove was just wide enough for *Windigo* to swing in, with clear cold water, and steep cliffs on the mainland, which we climbed. On top, the beautiful moor scenery spread out before us.

As we departed at dawn a young boy rowed his skiff out to watch us leave. His dreams at that moment must have been similar to each of ours at one time or another, of sailing off on a beautiful ship to see the world. *Windigo* was well past him before he seemingly let go of those dreams, and raised his arm in a farewell wave.

I also recalled Harbor Le Cou and its waterfall, where Rick found a large air pocket between the falls and the rock wall behind it. What a sensation to stand in churning, knee-deep water with your back pressed against the rock and water cascading past, only inches in front of your face.

We could revisit those places or find new ones. I reread the Cruising Guide and checked the charts trying to decide where to head. The final destination, as usual, depended upon the weather.

A thick fog covered Port aux Basques when we departed. It grew even thicker as we felt our way out, from buoy to buoy, toward open water. At the outer bell I realized we would have to motor along the coast, running very accurate courses and distances, for this twenty-knot wind was from ahead. It would be foolish to beat along the coast in fog this thick, since there are practically no navigational aids and *Windigo* has no radar.

The alternative was to abandon the south coast, and cross Cabot Strait today. The wind's direction and strength were ideal for crossing the one-hundred-mile-wide straits. Returning to Port au Port wasn't even considered. We all wanted to go sailing.

Within an hour of setting the sails we broke out of the fog. What a delightful day—sunny, even warm, and a good wind. Gradually the fog bank behind us disappeared, revealing the Newfoundland coast bathed in sun. By noon the wind had died, leaving us with another decision. Motor for perhaps twelve hours to cross the Strait or turn back. Our plans changed again.

Heading for Grand Bay, a large harbor on the western side of Port aux Basques, we enjoyed a light-wind sail. The chart shows the depth to vary in Grand Bay from ten to twenty-five feet. Its scale is too small to show any depths in the channel, just three rocks that are nearly in a line, that we would have to thread through in an S-fashion. Giving credence to the channel's feasability was the government's recommended anchorage symbol on the chart for Grand Bay. It looked interesting. The conditions were nearly perfect for "gunkholing": very light wind, tide nearly low, and no swells.

Nearing the harbor's entrance we dropped the sails and prepared to enter. Many townspeople were out enjoying the water also. Two small sailboats passed us, a canoe paddled along close to shore, and a dozen or more dories were out with men and boys fishing. Many more people lined the rocky shore to enjoy the afternoon. We chuckled among ourselves that today would surely be considered their "summer." I'd been told that summer comes to the south coast anytime between the end of June and mid-August, and it lasts for one day.

With the sails furled we proceeded, very slowly. I had no way of knowing exactly where the channel was. Before advancing far *Windigo* touched bottom and stopped. The engine, in reverse, was not enough to back us off even though we had grounded very gently.

While the crew readied the anchor I wondered which side to put it out on. Where was the deepest water?

Two men fishing in a skiff nearby were paying more attention to us than to their lines. I called to them, asking where the deep water was. Both men pointed to our starboard, then offered to take the anchor out.

With it set at right angles to *Windigo*, we took a strain on the anchor line. *Windigo's* bow swung around easily but she did not move forward. Winching in the anchor line only dragged the anchor toward us, instead of moving us toward the anchor. Again the anchor was reset, but again *Windigo* didn't budge.

Navigational markers were scarce along the coast of Newfoundland, and not always reliable. This was one of the few operating lighthouses on the south coast of Newfoundland.

Since the tide was nearly low there was no point in straining boat or equipment. We could easily relax and wait for the incoming tide to lift us off, in something over an hour.

During this wait I asked the two fishermen who had helped us if they would like to come on board. They accepted eagerly. Our conversation finally turned to the question foremost on my mind. "Is there enough water in the channel for *Windigo?*" Before I could mention her nine-and-a-half foot draft, Tom, the spokesman of the two, answered that there was "Plenty of water, sure, plenty of water." In the old days, it seemed, lumber schooners much bigger than this boat sailed in and out of Grand Bay "fully loaded and at all tides." Tom's friend Len nodded his agreement. "But," Tom quickly added, "you must be well over on the right hand side, close to this first island. Then when a particular rock is abeam you head directly for the outer corner of the government pier. You must not be more than forty feet from it while passing by, for a rocky shallow extends well across from the far shore." He continued the instructions, ending with "sure, there's plenty of water."

The directions sounded complicated enough and Tom knowledgeable enough about the channel that I asked him to take *Windigo* in. This startled him for a moment, then he said, "why not—there's plenty of water."

So, when we were finally freed from the bottom and ready to proceed, I turned the wheel over to Tom. I stood leaning against the mizzen mast, paying close attention to our course, for without Tom I'd have to get us out in the morning. Tom pointed to the identifying rock to starboard, then turned smartly toward the government pier when it came abeam.

The town's radio station had already mentioned that "a large American yacht was aground off Grand Bay." Little did they know what was yet to happen. The government wharf was crowded with the curious, anxious to get a closer look. Children and adults alike stood on it shoulder to shoulder, pushing forward for a better view.

On passing the inner end of the wharf I began to relax—we'd made it without incident. Tom, I guess, thought the same for his shoulders relaxed as he exhaled a sigh of held tension. At that moment *Windigo's* bow rose in that unmistakable way a boat reacts when its forefoot rises up on a rock. Tom knew the meaning also. His expression changed instantly from relaxed concentration to total disbelief. He was far more surprised at our grounding here than I.

My attention immediately turned to our predicament. *Windigo* was in no immediate danger. We hadn't hit hard and the tide was rising and would eventually lift us off. The current, however, would be increasing to two-and-a-half knots through this narrow channel, pushing *Windigo* farther up on the rock—perhaps over it, perhaps not. We would surely get off sooner if we could hold *Windigo* in position.

Two heavy lines secured our stern to the pier. Len used his skiff to place two anchors to help hold us. In this manner, with *Windigo* held securely against the increasing push of the current, we waited for the tide to lift us free.

Windigo's stern was so close to the pier that children reached out and touched the end of the mizzen boom. Conversation there was in low voices, wondering, I guess, what was going to happen next.

I wasn't sure myself. Should we continue on in or retreat? I decided to retreat and anchor off the harbor for an early start next day, if we could turn *Windigo* around in this narrow channel at maximum current. We put out more lines to the wharf and to other anchors, getting ready. Two unknowns remained—what was the water's depth above the rock, and would the anchors, lines, and pier pilings hold as *Windigo* swung broadside to the current. If any of these let go we could be in trouble.

When the moment came the lines holding *Windigo's* stern were slackened. She pivoted smoothly around her bow and, except for a moment's grounding again on the very rock we'd just come off of, the maneuver went precisely as planned. But I will always remember Grand Bay as "Plenty of Water" harbor.

4 *Bird Rock*

Our expedition to Bird Rock, the northernmost of Quebec's Magdalen Islands, began with a lovely afternoon sail down St. George's Bay, Nova Scotia. At sundown the tip of Prince Edward Island could just be seen out to the west, while the high mountain range along the Cape Breton Island coast stretched out for miles to the eastward. By sailing all night I hoped to reach the Magdalen Islands around sunrise.

On board was an expedition put together by Tim Pfiffer, a student of ornithologist John James Audubon's work. Tim's purpose was to follow Audubon's 1833 trip to Bird Rock on the seventy-five-foot schooner *Ripley*, to find the birds, as he did, and to photograph them.

I took over the watch at 3:00 A.M. Our course was still 355 degrees. The night was clear with stars twinkling high overhead. The luminous band of the Milky Way stretched across the sky to the north, and the crescent moon had long since set. A ten-knot breeze was blowing over the starboard quarter, pushing us along easily. It was a delightful night for sailing. I felt fortunate to be heading to this seldom-sailed-to group of islands.

A five-second flashing light with a range of fifteen miles was what we were heading for, on Ile d'Entrée, the highest and southeasternmost island of the group. The earlier watch had pointed to the only light they had seen, a steady light some 25 degrees west of our course. I didn't think much about it, but did keep track just in case it turned out to be a ship coming our way. Before long, I realized it was in fact the light we were looking for, despite its being listed on the chart as flashing rather than steady. A note on the chart also mentioned magnetic disturbances in these waters, and possibly that's why *Windigo* was off course. We jibed over and trimmed the sails to head for the light, which faded as dawn broke.

The wind also disappeared when the sun rose. High clouds replaced the stars, and a ground haze reduced visibility to less than five miles. We approached Ile d'Entrée slowly under power, maneuvering around tricky sand bars. The sleepy town was beginning to stir. Green-carpet fields sloped gently down to the water's edge from the cliffs of the island's far side, dotted with bright-colored houses and crisscrossed by stone walls and hedges. The church's steeple bell rang the hour of six. Cows wandered along what appeared to be the main street with a boy and his big white dog keeping them going. On the point of land now behind us was the lighthouse that had guided us here, freshly painted white with a bright red roof. An inviting place to stop—next time.

Our course lay now across Pleasant Bay to Cap aux Meules, where recently a big deep-water harbor has been built. Two huge breakwaters reached out from the shore, overlapping at their outer end to provide good protection. We entered, not knowing whether there was space for us to tie alongside or even anchor.

Luck was with us, or so it seemed. The whole north wall of the harbor was free, well away from the busy ferry dock and fish plants. We tied up and all went below for breakfast.

The conversation turned to plans for exploring Cap aux Meules today. Bird Rock was forty miles to the northeast, a good trip for tomorrow if the weather permitted.

The Magdalen Islands comprise eight islands, six of which are tenuously linked together by sand dunes and bridges. The islands have miles of white sandy beaches backed by red sandstone cliffs. Many of their fourteen thousand residents are fishermen, who freeze and ship out quantities of cod, mackerel,

Windigo's crew explored many small fishing villages like this one on the northeast coast of Cape Breton Island, Nova Scotia, and often she would be one of the few yachts to visit all year.

lobster, and scallops. They also smoke herring in huge long barns near the shore. We could see these sheds from *Windigo* with their twists of smoke rising lazily skyward.

For the summer tourism trade, the two-hundred-eighty-six-foot ferry *Lucy Maud Montgomery* makes the seventy-mile trip from Prince Edward Island to Cap aux Meules twice a day. Scheduled airplane flights come daily, bringing people to the small hotels to enjoy the sun and beaches. We went ashore to explore, and everyone we passed, whether in cars, on bicycles, horses, or on foot like ourselves, gave a wave and a cheerful greeting—always in French. The group that had gone birding on the island's northeast end came back exhausted and enthusiastic about their finds. One day's stop at Cap aux Meules was far too little, but our time was short. Tomorrow's weather forecast was for another settled day—an excellent chance to get close to Bird Rock.

Back aboard *Windigo* we realized why the north wall of the harbor had been free. The area next to its dock was undergoing construction and all the ground cover was gone, leaving just loose fine sand which the local breeze was blowing onto *Windigo*. Sand now covered the decks. It was ruining the varnish and filtering below, even through the closed hatches. We hastily investigated alternative harbors and headed for Havre de La Grande Entrée, a large landlocked bay at the north end of the chain of islands, and well along toward Bird Rock.

With Cap aux Meules barely astern the cleanup operation got underway. The fine sand was already being ground into the teak decks and tracked all over the boat. The salt water hose, a bucket, and a deck brush were put to work. Anchor line and docking lines were towed astern. We finished cleaning up the awful stuff by the end of the day.

It wasn't far now to the bell two miles off Grand Entrée. The chart shows sufficient water in the channel, and a lighthouse on the point at the cut, around which we would turn tightly, and two black spars to be left to port to keep us between a sand flat and the government pier. Our anchorage was to be about two hundred yards from the lighthouse.

We got as far as the first of the two black spar buoys, and could see the anchorage only a short distance away. It looked straightforward. But the second black spar simply wasn't in place. This didn't bother me; I could use the shore and other markers as reference points. People on the pier and on fishing boats turned to watch us. One man seemed to be waving *Windigo* over, to tie alongside I assumed. This didn't interest me after our sandy experience at Cap aux Meules.

On passing the first black spar we ran aground. Our speed had been very slow, but still we could not back off with full reverse. We quickly launched the dinghy to take the anchor out so we could pull ourselves off. But before it could be set, the man who had waved to us from the pier came out in his lobster boat, took our bow line, and easily pivoted *Windigo* around. He gave his engine full throttle, even though his bow was headed straight for the government wharf just yards away. Still *Windigo* didn't budge. Whereupon I added *Windigo's* full power to the effort, knowing the possible results if she broke free suddenly and headed for the wharf herself. After agonizing minutes of churning the water muddy around both boats, *Windigo* moved forward slowly. We were free.

When the lobsterman cast loose the tow line he suggested we tie up to the government pier, as it had enough water for us. He then asked why I was so far over, away from the pier. Pointing to the black spar he told me it is the mast on a sunken boat that is out of water at low tide. Apparently the real black spars hadn't been there for a long time, if ever.

It seemed as if the whole town was on the dock to look us over. I was surprised to learn that only twelve yachts, cruising boats, had visited the whole of the Magdalen Islands the year before; probably only a fraction of them reached Grande Entrée. This is an English-speaking community so our conversations with the locals were easier than at Cap aux Meules. We talked awhile, but it was well after 9:00 P.M. and getting dark. Everyone was starved and tired. We didn't stay topside for long.

My alarm, set for 6:00 A.M., seemed to go off as my head touched the pillow. The weather was holding, the lines were cast off, and we left without incident. We weren't the only ones with an early start. Two dozen lobster boats were already working off Old Harry Head hauling their pots.

Bird Rock was now about eighteen miles away. Our first view of it was of its top, emerging in various shades of grey from the haze; we weren't sure it actually was the island when it appeared. Nearing, we clearly understood what Audubon meant about his approach, when he "thought it was covered with snow," but as he approached "half the snow got up and flew off while the rest remained." Bird Rock is one of the few nesting areas for gannets, a large white bird with a six-foot wingspan. It is also the home of kittiwakes, murres, razorbilled auks, and the puffin.

Explorer Jacques Cartier named them Isles des Margaux in 1534, after the gannets, which with the other birds were "as thick ashore as in a meadow with grass." His men killed a thousand birds in a very short time for food, a process that continued pretty much unchecked until the presence of lighthouse keepers began to protect the birds.

In 1833 as Audubon approached Gannet Rock, as it was still called, the beautiful weather suddenly changed and they were hit by a fierce storm. They

Sighting Bird Rock, James Audubon said that at first he "thought [the island] was covered with snow, but half the snow got up and flew off while the rest remained."

launched the whaleboat and headed for shore. Audubon himself remained on board the *Ripley* and began his own distant observations. The whaleboat, unable to land, returned to *Ripley*. With all safe on board they headed for Labrador (the part we now call Quebec) under bare poles.

Our luck was better than Audubon's. We circled in close under the cliffs for a good look at the nesting birds, and moved around to the island's north side to anchor. There was still no wind and only a slight leftover swell which barely rocked *Windigo*. Ideal conditions for trying to get to shore.

The island's two lighthouse keepers came down to the decrepit wooden pier. They lowered a rope ladder to us in the dinghy. *Windigo* rode on a calm sea not far away, but waves two feet high were crashing in on the rocks and under the pier, a result of the shallow water and currents. The dinghy was tied bow and stern to keep it from being smashed to bits on the rocks.

The climb up the nearly vertical stairway to the top of a sheer rock wall, one-hundred-five feet above sea level, was breathtaking. Fortunately for those who got tired half way up, the entire face of the rock is filled with nesting birds. Everyone had excellent excuses for a rest, to photograph birds almost within arm's reach on both sides of the stairs.

Bird Rock lies along the heavily trafficked shipping lanes to Canada's St. Lawrence River. Its high, flat-topped configuration is an obvious location for a lighthouse. There is one atop the rock today, and two lighthouse keepers live there with their dog. They told us that they rotate assignments with two others, one month on, one month off. In summer their families join them on the Rock, but otherwise wives and children live on the Magdalen Islands. Both men recall the days of making the trip in a lobsterboat, along with all supplies, but today they fly back and forth by helicopter when the weather permits.

The lighthouse keepers provide an additional and unique function on this island. They mean protection for the birds, an important difference between Cartier's and Audubon's times and the present, and a far better circumstance for the birds than what is usual today.

Claudia and Roger, the expedition's ornithologist and official photographer, could have stayed indefinitely. They had seen all that Audubon had promised. The mass of moving life on Bird Rock was incredible, from adult birds fishing near the island, to adults sitting on nests, to speckled eggs just breaking open, to fluffy balls of feathers dazzled by their new world, to slightly more mature young, necks stretched out, mouths wide open for food.

I had remained on board *Windigo* while the others explored ashore, just in case someone was needed there quickly. It was anything but a secure anchorage. Odd jobs kept me busy; there are always things to do on a boat. There was also the weather forecast to listen to—a twenty-five- or thirty-knot northwest wind predicted for tonight, and a call to Boston to make on the SSB (single-sideband) radiotelephone. I stood in the dog house, talking on the radiotelephone, looking out the companionway at the hundreds of birds flying and diving around *Windigo* and Bird Rock. The birds soared in circles one hundred fifty to two hundred feet up, then all of a sudden tucked their wings back alongside their bodies and plummeted into the water, making no splash, in perfect ten-point dives. More often than not each bird surfaced with a fish held sideways in its bill, and flew off toward Bird Rock, presumably to feed one of those hungry young.

I ended my intrigue with the birds and call to Boston quickly when I realized the dinghy had broken away from the pier and was crashing into the rocks.

Several long loud blasts on the fog horn brought people running. Ted, the crew member first down the steps, rescued the dinghy after he slid off the slippery rocks into the water. The water was now so rough near the pier that only two people could be safely carried in the dinghy. Ted brought Claudia out first, then another *Windigo* crew member named Scott took the dinghy back in.

Someone suggested he approach the pier from the other side—it seemed smoother. Perhaps it was, perhaps not—regardless, the dinghy and Scott turned over. The dinghy was caught upside down under the pier with the oars floating off in different directions. Scott surfaced greatly surprised, as it all happened so fast, and instantly apprehensive in this cold, wild situation. Realizing he was alright and that shore was within easy reach, he grabbed both oars and scrambled out on the rocks.

Ted and I pulled the inflatable Avon dinghy from its locker and quickly

Gannets nesting on Bird Rock.

Windigo's crew had to climb a nearly vertical stairway 105 feet up the rock wall. The entire rock face was filled with nesting birds, which they observed at arm's length.

pumped it up, and I paddled for shore. By the time I got there the dinghy had been hauled out from under the pier and up on top of it. Its fiberglass skin was bashed in in four or five places, but fortunately, it being a Boston Whaler Squall, it is foam-filled and could still float even with these holes.

The tricky problem was now to relaunch the Squall from eight feet above the very choppy water without swamping it or tipping it over again, then to get crew and cameras into it and away. It still seemed strange that the water by the pier was so rough, yet only twenty yards off the end of the pier the sea was flat.

Back on board, with everyone in dry clothes and the dinghies secured on deck, *Windigo* got underway. I didn't follow Audubon's example of "a double allowance of grog" as they got *Ripley* underway from Bird Rock. (That could come later!) He had headed north under bare poles. We now headed south under sail.

5 *The Avalon Peninsula*

For six long hours we punched into short steep seas and thirty-five-knot headwinds. *Windigo's* small jib and mizzen were straining hard along with the engine. Finally, the wave-lashed rocky shore of Newfoundland's Cape St. Mary's was safely to leeward. We bore off and eased the sheets, and shut the engine down. We took a moment now to look at the Cape St. Mary's cliffs, two and a half miles away.

Binoculars and telephoto lenses showed us a huge rock devoid of all vegetation. Even at this distance it stood out from the surrounding sheer, grass-covered slopes. The cliffs were distinctly white, from their rock top right down to the sea. The cliffs are a sea bird sanctuary, one of six gannet nesting areas in North America where hundreds of thousands of these large snow-white birds nest every summer. Murre and kittywake colonies crowd into the cliffs too.

Windigo was now heading across Placentia Bay off the Avalon Peninsula, the easternmost part of Newfoundland. The wind was still strong enough to send us along at nine or ten knots, with the tops of eight-foot waves slapping over the rail often enough to keep us in full foul weather gear. It was some sail. We were headed for an area of unlimited anchoring possibilities—the whole ninety mile western shore and head of Placentia Bay, much of it studded with islands and indented with watery arms.

We changed course to round Merasheen Bank, the beginnings of Merasheen Island. The water's depth shrinks from six hundred feet to nine feet in less than a mile to form the bank. It is ten or fifteen miles from the nearest land, but no buoys or lighthouses mark the bank—nothing. Without the full complement of Loran stations to cover this coast, readings here consistently placed us five to ten miles out of position and made the Loran unreliable for coastal navigation. Instead, I used a combination of navigational aids: the log for our distance travelled, the compass for the course steered, and the depth sounder to follow our progress across the bottom's contours as shown on the chart.

Our anchorage that first night was in Presque Harbor, just off the town of St. Kyran's and just west of Merasheen Island. We noticed two bald eagles soaring gracefully back and forth along the hill tops. The chart shows St. Kyran's to have a church, school, government wharf, and many houses. From far down the harbor we had seen the church, an impressive structure at the base of a hill, surrounded by open fields. Much closer now we could see that the church was in ruins. There wasn't a sign of human life ashore. An occasional weathered post leaned wearily out from the bank, the only indication that a pier had once stood there. We could only speculate where the long government wharf might have been. The town's buildings have all gone, either relocated or the wood reused elsewhere. Long grass or brush now grows in their foundation. An old root cellar built into the hillside is all that is left. We wondered why people had left this lovely place.

During the few minutes between going to bed and falling asleep my mind dwelt on this potential cruising haven. When discussing my trip to Newfoundland I had been surprised how many people had said they had been to Placentia Bay. Their time here was all during World War II when Argentia, on the Bay's east shore, was a major American naval and air station. But I found no one who had cruised here. Why did those who cruise the southwest coast of Newfoundland stay away?

In the morning, shoreside expeditions from *Windigo* took off in several directions. Hiking was easy along old cart roads but the going was extremely difficult through the woods or across boggy fields. One expedition climbed to the west for a swim in a lake on their way to Clattice Southwest, another abandoned

An abandoned but still graceful church dominated the empty village in a harbor in Newfoundland.

village. A second skirted the shore to pick wildflowers and gather shells and rocks. I wandered back to the big church, with its prominent view down Presque Harbor, and then wandered along an old road running across an isthmus. In the distance I could see several small islands backed by a mountain range. There was no sign of civilization to mar the completely natural surroundings. The stillness was incredible, and I wished I'd brought my camera to preserve the scene before me. The water looked refreshing. It was! The sun was warm enough to dry off in quickly.

We left Presque Harbor at low tide just after noon and found no wind outside and only a slight swell left over from yesterday's winds, so I decided to continue exploring and poke into tiny Toslow Cove. Through folksongs the cove had become the symbol of all small outports around Newfoundland, and its tricky approach became symbolic of coastal navigation. The two off-lying rocks shown on the chart were identified by slight swells eddying around them, still submerged at this tide. These rocks guard the entrance like hidden sentries, which is perhaps why the fishermen of New France chose this little harbor over all the others for its safety. On closing with the entrance we saw another rock that is not shown on the chart. I also began to wonder if *Windigo* could even turn around in the tiny harbor. I sadly gave up the idea of Toslow Cove for now.

We headed instead along an unnamed waterway between Merasheen's west shore and a string of islands tucked along it, exploring slowly with an eye for a tantalizing anchorage. Our interest was caught by Best's Harbor, a narrow arm of water that nearly splits King Island in two. We followed a straight two-hundred-foot-high cliff in, eased past a seven-foot shoal near the entrance, and circled tightly before anchoring in the middle of the harbor. *Windigo* settled back on her anchor and swung close to the rock wall to the north. Scraggy evergreens clung to crevasses nearly overhead.

In contrast, the shore to the south rose gradually from the rocky beach to broad open fields before reaching the woods. Several small buildings stood in the fields. In the doorway of one, three women stood watching us. Two piers extended from the shore, one of them piled with lobster traps. On the other stood a shack with a fish-cleaning table in front of it. In the fields, wildflowers added their bright yellow, white, and violet colors.

As we climbed onto the pier two curious cats came to meet us, as did the three women. The older woman, who looked to be in her fifties, told us she had grown up here, and moved away to the mainland along with everyone else during a resettlement program nearly twenty years before. She now lives in a "big" town on the coast, working in a fish processing plant. A few years ago her family built this hut on the site of her old family home. She was here now on vacation with her two daughters, and would stay as long as the weather held.

The second of our greeters on the pier told us more. She had been the school teacher here for eight years when about a hundred families lived in three or four connecting outports. The federal and provincial governments' resettlement program was instituted in 1965 at the request of the townspeople, to help entire communities relocate if at least ninety percent of that community approved of the move. The requirement became eighty percent a year later. At the time, more than half of Newfoundland's thirteen hundred coastal settlements had fewer than forty families, or about two hundred people, living in isolation on small islands or remote coves. Well over a hundred communities left in the program's first four years. This exodus was not even new: more than a hundred fifty other communities had been evacuated during the twenty years before that.

Standing on the shore of Best's Harbor I couldn't understand why a whole community would want to leave this beautiful place. What a fantastic spot. A return to nature. An ideal place to leave behind the hectic urbanization of North America. But listening to the school teacher describe the tedious, remote existence these people led here year round, their inability to leave its isolation at will as we can, I began to understand at last. The program's financial aid was in fact a golden carrot, equalling nearly three year's earnings for an average inshore fishing family. The human needs and desires were even more compelling. Rising aspirations for themselves and their children in education, medical, and municipal services led the inhabitants to realize that governments could not provide their small, inaccessible communities with services they now considered necessary. The program has allowed families the chance of a better way of life, the school teacher told us, which she believes they have, in general, benefited from.

Following a path through the fields along the Best's Harbor shore we passed signs of the old and some signs of renewal. The new wooden floor and partial frame of a small shack stood on a tiny point. Behind it, protected from the wind by some bushes, was an old dory pulled just above high tide. Beside it was a newer dory with an outboard secured to its stern. Children's voices were heard ahead. Rounding a bend in the path we saw young children playing beside a small, neat house. Their mother was busy hanging clothes on the line nearby, protected from the ruthless north winds by a stand of spruce.

The children's father we found cleaning fish on a rebuilt pier. He was reluctant to talk to us at first, but we gathered that he was bitter at what the government had done. Before the resettlement he had a general store, and he pointed a weathered hand to signs of its old foundation just above the pier, implying that life had been good then. He had been swept away with everyone else, but hadn't been able to adjust to the new transportation job found for him by the government. He is a fisherman again, returning "home" here to work from early April to October. But now the government is interfering with the fishing by

Lobster traps, stacked on the pier, provided a livelihood for the few remaining families in Best Harbor.

limiting the lobster season and the number of traps he can set. Having apparently had enough of this depressing conversation, he climbed down to his outboard-driven dory and went fishing.

Before too long the black flies chased us back on *Windigo*, where Phips, the doctor on board and an avid fisherman, had volunteered to fillet some fresh cod for supper. They'd been purchased from a fishing boat near Toslow Cove that morning. Phips set up operations on the pier's fish-cleaning table. Stripped to his red flannel undershirt, sleeves rolled up, the galley's sharp knife held firmly in his hand, he wondered aloud how to proceed. *Windigo's* young mate Colm eagerly joined the operation on the other side of the table; he had worked one summer in a fish market. Not until he was well into his second fish did we learn Colm had only watched others and had never actually filleted a fish himself. The local cat was there also and made out very well; he dragged away a skeleton, the head and tail still attached to the meat-covered backbone, and disappeared into the long grass. *Windigo's* cook Anne steamed our fillets, such as they were, in wine, chopped onions, and canned tomatoes.

I had always paid for the fish that we received, but several times my money wasn't accepted. One such time was later in Bay Bulls, on the peninsula's east coast. I had gone on deck at 7:00 A.M. to see what kind of day it was when an open fishing boat passed, heading in toward town. One man held a fish in the air as his boat swung back and pulled alongside. They asked if we would like some cod. I answered a quick "sure," then asked how much they were. The fishermen said we could have all they had, for they were going to throw it overboard when they got in anyway. At my puzzled expression they explained they hadn't caught enough fish that morning to take to market, a hundred pounds being the minimum they could sell. It seemed unbelievable that these three men who had gone out to pull their nets at 3:00 A.M. would throw their catch away. Their families and friends had eaten enough cod for one season, though, and there was nothing else to do with these fish.

During our ten-minute conversation one of the fishermen deftly filleted eight

Sandy spoke to disheartened fishermen and lobstermen about the resettlement program, which has emptied the tiny fishing village of people.

Phips and Colm filleting some codfish.

good-sized cod for us, using the galley knife that Phips had complained was not sharp enough. As each of a dozen other boats passed the three men they glanced up, checking to see how low in the water the boat was, and thus how successful their morning's fishing had been. It had apparently been a bad morning for everyone. They'd all go out again at 4:00 P.M. to pull their nets for a second time today, following a routine that is repeated daily in all but the worst weather. Whenever storms are coming they bring the nets in instead, lest they be torn loose from their moorings and ripped to ribbons on the rocky shore.

The wind was blowing well over twenty-five knots when *Windigo* cleared Merasheen's west shore islands at mid-morning, two days later. Under a sky still heavily overcast our course was set to the west, a broad reach with just the jib and mizzen, for Little Sandy Cove five miles away.

Plans changed as the sky ahead darkened. Showers obliterated the shore. The wind also changed, swinging into the north and dropping slowly in strength. We headed now for lunch in tiny Crabbe Cove, on Merasheen Island's northern end.

We entered slowly. My eyes were on the depth sounder. Lookouts were forward. Their eyes, however, were turned toward the quaint setting opening up on shore instead of on the water near us. Along the Cove's steep rocky shore was an old pier with three weathered houses on the grassy hillside beyond it. Near the pier stood two fishing shacks, one built with one side on the bank, and the other resting on tall logs somehow driven down into the rocky beach. Its doors were painted a bright green. A twist of smoke rose lazily from the chimney of one house whose clapboard sides and trim were in desperate need of paint.

Several skiffs and a mustard yellow dory were tied up at the pier, and on it were rows of lobster traps stacked three and four high and several men watching us. One of the men cast off and approached to ask if we'd like to tie alongside the pier. I declined—not believing there was enough water there for *Windigo*.

Our welcomer lingered. An easy smile stayed on his face as we talked. We noticed the contrast between the pieced-together fishing equipment in the bottom of his skiff, and the new thirty-five horsepower outboard on its stern. Another new outboard lay in the boat's bottom, carefully covered with canvas, as a spare.

We anchored in the middle of Crabbe Cove with just room to swing in. Our welcomer returned later and gave us four salted cod as "a greeting of welcome from Crabbe Cove" and apologized that this was all he had.

Not many hours later we had more company. A large black schooner steamed into the cove, pushing before her a huge bow wave. To my surprise she nosed right in beside the wharf with no hesitation. Her wooden masts and sails had been replaced by a diesel engine and by a yellow crane squatting on deck. The crane quickly reached out to lift four barrels off the dock, and swung them over and down into the schooner's hold. In minutes the fish buyer was off, hurrying to finish his rounds and return to the fish plant early—it was Friday afternoon, a time when many men leave the coastal towns and head back to the outports they left in the resettlement program. They were looking for companionship in surroundings they are comfortable with, and had come back to fish—their real way of life.

In the afternoon we left this pleasant place and moved on to Kingwell, a town in Port Royal Arm, on the island just east of Merasheen. The Sailing Directions indicated a government wharf with a depth alongside deep enough for us. At Kingwell I was surprised again to find few signs of the community; I still wasn't used to the chart being so wrong. We identified the government wharf, which is in ruins, and farther along the shore we found two newly rebuilt piers piled high with lobster traps. In the distance we saw large wooden tables that must have been used for drying cod in the century-old way of a good "shore cure"—light salting, very careful handling, washing, pressing, and prolonged sun drying to achieve the superior cure.

The low cloud cover we'd had earlier was replaced by whiffs of high white clouds and a warming sun. On board, Phips and his wife Jane began to sweep the shore with binoculars in search of birds. They soon spotted a peregrine falcon sitting in a tree top, and set up the telescope for a closer look at this swift bird. This was one of the two exciting sightings for these two avid bird watchers.

The other was later in Trinity Bay where they spotted a gyrfalcon outlined on the skyline high above us. That was a special day, for it was a first sighting even for them as it was for everyone else on board.

An incident happened now that I will not soon forget. Earlier that day in Crabbe Cove, two men had gone by in a partially decked-over flat-bottomed skiff. The younger of the two was forward, his head and shoulders sticking up through the forehatch as he coiled a line. The other man, older with white hair blowing in the breeze, leaned from an open pilot house window. Both pairs of eyes gave us a close inspection as they approached, returning our greetings, then continued slowly down Central Channel.

That small skiff now came into view, circled the harbor, and came over to us. *Windigo* was the largest yacht they had seen in Port Royal Arm. The old man had been the master of a sailing ship along this coast. His son George called him "Skipper," which we did also. Neither man could believe *Windigo* was built of wood—surely she must be fiberglass or at least fiberglass over wood. This was a common reaction in Newfoundland, where people are accustomed to seeing seams between planks on wooden boats, since it is nonfunctional and expensive to maintain their boats with a yacht's finish. Their boats are for rough work, constantly handling cargoes, heavy equipment, or fishing gear in all kinds of weather and sea conditions. It is only their newer boats, made of fiberglass, that don't show any seams.

At one point the Skipper placed his hand on *Windigo's* main shroud and looked aloft—remembering his years at sea. Later he pointed to where his house had been, "over there where that clump of alder now is." He recently turned seventy and had lived in Kingwell most of his life. Tears came to his eyes as he told us about Kingwell and the old days. The shadows grew longer as the sun went down behind the hills. It was time for them to go. George said to his father, "Skipper bye (boy) it's time to git goin now."

On board their boat again the Skipper handed us a dozen scallops, ones they had caught that afternoon. George demonstrated how to open them, and what muscle to keep, and suggested cooking them sprinkled with flour and fried in pork fat. The Skipper gave me more credit than deserved as he said impatiently to George "He knows how to deal with them. He's been around."

That evening, after hors d'oeuvres of Crabbe Cove mussels steamed in white wine with a dash of garlic, and a fine scallop dinner following, it was easy to imagine a busy prosperous fishing community surrounding this lovely harbor.

George and his father now live in Clarenville on Trinity Bay, north shore counterpart to Placentia Bay. To get home they simply trailered their skiff across the isthmus separating these two bays. But for *Windigo* to reach Trinity Bay, we had to sail all the way around the Avalon Peninsula. I wanted to see some of Trinity Bay and Conception Bay, two areas of the New Found Land that were "discovered" by Bristol and Basque fishermen during the late 1400s.

We anchored one night in Newfoundland's capital St. John's, a sheltered harbor on the peninsula's east coast, and left next morning in fog. We hoped to reach Trinity Harbor that day. It was a distance of over fifty miles and the farthest north we would reach on the whole voyage. The passage took the whole day, in fog and with the engine on most of the time.

We were to see interesting things near the end of it. Thousands of birds swarmed near the entrance to Trinity Bay. Small open dories worked in the straits with nets. Fishermen jigged for cod with hand lines in the century-old method, standing amidships with one line in each hand, jigging them slowly up and down slightly off the bottom, until a cod took a hook. Grooves worn by years of the lines' constant motion were clearly visible in the dories' rails. Two pilot whales were feeding close to Skerwick Rock, which was alive with terns as we entered the Bay.

Along Trinity Bay's west shore a light breeze rippled the water's surface, giving promise to a pleasant sail. The sky was cloudless, the sun warm. The wind died out completely after all the sails were set, though, leaving us to power again.

I studied the chart looking for an interesting place to stop for lunch. With just the chart, it was hard to figure which of all the coves to choose. The Cruising Guide has no descriptions for Trinity Bay.

I settled on Traytown Harbor on Ireland's Eye, an island about three miles long, whose narrow harbor penetrates inland between hills for nearly a mile, doubling back on itself and opening into a sizeable bay. I couldn't tell whether we could enter this final bay, because the chart showed a small island at its entrance—nearly blocking the channel—but the place still looked intriguing.

It was. From the harbor's two-hundred-foot-wide entrance we looked down the narrow waterway bordered by hills covered with low, weather-beaten spruce trees. The shore kept changing as we eased past it. The rocky shore revealed a continuous string of picturesque nooks and crannies along both sides. In awe, we rounded two nearly 90-degree turns. Half the crew had moved forward, just to see around the next point that much sooner.

There was no sign of human habitation anywhere. Then on the far shore a white church appeared, its faded red roof and steeple outlined against a very blue sky. "My God, there's a boat here!" someone exclaimed. It was the first cruising boat we'd seen since leaving Nova Scotia a month before.

Slowly *Windigo* drifted toward the little sloop, engine in neutral. Everyone had been silenced by the incredible setting surrounding us. I hadn't yet given thought to where we'd anchor, so Phips asked the young couple on the sloop about the water past the small island ahead. Their replies did not clarify things for us—the man first answered hesitantly, saying "There is no way of passing to the right of the island." A pause, then "There isn't much water on the other side either. Maybe ten feet." Then, more positively, "There is a shallow ledge that extends from the left bank."

Windigo's momentum carried her past the sloop toward the tiny island. I debated with myself whether to try it. Reason said no. But reason doesn't always prevail.

Speaking from the bow Phips broke into my thoughts to ask what the depth sounder read, for he could now see the bottom. He nodded when I replied fourteen feet, relating the water's clarity to its depth. Taking a deep breath I had Colm get in the dinghy to act as a tug boat should the need arise. I engaged the engine just for a moment, to get steerageway to approach the entrance parallel with the little island.

Windigo's crew stood by the rail and pointed to ledges reaching out toward us from both sides. The stony bottom was clearly visible. Depths fluctuated between nine and ten feet—very close. Suddenly we were though, safely in the small bay, surrounded by rolling wooded hills.

Beautiful as it was we didn't stay. The tide was falling. Not wanting to be trapped, we retraced our course immediately, before any of the conditions changed, to anchor safely out near the sloop.

After a swim and lunch part of the crew went ashore and picked wildflowers that had overgrown the small cemetery near the ruins of the church. Others climbed the grassy bog-covered hill behind. What an unbelievable view! Looking down the indented shore of Ireland's Eye, past countless little islands, we could see that many of the rock islets are connected to shore by seaweed-covered rocks at low tide. Silver-grey driftwood had collected along their edges. A few abandoned houses looked intact from this distance. Others were completely broken down. In another direction, *Windigo* lay serenely in a totally landlocked harbor. Beyond her we could see tree-covered hills, the harbor's entrance, and vast Trinity Bay.

We could have stayed all day, but there were more places to see and not enough time to see them in. Traytown has remained in my mind's eye as one of the most unforgettable places I have seen, a beautiful island, in a beautiful place, on a beautiful day.

6 *Sable Island*

The swing bridge across the St. Peter's Canal was opening as we rounded Handley's Island, departing Nova Scotia's Bras d'Or Lakes for Halifax, one-hundred-sixty miles to the southwest. The lock superintendent peered down from his station and called to me by name, asking if we wanted to go right through. (I was impressed. How on earth did he remember me?)

We followed two other boats through the Canal and tied alongside the lock. After the formalities the lock superintendent chuckled and asked why we had spent so much time getting under the Sandy Point cables heading *into* the Bras d'Or Lakes earlier in the summer. So that was how he knew us. He had watched it all from a river-edge place from which he could see we'd have no difficulty, and had no way to tell us this as he watched our antics of dropping the anchor and sending the crew ashore. His was a kind of concern and helpfulness that we encountered throughout our trip. That afternoon, incidentally, we had powered under the same cables without even slowing down, and with hardly a glance aloft.

After supper we departed, with a thirty-foot schooner in tow out to clear water. A light and unhelpful wind, an incoming tide, and an engine out of order made it hopeless for them to try sailing out of St. Peter's. Her crew was anxious to get back to Halifax for repairs. She was a pretty sight, yellow hull glistening in the path of the last of the sun.

Halifax was dead to windward. By sailing hard on the wind we were headed right for a speck on the chart called Sable Island. If the weather held, perhaps we could stop at this remote and dangerous place known as the "graveyard of the North Atlantic." For the two-hundred-fifty recorded wrecks on Sable Island, surely as many more have sunk there without a trace. We had learned a little about the island from Edward R. Snow's 1948 book *Mysteries and Adventures Along the Atlantic Coast*. The Sailing Directions issued dire warnings to keep well clear, even in calm weather.

The chart shows Sable Island to be about twenty miles long and a mile wide at its broadest part, and shaped like an archer's bow lying east to west in the water. Each end of the island is lengthened another ten or twelve miles by a sandbar so shallow that water breaks over it in all but the calmest weather. The island is simply the only above-water part of a huge sand bank two hundred miles long and around ninety miles wide, far away from the nearest coast, and made of particles of pebbles, coral, and shells.

Storm after storm has battered Sable Island, changing its configuration and position constantly. It was apparently much larger in the sixteenth century than today. Since its first lighthouse in 1873 the sea has swallowed six of them, as the whole island has shifted eastward. A 1766 chart of Sable Island also shows a harbor entrance. But a storm closed the entrance years later, as the story goes, and trapped two American vessels inside. There is certainly no harbor there now, nor does the island offer any shelter at all. "It's worse than trying to find protection behind a razor blade," to quote Snow.

Windigo came within sight of Sable Island by ten the next morning. The wind had died and we were under power. The sea was glassy, the barometer steady, the Halifax forecast was for settled weather. We'd try a landing. But why were there two lighthouses where the chart showed just one?

The difference was unsettling. We approached cautiously under guidance of the depth sounder, watching the bottom shoal to twelve feet before dropping back down to substantial depths. These were the three bars we had just read about in Snow's book. *Windigo* never touched, and we anchored in fifteen feet of water two hundred yards off the beach, just after noon.

The water was crystal clear. From the deck we could look down through it to see the anchor dug into the sandy bottom. We could see the chain's whole length, lying clear of the fluke and running straight along the bottom to the anchor line, which in turn curved gradually up to us. A light breeze blew out from the beach but *Windigo* persisted in lying parallel to shore, a sure sign of the strong currents that plague Sable Bank.

After a quick lunch we piled into the dinghy and rowed ashore. There was no motion to *Windigo* where she was, but two-foot-high waves were rolling onto the beach. Quick footwork, with cameras held high, kept most of us dry in the landing. What a beach—out in the middle of nowhere, clean hard-packed sand and stretching out of sight in both directions, bunches of grass on the dunes. There was a jarring note, however: tire tracks ran the length of the beach.

There was activity at the lighthouses. We could see men working there—building a completely new lighthouse right next to the old one. The old one had been there about eighty years and was in perfectly good condition, but the wind had eroded its foundation, concrete on sand, and the whole thing was about to fall into a huge hole.

The men were from Halifax. They came out by helicopter for two weeks' work, then went back to civilization for a week. They lived right there at the work site instead of traveling all the sandy miles to the settlement at the island's west end, where fifteen people man the weather station and radio beacon.

The tough little wild horses of Sable Island know how to dig through sand for drinking water. They have lived on this island of sand for two centuries.

From the lighthouse we could see quite a few wild horses out in the dunes. We came across one of them later, pawing at the sand in a valley floor. Wondering what to expect from this untamed animal we approached carefully. Rick got to within thirty feet before the horse took off, and just where he had been pawing there was, about a foot below the sand, a puddle of water, dark and disagreeable but undoubtedly their source of drinking water. Not one of us volunteered to taste it.

There are thought to be three or four hundred horses on Sable Island. They live in herds that are very territorial, killing others that move into their area. When the Canadian Government flew hay in to them for winter the horses would have nothing to do with it, and the hay just rotted away. Another time Nova Scotia horses were brought here to interbreed with the wild horses, but they were not accepted and were soon killed. Sable Island's is a tough, tough breed.

The horses may well be descendants of those taken to the Island two centuries ago by John Hancock's seafaring uncle, we gathered from the *Mysteries and Adventures* book. And they in turn were preceded by cattle left behind in the 1500s by Portuguese and Spanish explorers, for the benefit of their successors, and grown to eight hundred strong by the 1630s. That astronomical figure was recorded by Bostonian John Rose, who built a little boat from his ship's wreckage there and sailed safely back to Nova Scotia.

Aboard *Windigo* earlier, we had faintly heard a roaring noise. It was loud at the lighthouse and getting much louder now as we walked across the island. Standing on top of the last dune overlooking the south beach we found its source, the real danger that the island presents. From a flat surface just a hundred yards offshore the sea built into five-foot-high waves that crashed onto the beach at an angle, then rolled powerfully down its length. The sea was calm today. It was frightening to imagine what this place would be like in a storm, or even just a thirty-knot wind. What would it be like when seen from a foundering vessel? It was impossible to comprehend.

Heading across the beach now we saw that the shore was dotted with logs and rocks. We advanced wondering what sort of odd and interesting wreckage we could find among this lot. Soon one log, then two more moved into the water. Instead of logs and rocks they were seals sunning themselves on the beach.

As we approached, they all wriggled down the beach and into the sea. Some protested loudly at our rude disturbance. From the safety of the water they were curious about us and great fun to watch. Their human-looking heads, with big round eyes, would suddenly pop out of the water and stare at us. When a cresting wave came the seals would surf right down its face, all the while watching us, perhaps wondering why we didn't join them when it was so much fun. At the last second, just before being bashed into the sand, the seals would duck their heads under and scoot back out beyond the breaking waves. What a great time they were having. Mark thought so and joined them, but they paid no attention to him at all.

On the same beach we did come upon evidence of two wrecks, but there wasn't much to be seen; perhaps the waves have scoured it all away over the centuries. On the north beach we were profoundly disappointed at another sight: plastic bottles, old shoes, and beer cans, the awful trash that floats on the oceans today.

The barometer was still steady, but now more than ever I wanted to clear the west end of the Island and its bar before night. It was time to leave this strange place. Later that night we realized we were the first boat to have seen the new lighthouse in operation. The old one had been dismantled that day and a temporary light had just been turned on in the new one. We heard the Halifax radio state that "the light on the east end of Sable Island will not have its normal range tonight."

With no wind we powered all night, and as the sun rose so did the wind. We happily changed to the peace and quiet of the sails, running before an easterly at nearly seven knots for most of the day, but the journey was really not comfortable at all. We were all weary from the prior night's sail and the fascinating day on Sable Island. Sleep was impossible. As each wave rolled by *Windigo* rolled too, shaking the mainsail, rattling every single sail slide along the boom. The sail then filled again with a resounding *whap!*, whereupon it all began again. Below, cans, bottles, plates, and everything else that could get loose slid from side to side with each roll. What a noise. Tracking all the loose things down took forever. Being below was like being inside a great big drum.

The sky had become heavily overcast during the afternoon. Halifax was forecasting strong northeast winds. The barometer had dropped, and visibility ahead was decreasing. The weather was definitely deteriorating.

The visibility grew worse as we closed with the coast, plus it was getting late. The wind was coming over the stern at twelve or fifteen knots, and added to our speed of seven knots, its true speed was around twenty. That's a lot of wind if you're closing with the coast in poor visibility.

A running series of Loran and RDF fixes showed us to be near the outermost buoy off Halifax Harbor around 7 P.M. By now, though, the fog was so thick we were sailing virtually blind. Sambro Light's forlorn fog horn sounded ahead to port. It came from the expected direction but we never did see or hear the buoy itself. There was another buoy ahead and clear of the shallows, and we could get a positive fix from that before threading our way blindly towards shore.

The lookouts stood near the mainmast to listen in quiet. Their sharp ears soon heard the buoy's faint whistles slightly to starboard. Changing courses for the sound we got to within twenty feet of it before our spotlight could give us a positive identification. Its flashing white light was just a fuzzy blur. It was the one we wanted.

Running before the wind we were nearly on top of the next four buoys before we could hear their bells or whistles, because the wind carried the noise away.

I was steering. I feel I can react faster to imminent danger if I am at the wheel. I can also keep my senses more highly attuned to the situation than if I were doing the navigating or something else.

We were in our own small world. Our masthead light was just a faint glow overhead, our running lights mere pinpricks in the fog. Droplets of moisture clung to eyebrows, glasses, hair, and beards. Bigger drops fell from the rigging. The fog signal we'd been hearing from Chebucto Head was now close abeam and shattered the quiet so suddenly that we all jumped.

Finally we were in. With land close all around us, the fog began to thin.

What an evening. We tied up at the Royal Nova Scotia Yacht Squadron dock just after midnight. We'd just completed six hours of critical navigation in some of the thickest fog I've seen. There were long hot showers ashore and then there was bed, for a very sound sleep.

1 Rogues Roost

Planning for my first trip to Nova Scotia and Newfoundland, I had asked everyone I could for knowledge of these waters. One question that I always asked was "What are your favorite anchorages?" I asked it knowing full well that I'm reluctant to tell anyone my own favorite places, lest I find a crowd there on my return. One frequent answer to my bold question was Rogues Roost, said to be a beautiful and protected cove that's a comfortable day's sail southwest from Halifax. Because the anchorage was so warmly recommended, and because I have friends whose boat is named *Rogues Roost,* I decided to take *Windigo* in if we could.

Canadian Chart 4385 shows little detail of the Rogues Roost entrance, but the Nova Scotia Cruising Guide does give enough detail for me to try. The weather was favorable and the tide had just turned and was coming in. We headed in slowly under power, picking our way past islands and hidden rocks now on both sides of us. I put the engine in neutral for a minute while I matched the land formations I could see ahead with what chart and Cruising Guide described. *Windigo* drifted to a stop. Taking a deep breath I engaged the engine, chart folded in one hand, Cruising Guide open right beside me.

Roost Island's bare rock ledge showed ahead to starboard, topped to just above the high water mark by hardy weatherbeaten evergreen brush. Barnacles and seaweed dotted the smooth rock from there down to the water, which was just above its lowest now, and the rock then disappeared under water nearly straight down. Another rock off one small unidentified island was awash at this tide, which was a great help in positively placing it. It's certainly easier on the nervous system than going in at a higher tide, when the rock is covered by a few feet of water, just awaiting a hapless keel!

We crept along Roost Island's north shore, off to starboard, with the rock awash only thirty feet away to port. *Windigo* could never turn around in this channel, and I certainly couldn't back her out. If we had to retreat now we would have to use the dinghy with lines to the islands and an anchor or two set out. We were fully committed.

There was ample width here to proceed, but was the water deep enough? The depth sounder dropped from twenty feet to less than twelve, then went back to nearly twenty-five feet again.

I had to decide whether to turn one way to what is labeled "Rogues Roost" on the chart, anchoring in about twenty feet with ample swinging room, or go the other way down a short channel whose depth is not shown on the chart, to an anchorage that opens up in the eastern shore of Roost Island. The Roost Island anchorage is small, hardly large enough on the chart to contain the "3" indicating the depth of water in fathoms (one fathom equals six feet) and just "large enough so that five or six forty-foot boats could raft comfortably for the night." It was this anchorage that I wanted to try, but I had no idea how deep the channel was.

Windigo headed for it. The channel is nearly a quarter of a mile long and narrows to eighty-five feet, not much wider than *Windigo* is long, before opening into the anchorage. Rock ledges on either side rise straight up with a few hardy bushes clinging in their crevasses.

We ran the gauntlet safely, all of us amazed that we hadn't hit bottom or sides, twisting our heads this way and that to see everything as it went by. *Windigo* slowly circled, like an animal before it lies down. We anchored in the middle of the cove and tied stern lines to boulders, to keep us well in place.

The day was a fine one: clear skies, a swim, ledges to climb, scenes for photographs each more beautiful than the last. From all the way up on the highest knoll we could see small islands leading to the sea, and hilly Nova Scotia stretching inland. From part way up on a ledge we could see *Windigo* reflected upside down in the smooth water of her cove. The sun's setting light danced in a path directly across to us.

Later as we roasted fish over a fire ashore, two small fishing boats came in to see what was beneath the tall mast that they must have seen jutting up over Roost Island. A huge black cloud also approached, hurrying supper along and us back on board *Windigo* for dessert. A downpour quickly completed our job of putting out the fire ashore. What a picturesque spot, snug as a bug in a rug.

I went back to Rogues Roost again a year later, after toying briefly with the thought of going into Terence Basin, just east of it, this time. Terence Basin has an intriguing mile-long very narrow entrance, with no less than twelve feet indicated on the chart, into what looks to be a good anchorage. The Cruising Guide changed my mind. One writer had abandoned his entering there when he saw another yacht hard aground in the narrows. Sounding at low tide he had found no more than three-and-a-half-feet at one point all the way across the passage. The chart and Cruising Guide descriptions did not agree. I was not up to finding out which was correct that afternoon. Besides, the seas had an uncomfortable funny long roll to them and an unusually high ridge of clouds had formed to the southeast, from which long faint finger clouds radiated. The clear blue sky of earlier had been diffused.

Entering Rogues Roost this time was as intriguing and spectacular as last year, except, of course, I wasn't nearly as nervous as I had been the first time. On the way in we saw six local fishing boats turned yachts, rafted together in a nearby passage, tied to both banks. Inside the Roost Island cove, a motorsailer and a small white sloop were tied alongside the rock ledge with an anchor holding them off. We circled, dropped the anchor near them, and tied the stern to boulders on Roost Island, in very nearly the same location as the year before.

During the day the engine had been overheating for some reason, so after the crew dispersed ashore I took the hatches off to have a look. The fresh water cooling system was nearly empty even though I had filled it recently. I filled it again and waited for signs of any leak. Almost immediately a steady stream started running down from under the heat exchanger. I figured that at that rate it would take only two or three hours to get low again, but that we could make it over to Lunenberg in the morning for repairs. We'd have to refill the tank every half hour or so and trust that the leak would get no worse.

Two more boats came in, C.C.A. vessels heading south from the Bras d'Or Lakes. The local yacht/fishing group disbanded and headed for home. My crew was either on shore or visiting on other boats. Finding myself alone I settled down to read, a seldom found luxury, and decided to add to my comfort by turning on the radio to a station with gentle music. How enjoyable—until the 6:30 news. The weather forecast said that hurricane Blanche had changed direction. Instead of heading east of Nova Scotia it was expected to be well west of that and to head up to the Bay of Fundy tomorrow morning, then veer across Nova Scotia. That was the first I'd heard about a hurricane. No one had spoken of it at the Yacht Club in Halifax. I realized now what those high clouds to the southeast were from, and also those long lazy swells.

Rogues Roost might have been fine for these smaller cruising boats, but it was no place for a boat the size of *Windigo* in a hurricane, even if we had had the place to ourselves. With headway *Windigo* can turn clockwise in almost her own length, but with no room for getting headway we just couldn't move in here without using anchors and lines ashore. And once the wind started really blowing it would be impossible for us to leave even if we did get turned around, threading our way out through the rocks at slow speed, susceptible to any gusts.

I began to feel caged, wanting to leave this wonderful place right now in the calm weather, while there was still time.

The crew began returning; they knew we'd be busy getting *Windigo* ready for the big winds. While the other boats took steps to get ready we retrieved stern lines and anchor. The last thing I did before getting underway was to fill the engine's fresh water cooling system, showing Scott what I was doing.

I'd already studied the chart and found what appeared to be a good hurricane hole further up Prospect Bay from Roost Island, a small cove on the northwest end of Purcell Island. The cove looked wide enough for us to swing in even with extra anchor line out. There wasn't going to be any extra room, though, and it all depended on how much water there turned out to be along the shore. If it didn't look suitable when I saw it we'd anchor off the north end of the island instead. The center of the storm would pass to the west of us, so the strong winds would first blow from the S.E. then shift to the S.W. as the center went past, leaving us in the shelter of land throughout.

I made my customary circle around the new anchorage when we got there, with a close eye on the depth sounder. It looked all right. Another boat, the yawl *Grafin* from Boston, was already anchored farther in. Down went our one-hundred-fifty-pound Yachtsman anchor with twenty feet of chain attached to a one-inch nylon anchor rode.

We set about securing everything from the expected devastating winds. Un-

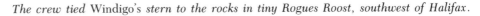

The crew tied Windigo's *stern to the rocks in tiny Rogues Roost, southwest of Halifax.*

hank the headsails and stow them below. Mainsail and mizzen sail covers on and lashed to the boom, to keep the wind from tearing any loose corner free and then ripping the cloth to ribbons in an instant. Everything else possible was removed and stowed below. By 11:00 we'd done everything I could think of, and we crawled wearily into our bunks.

My alarm woke me for a look around and the 4:00 A.M. weather report. The storm was still heading for the Bay of Fundy and was expected to pass Halifax around midday. The weather outside wasn't bad. The tide was going out. Dark clouds hurried past the moon ominously and the wind wasn't anything yet. There was a heavy feeling to the air.

I went back to my bunk and reset the alarm for 8:00 A.M. The weather forecast was still the same by then, but the weather outside had changed. Light rain was falling and the wind was building from the S.E., right off Purcell Island, just as we had figured. *Windigo* lay across the narrow cove with her stern very close to some rocks. The tide continued to drop and more rocks appeared nearby.

By 9:30 the wind was forty knots and more. I wondered if we had dragged the anchor. It was hard to tell whether we were dragging closer to the rocks astern, or just falling back on our line as the tide went out. Or was the tide simply exposing more rocks?

The depth sounder showed enough water directly under its transducer just aft of the mainmast, but the deepest part of *Windigo's* hull is well aft of that, much closer to the rocks.

We had pulled the big Danforth anchor out of the forepeak the night before, and laid it on deck set to be used instantly, all attached to thirty feet of chain and its own anchor rode. It was time to put it to use. The crew was all bundled up in foul weather gear and awaiting instructions. I yelled to them above the noise of the wind: I'd fill the engine's fresh water cooling system, then power ahead and to the right of the anchor already down. When I raised my arm Scott would count to three and on three they'd drop the Danforth and its chain over the side, making very sure that the line wasn't tangled on anything, much less themselves.

Before going below I started the engine to warm it up. The cooling system needed filling again. I'd already learned it took five tea kettles to fill it and kettle number four was almost in when a strange bump affected *Windigo* underneath me. Had we hit a rock?

I didn't bother with the rest of the water but dropped the kettle and raced for the cockpit. I put her in gear immediately and advanced the throttle. The crew forward were all looking aft; they hadn't felt anything because things were so rough on deck, but the sound of the engine's increased speed did reach them.

The propeller bit into the water, sending swirls of boiling water astern. I felt one more bump before we moved forward. That was close!

As we advanced the winds tried to take control of *Windigo* herself. Her high bow and her tall mast and all its rigging offered massive windage. I had only one try to put the second anchor where I wanted it.

We got as close to the right spot as I could get. I raised my arm. Scott counted and on three the anchor and chain went over the side. *Windigo's* bow was already being blown right around broadside to the wind. I hurried forward to let the anchor line out while Scott came aft to check the cooling system. We couldn't afford to have the engine quit now. I let out plenty of scope for the anchor before slowly snubbing up on the line. The Danforth held.

The wind soon began its swing to the southwest, and stayed steady at sixty-five knots with gusts to well over seventy-five. We held throughout it, paying out more line, watching the rain end but the water still fly by horizontally. What an incredible sight. The worst was over by midday. We decided to lay over a day to tackle the problem of the cooling system, and we were all just as glad at the delay. Several hours ashore with the telephone and the yellow pages and lots of help from Brian, a friendly man who lives ashore, and I still had no solution. It took Brian's ingenuity (some years ago he had driven a diesel bus and he knew its intricacies) and trips to an auto mechanic and a bearing store in Halifax, but we got the necessary parts. Back aboard *Windigo* Brian had the revivified water-pump reinstalled in fifteen minutes. It worked, with no leaks.

Mud, twenty inches thick, still stuck to the Danforth when we finally got it up the next day. No wonder it had held! *Grafin* had fared well and left at mid-day. We learned later that the sailboats that had stayed in Rogues Roost were safe too. I'd not soon forget any of this—the intricate channels twisting behind hidden rocks and rocky islands opening into peaceful anchorages, the waterways winding between tiny islands snaking to the ocean, the vegetation that fights to survive in the tough climate, and, amid it all, our safe encounter with seventy-mile-an-hour hurricane Blanche.

ATLANTIC OCEAN

FLORIDA

Bahama Is.

CUBA

Yucatan Peninsula

Greater

HAITI

DOMINICAN REPUBLIC

Virgin Is.

Belize City

Swan Is.

Antilles

PUERTO RICO

Antigua

Guadeloupe

Bay Islands

JAMAICA

Pointe-à-Pitre

Dominica

Leeward Is.

HONDURAS

Gorda Bank

Martinique

Barbados

St. Lucia

CARIBBEAN SEA

Quita Sueño Bank

St. Vincent

Windward Is.

NICARAGUA

Isla de Providencia

Antilles

The Grenadines

San Andres I.

Grenada

St. George's

Willemstad

Lesser

COSTA RICA

Curacao

Isla Orchila

PANAMA CANAL

Isla Los Roques

Punta San Blas

PANAMA

VENEZUELA

PACIFIC

OCEAN

COLOMBIA

8 *Antigua Race Week*

In the early morning hours of October 12, 1492, Christopher Columbus ordered his ships to heave to until daylight because the bright moon had shown cliffs ahead. San Salvador, as Columbus named the island seen that night, is part of the Bahamas and some twelve thousand miles from Cathay—his intended destination.

San Salvador and the Caribbean islands south of it—Cuba, Jamaica, Hispaniola among them—were reported to be as beautiful as any in the world, with a delightful climate. The land was fertile and mountainous. Flowers and fruit grew profusely. The rivers were full of gold that the natives wore as ornaments. Columbus was convinced he was within easy reach of India and the riches Marco Polo had described.

Columbus made several voyages to the Caribbean and was followed by a string of others within the next century—including English trader John Hawkins in 1562, and his cousin Francis Drake with his own ships in 1572. The settlements had a rough beginning but eventually flourished. Explorers, adventurers, navies, privateers, and buccaneers criss-crossed the Caribbean waters. Sugar cane, brought by Columbus, became a lucrative crop. Slavery came with the trade and became an industry itself. Some of the islands changed hands among the European powers four times during the eighteenth century alone.

The whole island chain that curves from the tip of Florida to the Venezuelan coast, from Cuba to the Grenadines, became known as the West Indies because of its original mis-identification by Columbus. The islands were also called the Antilles, after Antilla, the mythical continent that was once thought to exist east of the Azores. The large northern islands and the small islands that surround them became the Greater Antilles, while the Lesser Antilles start with St. Thomas and swing eastward and southward to Venezuela, and include the islands off that coast. In turn the Lesser Antilles are divided into the Windward and Leeward Islands, with Dominica generally considered to separate the two groups.

It was to Antigua, discovered by Columbus on his second voyage to the "Indies" and today several Leeward Islands north in the chain from Dominica, that *Windigo* headed as we began our exploration of Caribbean waters. We quickly found ourselves involved in an old island tradition: Antigua Race Week.

Antigua's English Harbor was once a major British naval installation and is today a center for yachtsmen. They anchor in Freeman's Bay or tie stern-to at Nelson's Dockyard, with its handsome old fortifications and the ruins of powder magazines and barracks. It isn't hard to picture huge naval vessels tied up for refitting. Some would have been stripped of their rigging and careened, dwarfing the men at work repairing the ship's bottom. Many of the old buildings are today being restored, one as a museum, others as apartments, offices, and marine stores. Two big capstans used to careen the ships are still in place. The Admiral's Inn, built of bricks that came to Antigua centuries ago as ships' ballast, is now restored as a hotel and restaurant.

In recent years the Admiral's Inn has held a grand New Year's Eve celebration that has drawn yachts from far away—including, one year, *Windigo*. A twenty-piece steel-drum band played all night, Calypso to Bach and Brahms. Dinner was served on tables set up on the lawn, with dancing on the terrace nearby. I wandered away for awhile to walk through the Dockyard and along the ridge to the old fort that guards the harbor's entrance. Looking out over the moonlit water, with the music from the steel drums carrying faintly over toward me, was heavenly. The festivities lasted until the early hours of the morning, and the beginning of a new year.

The day before Race Week began that April, *Windigo* had a visitor—Dave Simmonds, Chairman of the Race Committee. He informed me that we would be accepted in the Cruising Class if we accepted a seven percent penalty to our rating. The penalty was being applied to five other boats, he quickly explained, boats that like *Windigo* were designed as racing boats rather than the true cruising boats for which the class was intended. I accepted this calmly, thinking it made little difference to me if similar boats were treated alike. My main competitive interest in this week was to race against the famous seventy-three-foot ketch *Ticonderoga* boat for boat in the Cruising Class, with little concern for where *Windigo* placed on corrected time. Surely *Ticonderoga* would be one of the five assessed a penalty.

On learning she wasn't, I objected strenuously. A boat with her racing background—which includes nearly every race record there is—could certainly not be considered a "cruising boat" within the definition for this class.

As expected, I got nowhere. My choices were to accept the penalty and stay in the Cruising Class, change to the Racing Class without the penalty, or not participate at all. Dave Simmonds quickly assured me that the Race Committee hoped *Windigo* would race.

Grudgingly, we entered the Cruising Class with the penalty. There was no way I'd enter the Racing Class; setting the spinnaker with an inexperienced crew and the winter winds still blowing was out of the question. Besides, *Ticonderoga* was in the Cruising Class.

The starting line was perpendicular to the wind, so we had a running start with the wind directly behind us. My plan was to sail on the starboard tack nearly parallel to the line, with the wind abeam for the greatest boat speed. Then, we'd carefully time our turn to cross the line a few seconds after the gun fired, still with good speed. The plan was sound. My execution of it was not.

I didn't get *Windigo* into position soon enough, forcing me to cut one side of my planned route and head for the middle of the line on the starboard tack, with the wind over the quarter instead of abeam. *Ticonderoga* was ahead to starboard, sailing directly with the wind on the port tack. She was heading for the same part of the line that we were, but going more slowly.

The starting gun fired, its sound echoing off the rock cliffs of Fort Charlotte. We were across a moment later and changed course slightly for the first mark. *Ticonderoga* was just ahead, our courses nearly parallel, but we were steadily gaining and converging with her. We were on starboard so had the right of way.

On overtaking her, I could not resist the opportunity to call across "Right of way, I'm coming up!" My hail brought no reaction from *Ticonderoga's* afterguard. No one even looked our way. David Simmonds did look, however, from nearby in his thirty-foot sloop, and felt none too safe having done so. He was sailing the smallest boat in the fleet and was directly between us, about to be squeezed by two giants, with no place to turn. To his relief we both soon passed him, still converging. I really didn't want to head up, but couldn't let my hail go without any response. Besides, it would be fun to watch *Ticonderoga* jibe over to avoid us, perhaps causing some confusion in her crew.

Again I called for right of way. This time, after a pause, there was this astounding response: "You are not allowed to start the race on the starboard tack." What an absolutely ridiculous thing to say. It left me speechless. There was of course no such rule.

My attention to our sails' trim gave me the few seconds I needed for recovery, by which time we were fully ahead of "Big Ti" anyway.

I was glad to have started early in the event. The Cruising Class had been the first to go, and beforehand the whole hundred-boat fleet, all five classes, had been sailing around in tiny Freeman Bay. It was unbelievably tight. The boats had no pattern to their movements and most had up only their mainsails until just before the start, which allowed them great visibility forward and not much speed. Nevertheless, there were many near collisions.

We saw one incident materialize. In the center of the Bay the forty-five-foot sailboat *Optimist* was sailing slowly toward the starting line. Under just main and

English Harbor, Antigua, was the starting point for our first race.

mizzen both *Ticonderoga* and another big ketch *Miss II*, an Ocean 71, were turning in a tight circle in the same area, but in opposite directions. From my safely distant vantage point it looked as though the seventy-footers would crash, crushing poor *Optimist* between them.

How she escaped I do not know. Moments before the crash a great black cloud of smoke erupted from *Ticonderoga's* stern as her engine got full-throttle—in reverse. Shuddering to a stop but still turning toward *Miss II*, *Ticonderoga's* long bowsprit swept over her deck. Some of *Miss II's* crew jumped clear. Others dared to exert their relatively puny strength to push the two massive moving boats apart, to keep the bowsprit from catching *Miss II's* rigging. It was a close call!

In the aftermath, I recalled that at the skippers' meeting the evening before, *Ticonderoga's* skipper had suggested the starting line be changed because the fleet had grown too large for the traditional one to be a safe start. The suggestion was received well by the competitors but with disfavor by the Race Committee, because the event was such a fantastic sight for the many spectators ashore on the old fortress and atop Fort Charlotte. Commercialism prevailed for another year over safety and seamanship.

We were nearing the end of the first leg of the race, westward along Antigua's south coast to Cade Reef Buoy, a special race mark. The wind was directly behind us. *Windigo's* genoa was set to windward, held well out with the spinnaker pole, with main and mizzen pulling strongly. She sailed on effortlessly, wing and wing like a soaring bird, sails out as far as they could be.

Three other seventy-footers followed us along the outer side of Cade Reef, each trying to take the wind from the one ahead, each trying to keep her wind clear from those trying to sail past from behind. One easy way to protect your wind is to head up, forcing a boat trying to steal your wind to head up too. The disadvantage of forcing another boat is that you don't head for your mark, and in this case it meant all of us turning toward Cade Reef instead of safely along its outer edge. The four boats played tag with each other's wind, gradually working closer and closer to the reef. Here was a new dimension to the run—a game of chicken with the coral heads that extend out from the main reef.

The reef was clearly visible a short distance away, as a darkness in the light green water. The sun high behind us made the coral heads easy to see, but only with experience can anyone judge the depth of such clear water over them. We were lucky. An Antiguan dinghy racer had joined *Windigo* for the Race Week series, and now stood in the bow to guide us away from danger. As far as I know, none of the boats was tagged by the coral.

After the first mark we beat right back along Cade Reef. It was exciting, dodging the coral again and sailing back through the fleet heading for the buoy we had just rounded. Boats in the two racing classes flew their bright-colored spinnakers and bloopers, many with intriguing or outlandish designs. Sometimes we were on starboard and had the right of way and they all had to give way to us. Other times we had to keep clear of all the rest of the fleet, running before the wind toward us at about fifteen knots. The big number two genoa was just the right sail for *Windigo* in this wind. Her lee rail was down but not in the water, our speed seven or eight knots. The weather was clear and warm with puffy white clouds drifting by overhead. It was a perfect sail.

Our frequent tacks gave the crew a real workout, particularly those on the "coffee grinders"—the two complex and powerful winches that *Windigo* has for trimming the headsails. Each winch has a pair of handles that turn its drum, and each pair can be operated by two people turning them to tighten a sheet and trim the sail. The two handle units can be operated separately or, by shifting a lever, together to combine the strength of four people on one winch. The winches are also geared; the highest gear is used when the wind is light or as the sail is just beginning to fill. As the sail fills and pulls harder on its sheet, the winch gears drop down to give more mechanical advantage to the crew.

Working the winches is really quite simple, especially when demonstrated peacefully at anchor. It's more confusing underway, with distractions like trying to stay amidships during a tack, safely beyond the reach of the flailing genoa sheet that snaps around like the back edge of a flag in a storm, but with the authority of a sledge hammer, even in a light breeze. Then add the challenge of racing, with speed absolutely essential, with competition at your heels or converging with you at a mark. The chance for lethal mistakes is constantly present, even with well-trained crews.

I had been seriously concerned about this before the race. Only three of us had ever sailed on board *Windigo* before. Our crew of eight were strong and competent sailors, but they didn't know *Windigo* and had no experience working together as a team. We hadn't even had time for a practice sail. The twenty-knot trade winds had been blowing day and night for the four months since January and there was no sign they'd let up now. The forces that *Windigo*-size sails create with this strength of wind is phenomenal. In such a potentially devastating situation I knew I'd have to be extremely careful. I had to allow plenty of time and space for each maneuver. I had to make sure each person knew his assignment and what to watch out for throughout it. Rick could handle this last part—if I gave him time.

So much for serious concern. To everyone's surprise and my great relief we awoke the morning of the first race to a ten-knot east wind that held for nearly the whole week!

Rick had in fact organized the crew into the foredeck gang, the coffee grinders, and the sheet tailers. The foredeck gang would handle the quick sail changes we'd need. The coffee grinders would of course work those winches to trim the sails, and the tailers would haul back on the sheets as the winches brought them in tighter until trimmed. That all left me pretty much alone in the cockpit to steer and tend the mizzen.

Our tacking had gone smoothly. The tack would start with my "ready about," which was usually given plenty early. Heading toward Cade Reef, which everyone could see, the crew was often in position well before I was ready. Then came "hard-a-lee" as I turned *Windigo's* bow into the wind. My part was done; now Rick took over. As the genoa began to luff he'd say "OK, let it go!" to the crew taking the sheet off the winch. Seconds later as the sail flapped violently across the foredeck he'd call "Pull!" to the one tending the genoa sheet on the other side, then "Go!" to the coffee grinders, who'd now furiously turn the handles to trim the sail in on its new side. As the sail filled and pressure built Rick would then say "Change!" to the coffee grinders, who in unison changed the handle's direction to drop the winch down one gear, then down again with the next "Change!", and then again, and the tack was done. Until the next time— and we'd do it all over again!

The crew had had plenty of practice, and now it was a long beat to the finish off York Island, well past English Harbor on Antigua's southeast coast. After clearing the eastern end of Cade Reef our local crew had recommended staying close to shore past Falmouth and English harbors. Whether this advice was for favorable current conditions or for a better slant of wind I never did determine, but it paid off handsomely for us.

Off Fort Charlotte Point just east of the starting line we had a comfortable lead heading for the finish. Two Ocean 71s were just off to leeward. *Ticonderoga* was converging from offshore. The big puffy clouds were lower now, and had developed dark undersides. The wind had dropped to around ten knots. Should we change to the light-air genoa, the largest genoa on board? Was this only a lull, or would the wind stay as it was? Or drop even further?

I decided to change headsails. We made a good sail change—less than five minutes to complete the job. Even so our speed dropped from six knots to just over two during the sail change. Our competition gained. No sooner had we gotten our speed back than we saw rain falling from the not-so-white clouds directly to windward. A distinctive light grey band extended from cloud to water, at a slight angle. I knew that the wind usually increases under clouds like these, and sometimes it changes direction. We were headed right for it.

The wind did increase. Would the light genoa blow out? I hardly noticed the rain in my worry. We saw first one boat change headsails then another. It was a long several minutes for me before *Windigo* came out on the other side of the rain shower, decks wet and steaming. The genoa survived. The wind now did change direction, letting us up nicely for the mark.

On a close reach now, with sheets eased, we were overtaking the Classic Schooner Class just off to windward of us. They were heading for the same finish line after sailing a different course. The schooners were of various sizes, shapes, designs, and ages and they were all sailing very close to each other. This fact only semi-registered with me as being unusual, for they were such a picturesque sight.

The sun was at our backs, shining on their sails. Most were old and grey. One suit of white sails stood out in vivid contrast with a Bequian schooner's antique red sails. I remember wishing that my camera had been in my hand, but there was time for no more than a glance at the schooners. We were nearing the coast rapidly and still hadn't found the finish line. It was somewhere to leeward, I thought, but couldn't see it under the genoa. So I asked if someone would go forward and look. There was no response. No one moved forward. About to repeat my request in a louder voice I realized *Windigo's* entire crew was standing at the windward rail staring at the old Beque schooner. Her entire crew, all females, was naked. No wonder the other schooners sailed so close to her, the smallest boat in their fleet. The girls cheered and waved as we passed, bringing *Windigo's* crew mentally back on board, a little sheepish at being caught staring.

The committee boat blended in with the shore so well that we got to within half a mile before finding it. The buoy end we finally spotted when we were within two boat lengths of the line. *Windigo* finished first, well ahead of the next boat, even further ahead of *Ticonderoga*, and we were delighted with the day's outing.

We competed in three more races, finishing first in all of them. My main interest in Race Week was to race against *Ticonderoga*, whom we outsailed in each race—which pleased me immensely. Admittedly the light-air running and windward work did not favor the big ketch, but even on her optimum point of sail, the long reaching along the west coast of Antigua, *Windigo* held her own. The biggest achievement was undoubtedly the crew's work; short tacking along Cade Reef, dodging boats and coral heads, and their smart sail handling of genoas winged out on a spinnaker pole or set flying as a blooper. It was a wonderful week with many lasting memories.

9 A Project Period

On two consecutive years students from New England cut short their Thanksgiving break to join *Windigo* for two weeks in the Virgin Islands for an oceanography and sailing experience. Their only requirement while on board was to critique the course at its end. One student wrote, "Most of us didn't think a lot of work would be involved, but I found this to be wrong." Others said, "The project was packed with super educational classes: snorkeling above the reefs and fish, learning to work together in seamanship and sailing on beloved *Windigo* . . . and the cockpit discussions. Many nights I didn't want to go to bed for fear of missing something." "Nothing was really bad about the whole thing, except rough seas during the night sail." "My confidence has grown by the challenges that were presented to us day after day."

This course was in two parts: sailing and seamanship using *Windigo* and two windsurfers as classrooms, and studying reefs and their environments. Rick and I could handle the above-water subjects, and Dick and Dan, two young high school biology teachers from St. Thomas, agreed to join us for part of the time to instruct a marine life program.

We spent the students' first day on board in Christmas Cove, fitting everyone with snorkel, mask, and fins. During the afternoon we snorkeled in water three to thirty feet deep. Most of us were looking for the first time at the many different multicolored fish and varieties of coral. Two days later Dick and Dan joined us and showed slides of the underwater world we would soon be seeing. They explained how reefs grow and what destroys them. They also covered the eventual growth of islands and possibilities of a salt pond forming.

The next morning we returned to Christmas Cove and went snorkeling in that area again. It was a big help to have seen the slides, but it was far more beneficial to have Dick and Dan in the water with us, identifying the marine life.

In 1869 the steam-powered square-rigged ship R.M.S. *Rhone* sank off Salt Island. Today her stern lies in thirty feet, easily seen by snorkelers. The rest of her is in much deeper water and we could not see it, but we did snorkel over the stern and were fascinated seeing part of the huge propeller rising from the sand, the butt of the hollow metal mast, and the stern itself. A wide variety of colorful fish swam throughout the wreck. Several students had brought bread, which some fish ate right out of their hands.

Salt Island, Virgin Islands, changes its appearance in its wet and dry seasons. Sandy and the crew got to know Beatrice and Clementine, who live on the island and hardly ever leave it.

Myriad sorts of fish were the fascinating subject of study for the students during the project period.

The previous summer Dick and his five-year-old son had camped on Salt Island for several weeks. During their stay they became good friends with Beatrice and Clementine, two sisters in their 60s—we guessed—who have lived there all their lives. Their children moved to Tortola many years ago to benefit from the schools and jobs there. Their youngest children now spend summers on Salt Island with their grandmothers.

The sisters were delighted to see Dick again. They proudly showed us where they lived, in very small one-room shacks in the shade of coconut trees, with conch shells neatly arranged as a border.

Throughout the Caribbean these shells, which can be found almost anywhere, have a wide range of uses. The very poor use conch shells as grave markers. Others use them, as we saw on Salt Island, to border paths around houses and gardens. The prettier shells are highly polished and used in many intriguing decorative ways. I have one at home, its curled end cut off to be blown as a fog horn, similar to one we heard later in Martinique.

Five or six men also live on Salt Island. They moved from Tortola after retiring. They kept very much to themselves. Beatrice and Clementine, on the other hand, were very outgoing, and joined us on the beach for supper around a small campfire. They hardly ever leave the island, and probably don't read, but still they were very well informed about world events—thanks to the radio—and were eager to discuss them with us. We had trouble understanding their Creole English, but with Dick and one of the students who lives on St. Thomas interpreting for us, we had a very interesting and enjoyable evening.

From Salt Island we sailed on, to the tip of Virgin Gorda, anchoring off the "Baths"; a popular lunch stop for many charter boats. On the beach huge boulders, geographically totally alien to the Caribbean, had been thrown together sometime in the distant past. It is now fun to climb over, under, and around

Students study reefs, fish, and seamanship, using Windigo *as their classroom.*

these large rocks as the sea washes between them, often leaving behind crystal clear pools. Some pools were warmed by shafts of sunlight. In others the water surges back and forth as waves roll in, then recede.

Later, while sailing to Virgin Gorda Sound, our cockpit discussions about the underwater community, navigation, and the sail's functions continued. After anchoring in the lee of Saba Rock, Dick and Dan swam with us to an island-bordering reef where they showed us the difference in the reef's outer edge and inshore side. We learned that fast-growing coral, like elkhorn and staghorn coral, grows on the outer edge. Great chunks of this coral are broken off as storm-driven waves crash onto the reef. They then continue to break up in the water's continuous motion and finally end up as sand particles scattered somewhere behind the reef, perhaps near slow-growing coral, such as brain and star coral, or the variety of soft coral that swung back and forth not far below us.

On another day we swam near Great Dog Island, looking at a very different type of coral community.

When Dick and Dan had to return to their teaching jobs, our emphasis reverted to above-the-water subjects. They included exploring the tourist shops in Charlotte Amalie, climbing from Cinnamon Bay across St. Johns and back, and visiting the historic Annaburg Sugar Mill. Interspersed was more sailing, not only on board *Windigo,* but also on the windsurfer. It took even the accomplished sailors some time to master these over-sized surfboards with a sail.

I know they took heart in the description of my first attempt at windsurfing only a month earlier. *Windigo* had been anchored off Red Hook having recently arrived in the Caribbean. The wind was steady, blowing twelve to fifteen knots—too strong for a beginner. But I felt it was time to learn about this new sport that was beginning to sweep across North America and Europe.

Rick was already an accomplished windsurfer and after a demonstration he sailed off on one board. I set out on the other, drifting slowly toward shore some 200 yards away. I'd stand on the board, just as Rick had done—so I thought—only to fall before lifting the sail up. This happened time after time. Occasionally I did get the sail upright, but only for seconds before falling once again.

My frustrations mounted steadily. Rick sailed over in an effort to help, but I wasn't receptive. Particularly to instructions that I thought I was following, that always led to my falling yet another time.

Well after Rick returned to *Windigo* I sailed back to her too. I was exhausted and still frustrated at not having conquered this basic little sailboat; yet I was elated at having sailed back instead of needing to paddle back. With more practice my windsurfing improved rapidly. Those students who also persisted began to get the hang of it too.

After a thirty-five-mile night sail Rick took a dinghy load to the underwater National Monument off Buck Island. Leaving the dinghy anchored they snorkeled, following the well-marked underwater trail—complete with underwater labels—through the colorful coral gardens. Many multicolored fish passed their face masks, some very close. Their attentions were attracted by different sights, and as invariably happens, the group began to separate. That is, until Rick found himself face to face with a big barracuda! All the students had lined up behind him. Slowly they backed away, deciding they had seen enough.

No matter how often Dan told us, we all found it hard to believe that barracudas will not attack a person—unless, of course, the fish is cornered, or it may strike something that glitters or shines, like a watch. Every time I saw a barracuda face to face in his environment, I had to keep repeating to myself that it was only curious and not hungry. I was never convinced as the fish lay motionless, suspended in the water. Its long narrow head appearing to be two-thirds mouth was always slightly open, showing two rows of razor-sharp teeth, the eyes watching me intently, its body poised to strike. None ever did though.

One day at the end of the project period the wind was blowing hard, a perfect day for action photographs. Rick climbed to the top of French Cap Cay, 150 feet above the wild seas, laden with cameras and film. We passed close to the offshore cay's rocky sides a dozen times, sailing hard on the wind with seas washing over the lee rail and spray flying over the windward rail. It was an exhilarating time for us.

With Rick back on board the crew relaxed for the ten-mile sail to our evening anchorage. They were tired, but happy—they knew they had done a good job tacking *Windigo* without Rick's supervision. What a difference two short weeks had made.

Enjoying this sail one student carefully worked his way forward on the slanting wet deck to the bow. Holding onto the headstay he faced forward, with the wind blowing in his face, his hair flying. He could have thought of himself as Columbus. The bow of a sailing vessel has given many a person this feeling; the noise of the water against the hull and wind blowing in the rigging has a magical way of removing one from the rest of the boat, transferring one into the past, or even into the future.

How well I know this feeling, having spent many hours on *Windigo's* bow, and how I remember lying there during a race on the Bras d'Or Lakes the prior summer. We were reaching at nearly nine knots with the spinnaker straining. Someone else was steering while I wandered the deck, checking the sails' trim. Then I moved forward to lie on the genoa folded in the bow. What a spot!

What a sight! As I looked up, the huge red and blue spinnaker spread high above me all the way to the masthead. Only the red wind pennant was above it, standing out straight in the wind. Looking aft, along the sloping deck, I could see parts of the other three sails, pulling like race horses, the sheets holding them ramrod tight. Four people stood by the coffee grinders amidships ready to trim the spinnaker when needed. I was supposed to tell them when to trim and how much, but I'd already over-trimmed the sails and had lost myself in my own thoughts. Thoughts about *Windigo*; her feeling of incredible power and grace and responsiveness to a light touch on the wheel. The gurgling, swishing noise of water curling into a foaming wave to leeward all but muted the other sounds. Combined it was a real thrill—what sailing is all about.

Off French Cap Cay the student's thoughts in the bow were short lived, for others quickly joined him. Hanging on they shouted with glee anticipating the next wave, their soaked bodies glistening in the afternoon sun. Delight was in their eyes as *Windigo* rose over wave after wave, sometimes crashing into one, sending spray flying. Occasionally *Windigo* buried her bow in a wave so that foaming water pulled at the students' legs before it pushed aft, down the sloping deck.

What better way is there than this to end a trip to the Caribbean? In the morning the students would all fly north to cold winter weather. They would take with them their tans, many memories, a better knowledge of coral's progression and of the many colored marine life that surrounds it, a developing skill in sailing, and, for many of them, a better understanding of themselves.

10 *Mum*

On a dark moonless night, with a multitude of stars out high above the French island of Guadeloupe, crickets chirped in the grass nearby. "No, Madam," the taxi driver said to his two female passengers, "I cannot change American money." At this point, an American voice was heard outside the taxi: "How much is the fare, I'll pay it." That's how I greeted my mother at the Hotel Arawak. She had arrived two days early to see some of Guadeloupe before joining *Windigo* for a week with friends.

I certainly had inherited from my mother her love of travelling, of seeing different people and far off places. Another similarity is our love of the sea, which she had grown up on—as had I. For both of us, this was our first trip to the Caribbean.

The eastern part of Guadeloupe is flat and dry, actually a separate island from the western part, which is mountainous, lush, and well cultivated. Fruits and vegetables grow big and juicy in this part, and are brought daily to the open air market in the center of Pointe-à-Pitre, the commercial center of the French islands. The market is a bustling four-block shopping place half of which is covered by a high, curved roof, open on all sides, with the other two blocks a square with fountains, a statue, and benches. The square is packed during market time with extra fruit and vegetable sellers. Markets on other islands also had a section for fish, poultry, and meat, but I stayed well away from these fly-infested stalls and strange cuts of meat. It was the fruit and vegetable sections we enjoyed, particularly this one in Pointe-à-Pitre.

The market women were delightful to us. The place hummed with the give-and-take banter of island housewives and women vendors—bargaining across tables stacked with fresh produce. Rick had the fruit and vegetable list, and when I got back with the wine, cheese, and meats I had bought elsewhere, I stood guard over the growing pile of fresh produce Rick had collected, while he went off for more. Each woman around me had perhaps six feet of table top on which she neatly stacked her own fruits and vegetables. On both sides of her were other women with their piles of fruits and vegetables, usually identical ones but sometimes with an added fruit or vegetable. If one woman was off for a moment her neighbor happily sold from her stand, handing over the money as soon as she was back. All worked cheerfully together.

Having grown up by the ocean, both Sandy and his mother have a great love of the sea. Together aboard Windigo, *they visited the Caribbean and the Sea of Cortez for the first time.*

Rick had a great time, with his few basic French words and a French-English dictionary in hand. He wasn't sure whether to "bargain" on price or not, nor was he sure what many of the vegetables even were. One slightly built market woman who didn't have what he wanted took him around to other vendors to find it. If she didn't like the product or the price she wouldn't let him buy it, but went on looking for something better. Another market lady, much larger and the proud owner of a straw hat at least four feet in diameter, was always smiling. Unlike most of the market women, who turned their backs on seeing a camera, or shook their fists and disappeared in the crowd, she enjoyed posing for pictures.

Guadeloupe itself is not a favorite island among yachtsmen, principally because it has no good, easy-to-reach harbors. The most frequently visited harbor is De-shayes, at the island's northern corner, protected from the winter trade winds and an ideal landfall or jumping-off spot for Antigua. Guadeloupe's capital Basse Terre, on the southwest corner, is on an open roadstead. Don Street's description of it as "open rolly, steep-to and the bottom littered with anchors, cables, and water-logged timber" kept me away.

On leaving Pointe-à-Pitre the light wind and calm seas were perfect for my older than usual, nearly all female crew. Running before a light easterly, from Marie Galantes to the tiny Isles des Saintes, my mother took her place on the coffee grinders for sail trimming. These conditions were also ideal for exploring the east side of the island, which would be unattainable with the relentless winter trade winds soon to come.

The sun was bright, the weather warm. What a joy for those who had just arrived from cold New England. Lightweight long pants and long-sleeved shirts kept us comfortable, with hats as protection from the intense sun. The sail's shadow on deck was welcome. No one wanted to spoil the trip with a sunburn.

Baie de Pontierre, a little bay on the easternmost shore of the Isles des Saintes group, looked delightful on the chart. Street's comments were less reassuring, mentioning "a rock with only four or five feet of water over it smack in the middle of the channel." Some people wonder if a rock is really there—they have entered without incident. Don reassures his readers that it is: he saw it clearly from a hilltop and, just to double check, circled the bay in an airplane.

Windigo approached the bold rock entrance slowly. Close to the channel's western side we all searched for the rock. The sun was overhead but not really behind us, so it was difficult to see the color variations in the water that show changes in depth, particularly rocks or coral heads. We entered without mishap and without seeing any rock, and anchored in twenty feet of water.

Baie de Pontierre is completely landlocked, giving great protection from the wind in all directions, and from the sea except for easterly swells that would surely bounce off or bend through the channel. A narrow white sand beach circles nearly half the harbor. We noticed a lean-to and a table with benches just back of the beach, under some palm trees, and a path winding up the slope behind the trees and disappearing over a ridge between two hills. Goats were grazing on the hillside.

In contrast, the outer half of the bay is solid rock, thrown vertically, to form a narrow wall sixty feet high and interrupted by broad cracks in several places. The bottom of the bay is pure white sand, with parts of its shallows covered by turtle grass and an occasional conch shell. Baie de Pontierre's colors were of the picture-postcard type that day, bright blue sky with shades of light blue-green water over a sand bottom, backed by a long, blindingly white beach with the soft browns of rock, dirt, and thirsty vegetation. What a beautiful spot. We had it all to ourselves to savor. A swim, lunch, and a short rest were followed by a walk ashore and swim back to *Windigo*.

The sun was high in the sky behind us as we left, but a light breeze rippled the water and our underwater visibility wasn't ideal. We neither hit nor saw the mysterious rock on the way out. Powering around the island we anchored off the delightful little town of Bourg des Saintes, on the opposite side of the ridge from where we had eaten lunch. The town's main street has several small squares with statues surrounded by well-kept flower beds. Two small old churches dominate the street. Children hurried by in small groups, smiling, laughing, and looking at us. Their schoolbooks were held together with a leather strap and slung over their shoulders.

Our mouths watered at the size of two crayfish being carried along the beach by their antennae. Each was as big as a good-sized lobster, at least eighteen inches long. I'd have purchased one or both if I could, but my French is limited to other words, and it wasn't until much later that we had a chance to try some. Four crayfish and a salad were more than enough for the ten of us. My comparison of them with the Maine lobster is that crayfish are not as rich and have a more delicate flavor. Most definitely one is better than the other; in Maine the lobster, in the Caribbean the crayfish.

Our sail south to Dominica was a fine one, wind was about fifteen knots on the beam with all sails set. My mother took her shift at the wheel and clearly enjoyed it. We covered the twenty miles in less than three hours. As we rounded the point into Prince Rupert Bay, off the town of Plymouth, boys in three small rowboats came out to meet *Windigo*, trying to outmaneuver each other to be first alongside. They were the local entrepreneurs, greeting us with "Hey skip, do you have a job? Do you want bread or some fruit? Do you want any laundry done?" My first concern was to anchor without them hanging on to *Windigo's* rail and their sturdy little boats getting swamped or gouging *Windigo's* topsides. I asked the boys please to stay clear until we were settled, and they did.

At anchor I sat on the rail chatting with them. It was English this time; Dominica was a British possession until its independence in the 1970s. The boys were well mannered, which impressed me. I had no jobs on board and we needed no food just then, so I asked them what there was to see ashore. There were ruins near town worth seeing, they suggested, or they would row people up the Indian River. Since Street's book had suggested a dinghy trip up this river, off went four of my crew in two of the boats. Stone breakwaters mark the river's mouth, and upstream the jungle trees overhang the stream making it cool and peaceful, with shafts of sunlight filtering down and wonderful varieties of birds singing against a background noise of water gurgling along the banks.

Meanwhile I had to find something for the third boy, Philip, so I got him to row me ashore and act as guide. Philip was about twelve years old, and as we walked along the beach he gave little notice to his friends playing there. First he took me to the Police Station to clear in with customs, then to several shops in search of bananas. For some reason we never discovered, there were none in town.

We then went in search of a friend of Philip's who owns a taxi. Just a block inland from the beach we walked along a soft sand road through the residential section of town, with small wooden planked homes squeezed together along both sides, palm trees giving shade. The very young played in the street naked. The old people sat on porches talking. I had no qualms about walking through their neighborhood, perhaps because I was with Philip. His friend wasn't home but his car was, and soon the friend as well. He agreed to take part of the crew overland to Roseau in the morning, on Dominica's southwest shore, while the rest of us made the trip on *Windigo*.

The overland party rejoined *Windigo* at the Anchorage Hotel, a mile south of Roseau. A stern anchor held *Windigo* off the rock shore while the bow was tied to a palm tree beside the Hotel's porch. Proprietor Carl Amour and his wife couldn't have been more hospitable. They also warned us about unrest in Roseau and advised not going there after dark or out of the main shopping area at any time. How different the atmosphere was here from what it had been twenty-five miles to the north.

In the morning we got underway for Martinique, next south in the island chain. *Tanra,* a small sloop from Salem, Massachusetts, had left earlier under full mainsail. She returned under power just as we were retrieving the anchor, shaken by the fierce cold-air squalls that oftentimes sweep down Dominica's mountain sides. A large yawl, which turned out to be the eighty-foot *Fantango*, now passed half a mile offshore under full sail. We watched a squall hit her, laying her on her side momentarily until her genoa blew out. She continued on under staysail and reefed main.

Leaving our well-protected anchorage I set only the number three genoa and mizzen until we cleared Dominica. At times the wind was so light we stood still in the water, while at other times we sped along with the dinghy planing in our wake. The wind was so strong sometimes that I bore off to run with it to reduce its force. I fully expected the wind to drop once we were clear of the land but it never did. It steadied at twenty-five or thirty knots, with the waves at least six feet high. The weather was nothing like just two days earlier on our pleasant sail to Dominica's northern end. The winter trade winds had arrived.

As we headed for the west coast of Martinique the wind and seas were abeam. *Windigo* enjoyed it all but the dinghy was having a wild ride, taking off down the face of a breaking wave, nearly catching up with us, well off to leeward with its tow line slack. When it finally lost the wave it would turn almost lazily until the tow line snapped tight, and then be jerked around to follow in our wake again.

The dinghy could never survive these antics for the twenty-five miles to Martinique. Somehow we had to get it on board, and we did. It wasn't as hard as I feared. We dropped the sails and ran off before the wind and seas, then pulled the dinghy alongside and fastened a line to its bow and stern. Using the mizzen staysail halyard attached to the middle of this line, we winched the dinghy up and swung it around under the mizzen boom, to rest on its chocks.

For the comfort and safety of the older members of the crew on board, we

Fishing nets hung to dry on Martinique. A hundred men and women worked these nets through the harbor, chanting.

also reefed the mizzen and set it with just the small jib and staysail. *Windigo* was still going as fast as she had with the genoa up, but now she was sailing upright with the much lower center of force. Her motion was comfortable and she wasn't straining as she had been. It's a lesson I relearn occasionally, nearly always surprised all over again by the results—you can reduce sail and still go very nearly as fast, but with far less strain on the boat and with a far easier helm.

We entered Martinique, a French island, via the harbor of Fort de France. Learning what is wanted by each customs office in each port is quite an experience. The requirements often differ in ports on the same island or even within one port, depending who is on duty.

Generally the officials want to see the "ship's papers" and a "crew list." If you have prepared one copy of the crew list in advance, it seems they always want two or three. If you have three copies they want only one. Sometimes you can use any blank piece of paper, at other times it has to be on their special form. Entering Fort de France I had had the ship's papers and three copies of the crew list, the most any of the islands required. After waiting half an hour while the customs officer tended to another boat I was bawled out for not having the crew's passports—"This is France, we do things right here!" On my second arrival some weeks later the same customs official greeted me with "Bonjour, *Windigo*."

We continued on now to Petite Anse d'Arlet, on Martinique's west coast. Street's mention of the bay's "ferry communications to Fort de France" came to mind early the next morning, when I was awakened from a sound sleep by a series of three blasts on a horn. It was still very dark, only 5:30 by my watch. The ferry must be coming in for an early morning run, I figured, taking the villagers to Fort de France for church and Sunday in the city. Out on deck it was pitch black—no moon, not even any stars. No light could be seen on shore and the outline of land was barely visible. Nor could I see any lights on the ferry coming in. I hoped they had picked us up on their radar, and I would have turned the spreader lights on so we wouldn't get run into, but the horn had stopped blowing. Returning to bed I assumed it had passed on the way to another village.

Half an hour later, with daylight just beginning to make its appearance, I heard talking on deck, English and French. A fisherman was alongside talking with one of the crew who had slept in the cockpit. It sounded like a pleasant conversation so I turned over. Moments later I heard the ferry's horn again so came up on deck; there was plenty of light for them to see us now, but I wanted to see the ferry and the bustle ashore that went along with its arrival and departure. Looking offshore my eyes finally found the source of the noise, a man standing in a dugout canoe blowing a conch shell. Four other canoes, each with one man in it, were fishing a hundred yards away from us. I moved aft to join in the conversation there only to realize neither speaker understood the other. The fisherman used Martinique French, pointing excitedly to the men fishing and then to shore where two lines of people led from the water's edge up the beach to the palm trees. Their gentle chant carried over the water to us in unison with their swaying back and forth. They were pulling on lines that extended out into the water toward the canoes, which I now saw were connected by lines of cork floats marking the edges of a big net being hauled in to shore. *Windigo* was anchored right in the middle of it all.

We got out of the way quickly and watched. Men and women of all ages, fifty or so in each line, pulled on the two lines from shore. A young boy carefully coiled the rope as it came in. Little energy was needed for getting the line in, just the simple slow rhythm of everyone leaning back against the net's resistance at the same time. People joined and left the lines seemingly at will. As the net neared shore the fishermen abandoned their canoes and waded in after the net, trying to keep the fish from getting free. I was surprised how few fish were caught with all this effort.

Ashore later, after breakfast, we walked through the village. The net was now hanging on tall poles stuck in the sand to dry. The dugout canoes were pulled up the beach on rollers, red and yellow trim bright in morning light. Some canoes had their masts upright and sails wrapped around them, others had big chicken-wire fish traps laid across the gunwales. What a picturesque sight it was, looking out from under the palm trees, with ancient wooden shacks, the dugouts pulled up on the beach, nets drying on their poles, and *Windigo* riding on the turquoise water.

Sitting beside me in the main cabin at anchor in Anse d'Arlet, just after lunch, my mother turned to me and asked if I remembered her comment when I bought *Windigo* and told her my plans. I sure did—she had told me in no uncertain terms not to take any "old people," for they are certain to have back problems, stomach problems, and other ailments, and wouldn't be able to get about the boat or help out.

And here she was enjoying every minute of it. She had toured the island in a taxi and talked with people she met. The sailing had been beautiful. She had never felt better, and next winter she rejoined *Windigo* in the San Blas Islands and for the passage through the Panama Canal, and again the following year in the Sea of Cortez and Baja California.

The author's mother and her friends did not flinch at the work required to sheet in the jib on the coffee grinders.

11 *Climbing*

With sheets eased we sailed north from the island of St. Vincent across miles of trade-wind-swept ocean toward St. Lucia, under reefed main and number three genoa. We were in the Windward Islands now, well south of Martinique. Spray flew across the foredeck, keeping it constantly wet but barely reaching us in the cockpit. Anyone who did get wet dried off in minutes in the warm air. The helmsmen rotated punctually, on the hour. The relieving helmsman's eye was casually glued to the cockpit clock, not wanting to miss a moment of his turn at the wheel, while the present helmsman savored the last seconds of his time.

The seas were big but far enough apart so that *Windigo* fit easily between them, not burying her bow or falling off the tops. In the lee of St. Lucia, the wind gradually died. The seas turned into long easy swells and finally disappeared. Changing to a larger genoa would have let us sail quietly in to our anchorage, but with the exhilarating sail we'd just finished we didn't care about a tame one. So as our attention turned to our destination—St. Lucia's Anse des Pitons—we motored in.

Some say Anse des Pitons is the most spectacular anchorage in all the Lesser Antilles. Petit Piton rises straight up from the Caribbean to 2,560 feet, and to its right Gros Piton rises about sixty more. Between the two peaks is a slightly indented bay. In its northeast corner, at the base of Petit Piton, is a sandy beach, our anchorage for the night.

Anchoring in Anse des Pitons is unique. The bow ends up tied to one or two coconut trees about thirty feet from the beach, with the boat held off the beach by a stern anchor in seventy or eighty feet of water. Getting *Windigo* into this position often took more than one try, because I wasn't used to judging when to drop the anchor overboard beside the shrouds in order for it to be correctly positioned astern, once we had moved close enough to shore for the bow line. We'd get the line ashore to its tree by swimming, or else in the dinghy, which was more practical but not nearly as much fun.

Ashore under the trees at Anse des Pitons are some interesting ruins of old plantation buildings, intermingled with an active coconut-cocoa plantation. We saw piles of coconut husks piled around sharp-topped stakes driven into the ground. Men held a coconut in both hands and struck it down on a stick to open

Jim Madden at the helm.

it, then pried the nuts from the cracked husks. The nuts would go by boat to Castries, on St. Lucia, to be made into the various coconut products we buy in supermarkets.

Inland, walking along a path under the trees and following the shore, we saw that underbrush had reclaimed parts of the path and the pastures. Men with machetes hacked away at the brush to clear it and burned the cuttings nearby in small fires. Cows grazed in the areas already cleared. Beginning to climb, the path wound past two houses with small children playing in front, who stopped their games to stare at us.

We headed on, and found the trail to the top of Gros Piton. Five of us started up, but before long only Rick and I kept going. At first there really was a visible trail, winding steeply through thick prickly brush that grew high over our heads. The slope started out steep and got even steeper. Somewhere we lost the trail, turning off onto a rain runoff, or washway. The dirt was loose, the rocks were loose and crumbly, the footing was awful. It was so bad and the slope so steep that we really climbed on all fours, with each hand pulling at the base of a bush, testing to see if it would break or pull out when we put weight on it. Then the feet moved up, searching for a hold that would support some weight too. It was hot, hard work, but the anticipation of the view from the top kept us going. What a sight it would be, Petit Piton with *Windigo* lying at its base.

After two hours of struggling we reached the top. The vegetation had changed dramatically—we were in a rain forest now. Huge mahogany trees towered over us, growing up somehow through tremendous boulders covered with slippery moss, with gaping holes between them. The trees were so big and thick with foliage that sunlight could hardly penetrate below to Rick and me. The temperature dropped substantially and I began to shiver. It was hard finding a tree with branches low enough to climb, but finally we did, and worked our way far enough out a limb to get the view we were seeking. Far down through the leaves there was *Windigo*, lying at the base of Petit Piton. It was quite a struggle, but what a sight.

The trip down was sometimes even harder than the climb up. We went straight down, wondering several times if we had stumbled on the path we had lost coming up. But always in a short distance it would disappear again. In a little under two hours we reached the point where the path had begun. We were hot, tired, and very thirsty. Back on *Windigo* the ensuing swim was perhaps the most welcome one I have ever had. As I floated in the deliciously refreshing water the dust and dried sweat finally soaked off with the aid of a good lather of Joy and a scrub brush. Two cool beers later I began to recuperate.

The Pitons, as is most of the Antilles, are the projecting remnants of an ancient mountain range that was once a nearly continuous bridge between North and South America. Many Lesser Antilles islands owe their origins to volcanic activity, and some of it is still going on.

We had seen evidence of it in the small museum in Martinique's St. Pierre, with its relics of the disastrous eruption of Mont Pelée in May 1902. St. Pierre had been the most important city on the island, in fact in the whole Lesser Antilles, until the eruption. The entire city was covered with ash and lava. Ships at anchor nearby were wrecked. More than thirty thousand people died. There was only one survivor, a prisoner being held in the depths of a jail.

Mt. Soufrier, on St. Vincent's northern end, is a lightly sleeping volcano that Rick and I climbed on another day. It also had erupted in 1902, killing thousands. Only three years before we were there it started rumbling again, but this time nothing happened beyond a volcanic cone being pushed up in the center of its crater.

A jeep took us the five miles through banana plantations from the sleepy town of Georgetown, on the island's east coast, to a trail where we started our climb. This trail wound its way gradually upward; finally the banana trees were replaced by a lush forest that covers the foothills. How different this was from our climb up Gros Piton only a few weeks earlier. This trail was well worn and easy to follow. Once we were above the forest the sun baked down of us as it did on Gros Piton, but now the strong trade winds kept us cool.

The view out on the foothills was fantastic; banana and coconut plantations dotted the green hillside while the windswept ocean reached out beyond. Along the shore a ribbon of white breaking waves rolled along the beach—a black beach, created from pulverized lava that makes up this part of the island.

The trail now turned into hard dry sunbaked dirt dotted with sharp-edged rocks. Looking upward I could see it crossing ridges, following rises and disappearing behind outcrops. A dozen barefoot children passed us, descending the mountain. They bounded down the trail without concern for their feet. Our self-appointed guide, a young lad from Georgetown, was also barefoot. I couldn't believe their toughness; my own sneakers were being cut to ribbons on these same rocks.

At the mountain top we found ourselves on a narrow crater rim more than three thousand feet above sea level and in extreme contrast to the huge mahogany trees on Gros Piton. Here the only life able to survive was a hardy lichen that gave the sandstone-colored earth a green tinge.

The crater's sides are practically perpendicular, dropping some fifteen hundred feet to a lake. In the center of it is a volcanic cone that formed in 1971 and

The volcanic eruption of Mt. Soufrier, on St. Vincent's northern end, caused an evacuation of 20,000 people in 1979, not long after Windigo's *visit.*

is still billowing white steam. Curiosity about the water's temperature led us to inch our way down to the lake, much to the anxiety of our guide. Incredibly, the water was cool, despite the heat being given off by the cone.

Back on the rim we ate lunch in the lee of a small concrete building. We learned later that the seismographic equipment in this building warned of an impending eruption in time for twenty thousand people to be evacuated before Mt. Soufrier tossed millions of tons of dust sixty thousand feet in the sky in 1979—on Good Friday.

We descended the mountain's western side, quickly disappearing into thick woods so characteristic of the Caribbean islands that are mountainous. These high, warm land masses reach skyward, blocking the moisture-laden trade winds, causing clouds to form, which often drop torrential showers, particularly on the island's western slopes, creating very fertile soil. This is in vivid contrast to the low islands, which are very dry with very bad soil so typical of the Grenadines, just to the south of St. Vincent and where we were headed.

On reaching the first town along the coast, we went straight to the nearest store for two quick beers. We were parched. Drinking our third beer more slowly, we inquired as to how best to get back to *Windigo*, anchored off the island's southern end. The buses, we learned, only leave before sunrise, just in time to get the farmers and their produce to Kingston for the market. Mr. Findley, we were told, might drive us there. When we found him at his home he was repairing a flat tire on his old yellow Vauxhall. In five minutes he was ready to go.

Every joint in the old car groaned as we bounced over the narrow pot-holed road that twists in hair-pin turns along the coast. We were back aboard *Windigo* in under two hours.

12 *The Grenadines*

The Grenadines comprise a string of small islands stretching fifty miles southward from St. Vincent to Grenada. They are a varied lot, ranging in size and topography from little Palm Island and Petit St. Vincent (P.S.V.), which are low and flat, to the much larger Carriacou and to Union Island, close by, which rises to more than five hundred feet. Good anchorages can be found on many of the islands and passages between them can be short or long, depending on your mood. You can make two or three stops each day, or take longer sails in the constant trade winds.

The islands stretch in a north-northeast/south-southwest direction so you'll have delightful close-hauled or broad-reaching sails in the winter easterly trades. This is in marked contrast with the Virgin Islands, where you'll generally be beating or running in these same winds. The Grenadines have vast areas of shallows, also unlike the Virgin Islands. The shallows are sometimes covered by coral and the rest are primarily sand banks, ranging from only a few feet under water to thirty feet. It is unnerving, at first, to sail over the higher banks at eight knots and watch the bottom rush by. Once you're used to it, it's quite a thrill.

Flying to the Grenadines seems almost as difficult as getting there by boat. Flights from New York land in Barbados, where you must spend a night before catching the unreliable LIAT plane to Grenada or St. Vincent. When we were there the LIAT operated just like any other small airline, with a considerable amount of flexibility. That is, lightly filled flights were often delayed until filled. I also kept hearing rumors that half the flights were going to be discontinued, or perhaps even all of them. I always took a good book along when meeting these flights. Actually everyone I expected to arrive in St. Vincent did arrive. But only one out of the many flights I met arrived on time, and some baggage for that flight didn't come until the next day.

St. Vincent's airport is unique, as are many of the landing strips in the Caribbean. Planes come in low over the water, across the trade winds, landing at the beach's edge. Upon touchdown full breaking power is applied. The planes shudder as they roll up the sloping runway and stop just short of the steep-sided mountain. Before a plane lands cows must be chased off the runway, which has the greenest grass on the island, and barricades and red lights must stop traffic on the main road, which runs right across the middle of the runway.

I've decided that a one-week vacation in the Grenadines really isn't enough. Ten days to two weeks will let you have two days to unwind from the flight down and from getting away in the first place. At the end of the trip, you need another two days to pull yourself together for the flight back to reality.

The second morning my brother was on board, he helped with the heavy work of getting *Windigo* underway—raising the anchor, stowing it, and setting the sails while I steered. Trying to make amends as he came aft I asked if he would like to take the wheel. His face fell as he asked "Do I have to?" He had been so busy at home that he hadn't read a book in a long time and now he wanted just to sit, relax, and read. He did, but I don't think he even finished the book during our trip. Once the unwinding begins, people are happy simply to sit and absorb the surroundings, suspended in Nirvana.

Another day, when we anchored in Charlestown Bay on Canouan Island, south from St. Vincent, someone noticed a small cargo boat being built under the trees alongshore. Four old salts in *Windigo's* crew discussed for fifteen full minutes whether to go ashore to see it or not. Finally they decided to wait until the morning because they were too relaxed just now. I reminded them that I like to get underway in the morning, stopping by mid-afternoon for a walk or exploration ashore before getting set for the night. The salts went in that afternoon after all, and had a fine time inspecting the vessel and talking with the men building it.

A few days later we were sailing north, planning on lunch and a swim in Friendship Bay on the southeast side of Bequia Island, still closer to St. Vincent, when we came across something else to watch ashore. Weather was classic Grenadines: a perfect twenty-five-knot sailing breeze for reefed main and the number three genoa, clear blue sky, temperature about 80. As we passed east of Petit Nevis one of the bird watchers, glasses to his eyes as always, noticed people on Petit Nevis. I was surprised; the island is uninhabited. We got closer. It was certainly people, lots of them. Smoke rose from behind the southwest tip of the island. The Bequians must be having a Sunday outing. Changing course, we swung around Petit Nevis for a closer look and then realized what kind of outing it was. Pulled up on the beach were two whales. Men with long knives were cutting off great chunks of meat. Other men were cutting long strips of blubber. Still under sail, we gradually passed by. It was time for a decision: do we stop and watch or go on to Friendship Bay for the anticipated swim and quiet lunch? We turned back. Leaving me adrift with *Windigo*, the rest rowed ashore with cameras and plenty of film. What a sight.

The day before, they learned, whales had been spotted from the whale watch high up on Bequia. Word passed quickly to the men who man the eighteen-foot, six-oared whaleboats. Once at sea the whaleboats were directed to the whales by mirror signals from the watch station. The two humpback whales were harpooned by that evening. They sank while being towed to Petit Nevis, fortunately in water shallow enough that divers could go down to insert an air hose in each one. Pumps inflated the whales till they rose to the surface again, to finish the tow to Petit Nevis for cutting.

When we arrived, one whale had pretty much disappeared. First it had been dragged half out of water up on a concrete skid by a great manual winch. Men knee-deep in bloody water cut off meat and tossed it up on the bank. At the same time the long strips of blubber were taken to huge iron kettles hanging over wood fires. It was a busy scene, with gangs of people working, many more watching, and kids playing nearby. There was food and coffee for all, and whale meat cut up into smaller chunks and divided among the Bequians. Some people were eating it right away, raw. It's not bad—I'm told.

Save the Whale followers need not turn their attention to the Bequia whalemen. The two whales we saw being butchered were the first they had caught in almost two years. They do it in the old way, harpoons thrown from rowed whaleboats, and only go after whales seen to windward of Bequia because they cannot tow a whale against the wind, seas, and current back to the island. The Bequians use all the meat, blubber, bones, baleen, and every other bit of the animal. Nothing is thrown away or left behind, except for a horrendous stench on this small island.

On *Windigo* we visited quite a few other spots in the Grenadines. One is the Tobago Cays. They're a group of four small, low islands protected by World's End and Horseshoe reefs, well south of Bequia and Petit Nevis. They are uninhabited and ringed with beaches and deep-water channels that wind through pastel shallows, studded with coral heads—another area for eyeball navigation. We anchored off the cut between two of the islands and got ashore by swimming, in the dinghy, or on the windsurfer. The wind and current funneling through the cut gave us some exciting windsurfing, often to the entertainment of the charter boats that visit the Cays. One day Rick and I sailed the windsurfers the several miles to Petite Tobago. We had to dismantle them and paddle across a reef over and back.

For the cruising crowd two other popular Grenadine anchorages are Petit St. Vincent (P.S.V.) and Palm Island, the low-lying islands south of Tobago Cays. P.S.V. is an attractive island with a fair anchorage and excellent sandy beaches. A swell hotel sprawls over its southeastern portion. Palm Island is also beautiful and has a modest resort on it.

I much preferred Clifton Harbor on Union Island, west of Palm, to these two. Anchoring in the lee of its coral reef put us within easy swimming distance, with the choice of an easy swim along the inside of the reef, or a more energetic

A small fishing boat off St. Vincent, with precariously low freeboard, used coconut shells as bailers.

swim along its deeper outer side. If you take care and if the seas aren't too big, you can swim back through the reef without getting cut to ribbons on it.

One day we watched local fisherman sail right through a very small channel in the coral. I climbed to *Windigo's* spreaders and watched one boat come in this way. The wind was around twenty knots. The tiny boat had three men aboard under shortened sail. From my vantage point the deep water stood out clearly, but I wondered what they could see from right there. Bearing away to enter the channel they let the main way out. They didn't bother loosening the hand-kerchief-sized jib. In the middle of the reef the channel bends, requiring them to jibe. Over came the main, the boom nearly wiping out the two crewmen. The sail filled on the new side with such force that with the weight of the boom and the men the boat very nearly rolled over. Water did pour in over the lee rail, but the men hurriedly shifted themselves to windward and got to work with coconut shell bailers. They jibed again before heading for the beach, and made it safely.

Canouan Island, one of the largest in the Grenadines, lies north of Union Island and the Tobago Cays. It is little populated, although during the 1890s many New Bedford whalers anchored in its lee. The island's west coast has a delightful tiny stopping place named Corbay Cove. Don Street gives it room for two boats, although they certainly cannot be *Windigo's* size. Our plans to anchor there changed abruptly one noontime, because the sixty-foot sloop *Glover* was already there.

One other day when heading for this cove we left Mustique Island with a crew of good sailors on board. The wind was great for a morning spinnaker run to the lee side of Canouan. I was on the foredeck directing the spinnaker set.

Windigo's spinnakers are not set flying. Neither are they stopped with thread or rubber bands to hold the sail together until it is up and ready to be "broken out." Instead, *Windigo's* spinnakers use zippers to accomplish the same thing. The two sides of a light zipper are sewn down the center of the sail, about twenty inches apart. The sail is bunched in this space and the zipper makes a sleeve to enclose the sail completely. When the sail is hoisted like a snake and everything is ready, the bottom of the zipper is pulled apart. The zipper teeth open up, just as so many zippers do unintentionally on jackets and pants, and the spinnaker fills.

On this day the spinnaker was hoisted to the masthead. The pole was set and the sail pulled out to its end. People stood by on the sheet and guy ready to trim them when the sail filled. As I pulled the zipper apart at the sail's bottom, its head began to twist around the headstay as we rolled in the swells. The more the bottom of the sail filled, the tighter the top of the sail wrapped around the stay. The combined racing experience represented on board at that time added up to a great many years, but no matter what trick, idea, or theory was tried, we could not get the sail unwrapped. The twists were overlapping on a spiral going up, not down; it had to be unwrapped from the top.

Working aloft wasn't that bad, but every now and then I had to stop work and hang on with both hands as a wave passed under us from an unexpected direction, rolling *Windigo* and swinging the masthead—and me—back and forth in a wide arc. I couldn't get the sail cloth loose even from up there; it was jammed too tightly. I gave up and tied a stout line around it all until we could tackle it again at anchor, and cut it off if we had to. I was mad and frustrated at myself for getting us into this ridiculous situation and went below to cool off.

Two loud reports brought me on deck instantly. The first was the spinnaker pulling off and out from the headstay all by itself. The second bang was the breaking of the stout line that I had tied things up with. Only two wraps still held the spinnaker to the headstay, and we undid these carefully and lowered the sail. Amazingly, the only damage was a few small tears near the top. Very much relieved, we had a delightful lunch in Corbay Cove.

South of Canouan is Mayero Island, with perhaps my favorite anchorage in all the Grenadines. The southeastern side has a big beach protected by a reef that is easy to sail in behind. We nosed *Windigo* in close to a steep-to sand bank to drop the anchor in shallow water, drifting back to lie in thirty-five feet. We had a peaceful lunch there one afternoon.

But my favorite anchorage is the one on Mayero's northwest side: Salt Whistle Bay. It is protected by reefs and is very shallow. For *Windigo*, it is suitable only when no swell is running, as we found out one night when we had to put a stern anchor out to keep the glasses from sliding off the table. A lovely sand beach curves around the head of the bay, which is backed by tall, carefully tended coconut trees. An extensive off-lying reef creates sheltered pools along another deserted long beach on its eastern edge.

In our explorations ashore we found two contented-looking donkeys standing under the coconut trees, near a path leading back through them. Following it we came to a muddy pool, a spring. The path continued on up the hillside, twisting around crumbling rocks sticking out of the hard auburn-colored dirt. On top of the hill, overlooking Saline Bay, live the inhabitants of Mayero Island. The island's school teacher has thirty-three students age five to thirteen; after that they go on to school in St. Vincent. He talked about some of his troubles: money, supplies, and books being the major ones.

When Columbus first sailed into the Caribbean the tough, warlike Carib Indians inhabited some of the islands. As Europeans settled here they needed laborers to work the cotton and sugar fields, so many a ship brought slaves here from Africa because the Carib Indians were too fierce to be made to do the work. When the African slaves here were finally freed in 1838, most plantation/slave owners gave each of their slaves one acre of land. But one person owned all of Mayero, and instead he agreed to provide for the slaves' needs in return for two thirds of what they grew. This worked well only for a while, and until just a few years ago the descendents of the slaves still on Mayero were living at a bare subsistence level.

What turned this trend around I don't know for certain, but I suspect it had a lot to do with the school teacher and priest. Life on Mayero Island isn't good now but the trend is upward. The church had raised money to build a larger water catchment, for water is the island's major problem. The only fresh water they have is whatever rain that can be caught, and the brackish-muddy spring water we passed near Salt Whistle Bay. During the few rainy months this spring becomes almost clear. It was now the long dry season and the spring was far from being clear. Only the donkeys drank from it, between loads of water they carried on their backs to the church for making cement, to build the catchment walls with. These same animals also carried fresh water and food supplies that were brought over from Union Island in small local fishing sailboats.

Since the 1838 agreement was based on what they grow the islanders can keep all the fish they catch. The men go off fishing from dawn to dusk. We bought some of their delicious crayfish. We also left a pile of magazines with the teacher. That was such a simple thing to us, but the magazines were highly cherished by the island children, who are eager to learn about other places.

One young Mayero boy named Thomas, aged about eight, met us on Salt Whistle Bay's beach one day when we swam ashore. He was delightful, wanting to show us all the things he could about his island. Later, when Rick was wind-

The Grenadine fishermen go off from dawn to dusk, catching crayfish.

surfing, Thomas slipped out of his pants and swam, like a fish, out from shore to watch this strange sailing craft. Rick hoisted him onboard the windsurfer, sitting him ahead of the mast. They sailed all around Salt Whistle Bay, Thomas hanging on with both hands, a great grin on his charming black face. Surely he was the first person from Mayero to try out a windsurfer.

Southernmost of the Grenadines is Grenada, with St. George's its main harbor and, for years, the yachting center for the lower Caribbean. The town is small, overlooking the cruise ships anchored off of it. The harbor itself is crowded, so once the affairs in town are dealt with I like to move to the quieter Prickly Bay on the island's south coast. For solitude, however, none beats Port Egmont, a little farther east near the head of this long narrow bay. A one-hundred-fifty-foot-wide passage suddenly opens between a mangrove peninsula and a steep rocky hillside. On my first visit here we proceeded through this cut very slowly, carefully watching both shores for hazards and not expecting to see, as we were startled to, two natives making love under the mangroves.

The Grenadines are a delightful place to lose yourself from the hectic life the rest of the world leads. The sailing in trade winds is exhilarating, swimming in the tepid water invigorating or colorful, especially if watching the myriad colored fish and coral, and the pace of life is relaxed and enjoyable.

13 *Frontiers for Cruising*

In 1960 there were about eleven crewed charter boats in the Caribbean, and no bareboats. Twenty years later more than a hundred crewed charter boats sail out of the U.S. Virgin Islands, and several hundred bareboats. The scene in the Windward and Leeward Islands has changed drastically. In the old days you probably wouldn't see another yacht all day and certainly there wouldn't be one anchored in the same harbor with you at night. Those who recall this type of cruising in the Caribbean have recently been seeking new areas to cruise in— areas in which the amenities now found throughout the Lesser Antilles have not arrived. Where fresh water can be scarce, if available at all. Where fuel is brought to the dock in drums, which were used for lord knows what the day before. Where food is available in varying degrees of quantity, but don't plan on a balanced diet. Where service for repairs, laundry, showers, and you-name-it hardly exists.

Three areas in the Caribbean are filling these requirements for cruising frontiers: the north coast of Venezuela, The Bay of Islands off Honduras, and near them, in the westernmost part of the Caribbean, the one-hundred-fifty-mile-long barrier reef in Belize. These areas are a long way from anywhere and can be difficult to reach and return from, but they have their own charm and are steeped in history. Columbus sailed along Venezuela's coast and north all through the Bay of Islands. Henry Morgan was only one of many buccaneers who used the Bay of Islands as a base, and many of the inhabitants there today trace their ancestors to his times.

On *Windigo's* passage from Grenada to Panama I scheduled one week to island-hop in one of these areas, the four hundred fifty-odd miles from Grenada to Curaçao. Curaçao is almost the last in the final swing that the Lesser Antilles take westward after the Grenadines. There we would resupply with food, fuel, and fresh water before making the six-hundred-fifty-mile passage to Panama. New crew would join us in two weeks, so there wasn't time to see as much of Venezuela's north coast as I'd have liked. There would be no stopping in Colombia en route to Panama; my insurance underwriters simply would not cover any part of *Windigo's* operation in Colombian waters. Bizarre stories of anything from prolonged delays to murder were told by sailors who had passed through that country. The consensus of opinion was—stay away.

On departing Grenada before dawn the main and genoa were set wing and wing. *Windigo's* rhumb line course to Los Testigos, a group of tiny islands ninety miles south of Grenada, was 255 degrees. By sailing 245 degrees, south of the rhumb line, I hoped the ten-degree difference would be adequate compensation for the current's strong westerly set. The day was unusual, with a heavy overcast. The wind was moderate, the seas calm. It was good to be underway again, away from the hustle of last-minute details and the never-ending list of jobs that could be done.

My calculations indicated that Los Testigos should appear on the horizon at 1500 hours just off the starboard bow. Two minutes before the hour *Windigo's* cheerful cook Rae, who was steering, quietly announced "There it is." The top of an island could just be seen on the hazy horizon. The island was in sight, but it seemed to take ages for us to reach it.

We finally had to motorsail in between the islands, using a tracing of the island group I'd made in Grenada from another boat's chart, since a chart was unobtainable. The last of the sun's yellow rays shimmered across the water as the anchor went down. Relaxing in the cockpit we enjoyed the fading red clouds that stretched across the Caribbean.

In the morning we went our separate ways, exploring a small island connected to Los Testigos by only a sand spit that waves were washing across. Rae and I found a goat path which we followed around the island. From a hillside overlooking the sand spit we watched the water in turmoil, continuously changing color, relentlessly furrowing out channels in the sand while filling in others. Breaking waves just two feet high couldn't seem to get across the spit fast enough and into deep water again.

On the windward side of the little island, we faced the full force of the trade winds. It was chilling. The water was wild here, deep dark green in color with whitecaps all over, and big seas crashing on the rocks below us, flinging white spume high up to be blown still farther up the hillside. Blow holes in the rocks sent water skyward with resounding whooshes.

The rocks up near us were full of cracks, holes, and crevices that we had to watch out for. Curiously peering over one nearly circular hole I was far more startled than the prehistoric lizard I saw stretched out sunning itself, well protected from the wind. The creature was about fifteen inches long and took off away from us, running on opposite legs, belly to the ground.

On the north side the goat path ended. We continued on, despite progress getting harder in the thickening thorny brush, and emerged on a small beach surrounding a cove. Clear turquoise water, a refreshing swim, and a nap on the hot sand made the chilling windward side of the island seem far away.

The trade winds pushed us along as we left Los Testigos, wing and wing again. Isla Orchila, next in the Antilles chain after Isla de Margarita, appeared through the haze by dawn. The deep water very close to its south coast made it a far safer landfall than Islas Los Roques, our next stop, twelve miles to the west.

Islas Los Roques is a group of sixty low sand cays surrounded by coral reefs and sand banks that spread over three hundred square miles. In rising seas we rounded El Gran Roque, a big hill on its northeast corner, and entered the maze of uncharted channels that wind through these sheltered waters, dotted with tiny low islands and charming anchorages. Most of the islands are no more than ten feet high and are made up of sharp coral nobbins. A low green sea grass covers many of them like a mat. Pockets of mangroves and palm trees struggle for survival. Coral rings the islands' windward sides, while sandy beaches abound along the leeward sides.

Pelicans were everywhere. I was fascinated by these big, seemingly ungainly birds. Particularly with their diving. The slow beat of their very large wings lifted them off the water to circle overhead, motionless—waiting to select their prey swimming below. When they find it they roll into a dive, wings still extended, and hit the water at a perfect angle. The pelican doesn't submerge when it dives, unlike most fishing birds; its body somehow just does a 180-degree turn when it hits the water and almost instantly the pelican is floating calmly on the surface, head up, bill extended to swallow the catch.

We had a fine time the next afternoon in the whaler, meandering through the mangrove-bordered waterways of Aves de Barlovarto, a day's sail west of Los Roques. We saw birds everywhere—brown boobies, zillions of them. A continuous cloud of them rose from the bushes ahead of us and circled overhead until the danger passed by. The young boobies, about a month old, stayed sitting in the trees, snow white bodies against the lush green leaves and bright blue of the sky. We found nests, built into the intertwining bleached branches with little furry heads peeking over their edges. Fascinating though the whole sight was, the smell was awful.

On the way back toward *Windigo*, I thought there was sufficient water for the whaler to take a shortcut over coral. The whaler's bottom cleared but the propeller struck several times before the engine stalled and the shear pin broke. We paddled back to *Windigo* for repairs. An extra shear pin and spare spark plugs are the only spare outboard parts on board, and it wasn't long before the motor was functioning again. I hadn't known what a shear pin was until a few months before, when I helped someone replace the shear pin in his outboard. But I did seem to have problems with propellers in this place, because getting underway in the morning the dinghy's painter wrapped itself tightly around *Windigo's* propeller. Over went the anchor to keep us from drifting onto a reef, and over I went with a knife. The painter was now eighteen inches shorter.

Willemstad, Curaçao, was now just seventy miles away. I wanted to reach there before dark for there was no chart of the harbor on board; having detailed charts of every harbor we might explore would be prohibitively expensive, and logistically not sensible. I knew the harbor was deep because big tankers use it, but that is little consolation when you don't know where you're going or what lights you are seeing. I also knew there was a pontoon bridge across the entrance and had no idea how that worked. It would be so much easier on my nervous system if we entered during daylight. We motorsailed much of the day with the easterlies behind us, and followed two small freighters in just as the sun went down.

The red-orange tiled roofs and white-walled buildings clustered on each side of the Willemstad entrance were a colorful scene in the last of the evening light. *Windigo* was directed to the east side of the channel, tying to the dike across the street from the customs office.

What a contrast, this island to the other Caribbean islands. Here efficiency is a way of life. Everything is clean and orderly, and the city has the feel of progress. Oil refining is the mainstay of the economy. Huge tankers laden with Venezuelan oil passed slowly by our berth. Each morning a short narrow quay, just astern of where we were berthed, was lined with small Venezuelan craft. Some used only sails, but most were also diesel powered. They were piled high with fresh produce brought over from the mainland the night before and sold right off the boats, in the shade of awnings made from sugar sacks and flour bags.

The sail from Grenada to Curaçao had taken us one week. If I were to do it again I would double that time, because there is so much worth seeing. For those not continuing west to Panama the trip back to Grenada can be difficult; the recommended route is eastward along the coast itself, south of the islands. In close to shore there's a favorable westerly current where the contrary wind generally calms down during the night. The Venezuelan government has built several big new marinas and is encouraging yachts to visit their country. The atmosphere is now favorable to make Venezuela and its islands an interesting cruising area, but only for those who want to get away from people and all the amenities that people provide. During the whole week from Grenada to Curaçao we didn't see another yacht, and only a few fishermen on Los Testigos and around El Gran Roque.

We left Curaçao with lockers bulging with fresh food, water and fuel tanks topped off, and spare fresh water bladders filled and securely tied on deck. Our destination was Panama, six hundred sixty miles away. The mainsail was held out by a preventor against a jibe, and the small genoa held to windward by the spinnaker pole carrying us nicely before the trade winds. *Windigo's* speed through the water was about eight knots, and with another knot or so of current we were making good time.

Rounding the northern tip of Colombia, well off the coast, we sailed nearly parallel with it. This is the area that makes these waters notorious for boats sailing eastward from Panama. An experienced captain told me he had never had such a rough trip in all his years at sea as the time he took a one hundred twenty-five-foot motor yacht from Panama to Curaçao. The northeast trades build big long seas, helped along by the current. Along Colombia's coast the trades continue to blow but now the waves get backed up by a counter-current that turns seas into breaking, boat-wrecking waves. One night on our passage we dropped all sails because the winds and short, steep seas made steering extremely hard at high speed. Even running under bare poles we were still going nearly six knots. We set the small jib at dawn and it was all the sail we needed until midday, when wind and seas subsided. Our landfall was on a dark coast the following night, pinpointed by Loran fixes and depth sounder readings. We hove to five miles offshore until daylight, when we entered Porvenir, in the San Blas Islands, for a week's stay before proceeding through the Panama Canal and on to the northwest.

It was on the return from Alaskan waters three years later that I took *Windigo* several hundred miles north from the Canal to explore the next areas of frontier cruising: the Bay Islands and the waters off Belize, also known as British Honduras, in the westernmost of the Caribbean waters.

Before sailing for the Islas de la Bahia—Bay Islands—we spent several days anchored in the flats off Cristobal, at the Canal, preparing for the passage. The main topic of conversation at the Yacht Club was an exchange of current customs requirements and fees at the islands along the route. This interchange of experiences is a way of life for the wandering sailor, because any guidebook with this information is out of date before it goes to press. I had wanted to stop at Isla de San Andrés, among the first islands off the Nicaraguan coast, but boats that had just come from there were charged high entrance fees and a fee for harbor lights—which didn't work, and buoys—most of which were missing.

Instead we headed for Isla de Providencia, fifty miles north of San Andrés and two hundred fifty miles northwest of the Panama Canal. It took us a little over thirty hours to get there, and closing with the south end of the island we felt our way in among the extending unmarked shallows, then followed the shore in about twelve feet of water to Catalina Harbor. Halfway along the shore a man paddled out to intercept us, demanding that he pilot us in. I politely refused. Quickly outdistancing him, even with our cautious speed, we left him cursing and shaking his fists in the air.

Baby brown boobies stand in the foreground on the tiny sand island of Cayos Cajones, where the chief structure is this lobster-freezing plant.

On rounding the outer corner of Catalina Harbor, with another mile of shallow water still to go, I was ready to accept the assistance of another pilot. This one came alongside in an outboard-driven aluminum rowboat. His dress was no more official than that of the man we had left waving his fists, but his attitude was significantly different. Besides, I was tired. We had been picking our way along with only two to five feet under the keel for over two hours. The light had been poor to begin with but now the sun was getting low and the light was really bad. The pilot guided us right into the cove off the town, which showed one and a half fathoms (nine feet) on the chart. He assured me he had taken an eleven-foot-draft boat right up to the pier. I was skeptical but tried not to show it. The depth sounder dropped to under ten feet and then refused to show any reading—the bottom was too close and soft to send back a signal—but we never did hit anything. The Customs and Immigration officials came out and performed their duties pleasantly. I ended up paying a "light and buoy fee" even though the island had no lights and two of the three buoys were missing.

Many an experienced sailor has lost his boat on the reefs we were headed for next as we headed north, through the vast Caribbean shallows that extend from the bulge in Central America east across toward Jamaica and Haiti. Strong trade winds and northerly busters combine with a one and a half knot current angling across the shallows to create oftentimes disastrous conditions.

Our departure was timed to get us to the trickiest area, a westward turn between two banks, during the middle of the night when Loran A signals could be clearly received; we were too far away from the transmitting stations to receive the signals during the daylight hours. In quiet seas and under full sail we passed Quita Sueño Bank unseen not far to windward. Not until 9:30 P.M. was there a good fix on the Loran, which was repeated every half hour throughout the night. With these fixes and with RDF bearings from Isla de San Andrés and Swan Islands I established our position pretty accurately, I thought. But the depth sounder was giving readings of fifty to sixty feet instead of the ninety I expected from the chart. Exactly where were we relative to Gorda Bank and the other shallow banks so far off the coast? I wouldn't have been here had the weather not been ideal—the water flat and the wind light. The weather doesn't always stay ideal, however, nor does it give many warnings before it becomes nasty.

The sunrise was spectacular astern. The water was deep again and I felt more comfortable. The depth sounder stayed on just in case.

It was that afternoon that we anchored off a tiny cay out in the banks and had

In the Bay Islands of Honduras, Windigo is tied up near the shrimp boats.

a swim around the coral heads close by. Two fishing boats were anchored nearby, crews not in sight. We rowed in to Grand Vivario, a very small island despite its name, whose sole inhabitant is Harold, a sixty-year-old hermit. Harold greeted us on the beach and invited us into his home, the only building still standing in a once-upon-a-time large seafood processing facility. Inside was the crew off the two fishing boats anchored near us. We declined drinks kindly offered from a dirty yellow bottle. Harold proudly showed us what he calls his "office" or "shrine"—one whole side of a room filled with cleaned and painted coral, some painted in fluorescent colors, attached to bleached driftwood logs and branches, all of it secured in a Styrofoam base. On the opposite wall, which Harold did not mention but didn't need to, were large posters of selected parts of the female body. The far wall was one big windowless opening, looking out to the fishing boats and *Windigo* at anchor. Harold had lived here for sixteen years and his wife was due back soon from a visit to New Jersey. It was all too much for me. I excused myself to walk around the island.

Windigo's crew followed shortly, as did some of the fishermen. They gathered immature coconuts and cracked them open for coconut water. The captain of one of the fishing boats told us they stay out three months at a time, fishing the Gorda Banks for lobster. This was Easter weekend, which I had lost track about, and that's why they weren't working. The rest of the fleet had gone the extra one hundred fifty miles back to port, Isla de Guanaja, part of the Bay Islands and our destination en route to Belize.

The Bay Islands lie within about thirty miles of the northern coast of Honduras: three main islands that are sparsely inhabited, three smaller ones, and many cays. Each island is surrounded by reefs and banks that rise steeply from the great depths. There are no detailed charts for these waters; instead, we used a combination of topographical maps and a tourist map, which sufficed for the short time that we could spend here before heading west to Belize. The wind was gentle and the weather warm; we stopped in the town of Roatan, the only port of entry in the Bay Islands, then visited the other harbors on Isla de Roatan's south coast for swimming and rest.

Belize's great barrier reef, second in size only to the Great Barrier Reef of Australia, runs north-south for about one hundred twenty miles and lies ten to twenty miles off the mainland. We reached the long, winding channel that leads through it into Belize City well after dark. I expected an easy entry to Belize City, whose lights we could see ten miles distant. It wasn't to be so.

The lighted bouy off the entrance could not be found. A high bright spotlight near where the first channel marker should have been turned out to be a drilling rig, located in the middle of the channel. This natural channel is one hundred forty feet deep by seventy-five feet wide and twists through the reef. Its steep sides rise to a depth of ten feet before gradually sloping up to less. The lights of Belize City drew us on. I watched the compass and the depth sounder, following the one hundred twenty-foot line along the channel's north side, as we crept forward slowly. We kept track of our progress with continuous compass bearings on the lighthouse off the entrance and the lights of Belize City.

Creeping along the one hundred twenty-foot line we rounded the first ninety-degree bend, looking for the lighted channel marker there. It certainly wasn't lit and we never saw it.

This was ridiculous. It was now 2:00 A.M. and we were groping along at one and a half knots with eight miles still to go. The weather was calm so I turned out of the channel to anchor in twelve feet, leaving the spreader lights on in case someone else was out.

What a difference a few hours made. The next beacon was right behind us—a three-legged tripod structure with one leg badly bent, the light smashed. Following the channel markers was easy now that we could see them. I discovered, however, that Belize was now using the same buoy color system as is used in the United States, red right return, instead of the English system, which is the reverse of ours and of that shown on the chart. Regardless of the system being used then, each marker was in an advanced stage of rust.

The water off Belize City is so shallow we had to anchor half a mile off—and still we were in water only twelve feet deep. Almost all of the country's commerce comes and goes by ship through Belize City. It is all lightered to and from the ships anchored offshore just the way we were, still in the lee of the barrier reef but in an expanse of water that can be awfully uncomfortable when it blows. Taking on fuel or water here would have been a major undertaking for us, but fortunately the tanks had been topped off in Roatan. When the clearing-in officials departed in their own boat we got underway too, and sailed south toward the barrier reef lazily under genoa and mizzen.

The outer edge of the reef is rimmed with small cays and coral heads that drop off sharply to great depths. The reef's top offers a broad belt of protected sailing in ten or twelve feet, dotted with sand cays with pleasant anchorages. Because of *Windigo's* nine and a half foot draft we sailed in the deeper water among the cays along the reef's inner edge.

Sailing here you must be constantly aware of the islands and shallows. Some islands are mangrove covered and impossible to land on. Others are full of coconut trees and are delightful. The inner channel runs between the reef and shore, with a depth of about thirty feet, giving good sailing on calm water.

Windigo sailed close to the steep-sided bank between Moko Cay and Laughing Bird Cay. Clint and Warren, two crew members who are avid fishermen, put out lines. We were all relaxing over fishing stories when something struck Clint's line. He forgot his story in mid-sentence and began working the fish in. It fought hard and surfaced twice, but when Clint got it alongside all that was left was the head. Jagged gash marks showed where something bigger had slashed off the rest. At about the same time Warren had a strike. Again, just the head. Speculation as to what had made off with our fish dampened thoughts of swimming.

On clearing out of Belize we headed for Horseshoe Reef, about forty miles east of Belize City. Powering over long lazy swells we rounded the reef's southern end, well marked by a rusted freighter stranded there five years ago, and headed for Half Moon Cay and its lighthouse. The water drops to a thousand fathoms within a mile of the reef, so we crept along close in looking for the reported opening. I sent the whaler in with a lead line to check the depth. The two-foot swell didn't help. We cleared the coral heads with just a few feet to spare, and anchored in sand off Half Moon Cay.

The lighthouse keeper greeted us warmly, happy to have someone to talk with since his wife and nine children were stranded in Belize by a gasoline shortage.

The view from the lighthouse is breathtaking. Looking out over the tree tops I could see the Horseshoe Reef freighter and, closer to us, three more ships, one of which had gone up on the reef only three weeks before. I gave little thought to the lighthouse itself until I realized there were four solar panels fastened to its south side. The panels had powered the light since 1978, trouble free, replacing

This lighthouse, on the south end of Half Moon Cay, off Belize, went from kerosene lanterns to solar power in one step.

a kerosene mechanism tended by three men one of whom had climbed the tower every hour and a half to wind it up.

Somewhere in the middle of Horseshoe Reef, we had heard, is a remarkable natural marvel called "The Blue Hole." It's a circular pit three hundred yards across that was once thought to be bottomless. Science now tells us that it is four hundred sixty feet deep. Divers exploring it found a huge underwater cavern. We went in search of the Blue Hole one afternoon, working our way along the twenty-two-mile-long sand- and coral-covered plateau that rises so incredibly from the ocean's depths. At varying depths the sand bottom changes color. Turtle grass growing on it adds a darker shade, and coral heads and shadows from passing clouds change the colors still more. The coral heads four feet down looked nearly the same as the turtle grass fifteen feet down. Telling the difference was critical, but after a while I got pretty good, even reckless, at times increasing our speed to five knots.

We never touched, nor did we find the Blue Hole. Instead of an extensive search on the reef top we anchored in twenty feet of water, completely out of sight of land, yet surrounded by many coral heads. They had been delightful to snorkel around, but caused me an anxious night, particularly when the wind increased to twenty knots.

The wind was down in the morning, but now the sky was heavily overcast, so I had to adjust my mental color-depth relationship for retracing the route back to Half Moon Cay. Again we made it without incident.

Departing this remote and interesting reef we headed north under full sail and covered the two hundred miles to Cozumel in exactly nineteen hours. Our speed had been assisted by a two-knot current, but still it was a great sail. Any time you sail two hundred miles in twenty-four hours, particularly with cruising sails, it is exhilarating. I anticipated more of the same through the Yucatan Channel and Straits of Florida, expecting to combine the full force of the Gulf Stream with favorable winds. Perhaps there would be three or four two hundred-mile days back to back!

It didn't happen. On the morning we left Cozumel the wind slowly shifted to ahead, and stayed there. The wind slowly increased to thirty knots and held. Off Florida huge thunderheads blackened the night sky, obscuring the full moon, then laced the heavens with jagged flashes. It took us five days to cover the six hundred fifty miles I'd hoped to sail in three, but that is the way of the sea.

It is the adventurous sailor who purposefully heads for cruising frontiers like Belize, the Bay Islands, and Venezuela's north coast, for these areas are a long way from anywhere, hard to reach and hard to return from. They are remote and primitive, yet have their own special charm and history. They are areas I will return to soon.

PART THREE
PANAMA

FLORIDA

Gulf of Mexico

MEXICO

CUBA

Acapulco

JAMAICA

Belize City

C A R I B B E A N   S E A

Gulf of Tehuantepec

GUATEMALA

HONDURAS

Quita Sueño Bank

San Salvador

NICARAGUA

PANAMA CANAL

Punta San Blas

COSTA RICA

Gatun Lake

Panama City

Balboa

Puntarenas

PANAMA

P A C I F I C

*Gulf of
Panama*

O C E A N

COLOMBIA

14 *The San Blas Islands*

Help! Travel agencies give us not a spark of response about flying from Panama City to Porvenir!" Few Americans have ever heard of the San Blas islands, much less know where they are, which is just north of the coast of Panama. Even fewer have gone there. And nearly all who do go there go in their own boats. Consequently *Windigo's* crew for the islands had difficulty learning how to proceed after arriving in Panama City on one of the daily flights in from the United States.

Through persistence the crew prevailed, learning to take a taxi from the International Airport the few miles to little Paitilla Airport, where small planes do fly regularly out to the San Blas islands. Some are single engine planes but most are twin and carry anywhere from five to nineteen passengers. They fly as often as there are people to fill them, starting with three flights a day, in sort of a miniature Boston-New York air shuttle service.

The little plane lifts off and climbs over Panama City, circles south over the Pacific and back north across Panama to the islands. I made the trip once and got to sit in the co-pilot's seat, wondering what all the dials were and itching to put my hands on the co-pilot's duplicate controls that moved ever so slightly in front of me. The plane disappeared in the clouds, heading for an unseen mountain pass somewhere ahead. The seats were filled with the San Blas islands' brown-skinned Cuna Indian women and pale tourists who were flying to the islands for the day. The small cargo area was jammed with boxes held together with knotted string and bags full of supplies and food. Breaks in the clouds showed mountain peaks rising above the plane on both sides. Looking down into the jungle-covered mountains, where the only paths are wild animal trails, I hoped the little plane would hold together for another trip.

Once over the mountains and out of the clouds I saw the islands spread out ahead. The plane was immediately forgotten. Island villages appeared as the plane descended, and sailing canoes looked like ants sailing on the crystal-clear blue water. The water's color variations were marked distinctly by coral, sand banks, and depths.

Windigo lay off Porvenir, which is the port of entry for the island and land area of Panama called Comarce de San Blas. It is also the residence of the Intendante, governor of the islands and their liaison with the Republic of Panama.

The San Blas islands are semi-autonomous and extremely independent, and even though *Windigo* had a cruising permit for all of Panama I had to go through the whole process again in the San Blas islands.

We stayed there for nine weeks with several crew changes, and one time when a change wasn't reported to the authorities quickly enough an armed National Guard soldier summoned me to the Intendante's Secretary's office—immediately. Ned, who had just joined *Windigo* with his family and whose Spanish is better than mine, joined me. We sat listening like school children to the Secretary, Señor Muno, as he explained in broken English that "This is Big Problem." They had to know immediately when people came or went. And furthermore two of the new crew had only birth certificates, not passports. Señor Muno showed us the Comarce de San Blas Constitution, which we couldn't read, but I think it said that persons without proper papers would be fined $100, $500 for a second offense. "The new crew should be sent back to Panama on the next plane and you," pointing to me, "should be thrown in jail or at least out of San Blas." A long pause, then, "This is Big Problem, you must understand."

Ned and I finally placated Señor Muno but he still made no move to stamp the new passports or make out a new crew list. Finally, a pilot who had just flown the Intendante himself to Porvenir now appeared, and all was made right.

Before getting back to *Windigo* that afternoon we sat in the shade of a small hotel's porch for an indoctrination to the "Comarce de San Blas"—the island group's formal name—given regularly for tourists visiting the islands for the day. La Comarce de San Blas consists of a narrow strip of land one hundred miles long on the Panama coast, together with several hundred islands lying offshore within about ten miles. The Cuna Indians had moved to the islands from mainland jungle villages in around 1825, perhaps to escape the jungle's infestation of pesty insects. Today fifty-one of the three hundred sixty-five islands are inhabited, while the remaining ones are used for growing coconuts.

As an extension of their old custom of body painting, the Cuna women began sewing designs into their blouses—"molas" in the Cuna language. The molas developed into a unique form of art, combining graphic imagination with marvelous colors and workmanship. Through constant misuse in the non-Cuna world, the world "mola" today has come to mean simply the appliquéd panel of a Cuna woman's blouse, rather than the whole garment, and it is these panels that Cuna women had hung on the hotel's wall and spread on the grass for tourists to buy. It was a good chance for us to judge the panel's differences in workmanship, design, and graphic expression and to find the most delightful ones. We purchased our share during our stay in the islands.

We rode to a neighboring village in the hotel's large outboard-driven dugout canoe, called a cayuco. Small bamboo houses were squeezed tightly together

Island advertising and a crew change at the airport terminal in Porvenir, San Blas Islands.

four or five deep around the island's edge, with sand paths between them and with still more molas hanging on lines for sale. The center of the island was open, surrounded by coconut trees that shade the homes, and two small native hotels where guests slept in hammocks. The Cuna women were selling carved medicine dolls, ceremonial canes, necklaces of thorns and seedpods or bone and shells, and model boats. We also saw offerings of bright strings of beads like the ones they wore wrapped around their own wrists and ankles in lovely patterns.

Windigo's first anchorages in the San Blas islands were the bigger ones, or the ones recommended to us by other sailors. Only forty miles of the hundred-mile coast have been charted, drastically reducing the area I was willing to explore. As time passed, I sought out new anchorages, and one of the best of these was a neat place between three small cays at the eastern end of Coco Bandero Cays.

The chart showed a reef extending between two islands where I had been assured there was adequate depth for *Windigo*—if we were careful. Coconut-treed islands appeared above the reefs along the Mayflower Channel, as we neared the closest of the small cays. We crept forward through the darker, deeper water, twisting between light-colored sand banks. We stopped gently, with *Windigo's* forefoot resting against the steep sand bank and fourteen feet still under the mast. We anchored and tied a second line from the anchor to a coconut tree on shore, lest *Windigo* drag the anchor down through the soft sand and drift onto the reef astern. Within minutes everyone was in the refreshing water and headed for the beach. The dinghy, loaded with cameras and towels, was towed in.

Sandy points extend from each end of the little island and narrow to thin bands running along its lee shore. We were grateful that the limbless trunks of coconut trees let a cooling breeze blow through, while crowns of palm fronds shaded the ground against the mid-day sun. The trees had clearly been cared for by their owners—undergrowth had been kept to a minimum, and only a few dry fronds lay on the ground. Ashes showed where other fronds and brush had recently been burned. We could see smoke rising from another island not far away, and on the mainland in the distance. Several coconuts planted in an opening had just sprouted and would someday tower overhead like the others. Young trees down near the water grew at an angle, reaching out from under mature trees for more light, trunks curving over the water before reaching skyward.

In all our San Blas islands explorations we were especially careful with the coconut trees. The islands are owned by all the Cuna people, but individual families own the trees and coconuts are their major crop and principal source of income. We were cautioned that taking a coconut, even one on the ground, would be considered as serious an offense as horse stealing was during the days of our wild west, or similar to poaching lobsters from a Maine lobster trap today. We once bought some coconuts for ten cents each, and also traded a couple of gallons of gasoline for coconuts with Señor Muno, who was down island in the government outboard-driven cayuco with insufficient gasoline to get back.

Another anchorage I kept going back to was Caobos Cay, in an island group well offshore, where we anchored in a delightful pool thirty feet deep right where the chart showed a reef to be.

Our first time near Caobos Cay the wind was fairly strong and a distinct current flowed past the narrow entrance to it. We went elsewhere instead of tempting fate, but I remembered the place. Next time we were nearby the wind and seas were calm. The water's color in the cut was deep blue, indicating enough water, but it looked different—much too blue. I didn't want to be hung up so sent *Windigo's* crewman Steve ahead in the dinghy with a lead line; there was plenty of water, thirty-seven feet in the narrowest part, and even inside the reef there was twelve to fifteen. It was a good anchorage. Since the mangroves were too thick for going ashore we swam, snorkeled, and took trips in the dinghy instead.

Still another time we took *Windigo* along the thin light-blue trail between

Cuna Island neighborhood, with thatched houses and a dugout canoe, or cayuco, alongside.

Caobos and another island. The view from aloft was spectacular: two green-topped islands no more than a hundred yards apart, white sand bottom extending from each in varying hues of light yellow, with occasional dark patches and pale blue. At anchor many of *Windigo's* crew began their San Blas islands windsurfing careers. Some careers also ended here.

In the islands the wind generally blew from the northeast at twelve to eighteen knots during the daytime, less at night. The winds gave good reaching along the coast, from island group to island group, usually in sheltered waters. We found one sixteen-mile section of the coast that has no such protection, though, and five miles off this shore the ocean swell became confused as it rolled over an irregular and shallowing bottom, leaving several of us feeling its effects. Relief was felt the moment we sailed into the lee of the Cabaza Cays, a group of islands in the eastern part of the chartered waters.

Thick undergrowth on the islands forming Snug Harbor there also effectively cut off the cooling wind, so I moved into a passage between two islands where the breeze would funnel through. Wind and the water flowing through the passage held us at anchor in the center. Lying in this tight spot, *Windigo's* mast was almost completely hidden from view by the palm trees surrounding us. Small mangrove-covered cays bordered the larger cay nearby, with waterways around them apparently teeming with fish. Men in two cayucos stopped setting their nets to watch us.

Late in the afternoon another cayuco entered the passage ahead, sailing before the wind and then deftly jibing around to stop next to *Windigo*. Its young occupant Jim explained that he was returning to Playon Chico, his island village nearby, after spending the day tending his coconut trees. He had learned English while working on tankers sailing the world for fifteen years before returning home. Jim promised to introduce us to the chief in the morning and show us his village.

From his lookout spot on the boom next morning *Windigo's* crewman Dan guided us out of the tight anchorage and threaded us through intervening shallows and small cays to Playon Chico. The village looked like a long straight-topped cliff twenty feet high rising directly from the water. It was actually thatched-roof bamboo huts all packed together at the water's edge. Cayucos were pulled up on tiny specks of beach. Frail outhouses stood on stilts over the water. Brightly colored molas hung on lines, fences, and bushes to dry or adorn the Cuna women who turned up to watch us pass. As we anchored seventy-five yards off this intriguing village half a dozen cayucos put out from shore, each carrying two or three children. They circled *Windigo*, looking up at us with big eyes. Smiles spread across their faces as they talked among themselves.

At the town landing we tied the whaler up near a Colombian trading schooner unloading food and materials needed in the village. Jim met us here

Crew leans out to windward to hold up the mast as this laden dugout rushes home from the mainland.

107

and explained that visitors to Playon Chico had to be approved by the chief before they could see the island and purchase molas. He led us to the Council House, a large windowless bamboo and thatch building, dark and cool inside with rows of benches lining its walls. Hammocks stretched between the poles that support the roof.

The village chief officiates at nightly meetings here with his council, we learned. Laws are made and disputes settled here. The councilmen chant songs that tell the old village stories and that tell how to act under every circumstance.

The chief was sitting in one of the hammocks talking with some other men, and when Jim greeted him and told him about us he just kept talking to the other men. We stood waiting, not understanding a thing they said, until finally Jim turned to us with the word that the chief had welcomed us to the village.

Outside we wandered down Playon Chico's straight sand streets, packed hard by the daily comings and goings of bare feet and swept clean with twig brooms. Word of our arrival spread fast. Women shyly brought molas to their doorways for us to examine. This of course slowed our progress to a snail's pace, but brought us wonderfully into contact with these people. The Cunas are the second smallest people in the world, so their blouses are too small for North American women to wear. Our interest in them was thus not for wearing, but for decoration.

These blouses had begun generations ago with simple abstract patterns and progressed to island scenes, but today molas also depict space flights, political scenes around the world, sports events, whiskey labels, tools, and virtually every Cuna activity. Some are put together with relatively little effort—made to be sold, not proudly worn by their maker. Others are extremely detailed. The good ones take hours of skill and patience: The corners must be sharp and smooth, the thread colors matching, the stitches tiny—even hidden, and no areas must be neglected. The women's critical appraisal of their own work has created inter-island rivalries and pride, and turned their work into a form of art.

In our nine weeks in the islands I bought forty panels, from a well-worn faded old blouse with a simple geometric design and soft colors to a bright color-ful panel of a bird in a bamboo basket. Two of my favorites now grace *Windigo's* main cabin as pillow covers.

Each of the San Blas Islands we explored seemed to have a different attitude toward cameras and being photographed. On Playon Chico Jim happily posed holding a grandchild, with his wife and daughter, in front of their bamboo house. All ages watched me curiously and edged forward right into the picture. Later I knelt down to take a picture of Steve sketching a scene with three boys intently watching his work take shape. Four other young guys clustered around my shoulders trying to look through the camera too, so I held it while they took

The newer mola is a complex and colorful design of animals and birds, made here into a blouse.

This old mola has a simple geometric design.

turns peering through the viewfinder. I wish we had had a Polaroid and could have left them some pictures.

On another island near Porvenir, where tourism had left its mark, we had been allowed to take pictures of people only if we paid twenty-five cents for each person in each picture. One boy chased Jack for his twenty-five cents when Jack took a picture of the boy's monkey. He wasn't paid.

It was on Playon Chico that a woman selling molas—not as shy as her friends—beckoned me inside her home when I didn't want to buy the blouse she was showing. Using a long pole she deftly lifted several more off a beam high in the ceiling. At least twenty more blouses were draped up there, all turned inside out. My eyes adjusted to the windowless rectangular room, which light entered only through the door openings in each end. It was cool and comfortable inside, welcome relief from the intense midday sun. Blocks of wood served as seats around a crudely made low table. In the far corner, coals glowed in the fire pit and a few cooking utensils hung on the wall nearby. Hammocks were drawn up in the middle, where three or four generations slept under this one roof. A conglomeration of plastic bottles grouped in the corner stood upright full of water or on their sides empty. Two earthen jugs sunk in the sand were also full of water.

Steve often had a following of island children while he was sketching (left), or handing out Goldfish crackers (below).

Twenty-five to thirty children followed us as we walked on. Many of the women did as well, interested in which molas we had bought as much as they were in us. Wanting to share something with these delightful kids Steve had gone back aboard for some goldfish cocktail crackers, and now, hunkering down level with the youngsters' shiny brown faces, he held out a handful of them.

The nearest child had never seen anything like it before and had no idea what to do. Quickly Steve popped a couple into his own mouth, eyes twinkling as he chewed. Then he stretched his arm out again. This time two cautious hands picked up one cracker each and hesitantly returned to their respective mouths. The other children watched intently, eyes wide, mouths open, breaths held, waiting to see what happened. The two hands came back right away for more goldfish and Steve was nearly bowled over as the other children moved in too. Within minutes all the children on the island must have been there, pushing in on Steve. He was now standing, towering over their heads, dispensing goldfish into eagerly outstretched hands. The children gradually grew in size and age until all mola-making on the island must have stopped. Teen-aged girls were now crowding in, backing Steve, cracker box held high above his head, into a bamboo fence near the water. What a memory!

Heading back to *Windigo* later we came across the only open space on the island, a basketball court. I thought this a little incongruous for the second short-est people in the world, but they are an agile athletic people who love sports. The kids stayed with us right to the pier, sitting astride turned-over cayucos, waving farewell as each dinghy load returned us to *Windigo*. As the last trip was loading one lad ran up, holding out a camera that had inadvertently been left behind. We were tired from the activity ashore, glad to relax on *Windigo*, and very sad to be leaving these warm people.

We had one more afternoon, though, when Jim sailed out the next day with two of his grandchildren. He said yes to my request to sail his cayuco, and gingerly I climbed down to join them. Sitting in the stern I held the paddle in one hand and the main sheet in the other, and set off. The two children sat side by side amidships, holding hands and looking concerned, while Jim stood smil-ing, holding the unstayed mast. With no keel and no centerboard our leeway was so great that the water kept the paddle securely pressed against the hull. Much to Jim's amusement it took me two tries before I was able to tack and head back.

Señor Muno, Jim, and the shy and playful Cuna women were by no means all the memorable people we had met in the San Blas islands and were reluctant to leave. There were also the boys sailing cayucos who challenged our wind-surfer to a race, all the islanders who waved greetings to us as we sailed past, and even the four Cuna ladies who paddled out to *Windigo* to sell molas, howl-ing with laughter at their own remarks, which probably would have left us in-sulted or blushing had we understood them. And there was Denny, whose tiny daughter clung to his leg while we took their picture.

These Cuna boys often challenged Windigo's *windsurfer to races with their cayucos.*

Windigo and the crew stayed anchored in the San Blas islands while I flew to Panama City to make the arrangements for transiting the Panama Canal, far nicer a wait than in the commercial environs of Cristobal. At the Marine Traffic Control Office in Balboa I said that I wanted to go through the Canal east to west on a particular day. The Captain looked up at me and slowly shook his head, asking "Do you want to transit northbound or southbound?" Frowning in puzzlement I explained I wanted to go from the Caribbean to the Pacific. "Then you want to go southbound," he stated. He showed me on a map that the Canal runs nearly north-south and that in fact the northern end is west of the Pacific end, so my "east to west" request had really been backwards. There was a lot to learn in a hurry about this whole procedure.

The rest of the preparations did go smoothly. *Windigo* had transited the Canal before under an earlier name, so they had all her particulars on file. If they hadn't, we'd have had to spend several days in Cristobal for measuring and scheduling. As it was I made all the arrangements to transit the Canal—southbound, Sunday, February 4—before flying back to *Windigo* that day.

An unpleasant repair is made.

Studying David McCullough's book for the canal transit.

15 *Transiting the Canal*

Sailing between the breakwaters into Limon Bay, just inside the Canal entrance mid-afternoon on February 3, my apprehension about the next twenty-four hours was growing fast. Crews waved as we passed ships of many nationalities waiting their turn to transit the Canal. I wondered about our passage; would *Windigo* in fact go through in the morning, or would we have hours of waiting instead? What problems would arise in transit? I'd read as much as I could find about the procedures for yachts, much of it written because of damage that resulted. We anchored in "the Flats," an anchorage reserved for yachts, and called Cristobal Signal on the radiotelephone to advise them of our arrival and intention to transit the Canal.

An hour after the call a Canal Company boarding officer arrived to process us. He checked on his hand-held radio with traffic control in Cristobal. Cristobal had no information about it so called Balboa Traffic Control. My spirits sank; troubles already. Then they rebounded as word came that we were indeed scheduled to go through in the morning, that a pilot would board us at 8:00 A.M., and that we must be ready when he arrived. The same regulations and paperwork apply to the smallest yacht as to the largest ship, all in multiple copies. It was late in the afternoon by the time the boarding officer had everything in order and called his launch to take him off.

Outboards are forbidden in the Canal Zone, except with a special license which was impossible for us as non-residents to get. But we could row ashore, or sail in on the windsurfer. These methods of getting ashore are of course far more dangerous in the congested area than a maneuverable outboard. The cost for a launch in or out was $35 for the half-mile ride, too expensive for our blood. Regulations also required that we row to the pilot's landing between Piers 6 and 7 and nowhere else, but the landing was covered with oil and there was no place to tie the dinghy up to anyway. The regulations were relaxed temporarily a few years later, and we did use the outboard then to run back and forth to the yacht club nearby.

The remainder of the afternoon was spent preparing *Windigo* for the transit. Four hundred-foot lines were required, as were four line handlers who could tie bowlines quickly; the crew spent an hour practicing. The whaler was lifted on deck and secured, as was everything else. Over cocktails in the cockpit we watched ships appear around a bend in the channel leading from the locks, coming into the Caribbean. They were all types and sizes, some low in the water, laden with goods, others high and empty. Most unusual of all were the high-sided car-carrying transports, whose maneuvering characteristics, particularly in high winds with their acres of windage, must have been awful. *Windigo's* crew went to bed eagerly looking forward to the next day. I wasn't eager at all. I was wishing we were already safely on the Pacific side.

By 8:15 A.M. our pilot hadn't yet arrived. By 8:30 I was concerned and called Cristobal Signal. "He will be along shortly, don't worry." Louie did arrive in about another half hour, but we weren't scheduled to enter the locks until 11:15 so we could relax in the cockpit with coffee and hear about what lay ahead. We got underway at 10:00 to follow *Leo,* a large Monrovian freighter, toward the locks.

The Gatun locks appeared ahead on rounding a bend in the channel, the same bend we'd been watching the day before. From end to end the locks measure nearly a mile in length. Two sets of locks operate independently of one another, side by side, in either direction. Each set has three chambers separated by huge steel doors, each chamber a step up from the next, to move ships up or down between the levels of the Caribbean and the man-made Gatun Lake in the interior of Panama.

A freighter moved into one chamber, still at sea level, and was dwarfed by that chamber's high walls. Right beside it in the other set of locks was another ship coming from the same direction, sitting like a duck in its own small pond, the water nearly level with the top of its chamber's walls and well above sea level now. It was all an awesome sight, an unbelievable engineering feat, as we had read in David McCullough's *The Path Between the Seas.*

Leo moved slowly into the lock when the ship ahead had moved into the next chamber. Heavy steel cables controlled by electric engines called "mules" moved *Leo* forward, holding her in the center of the chamber. We moved in behind her. Instead of mules handling our lines, four men high above us on the lock walls threw a monkey's fist down to receive the four hundred-foot lines, which we tied to it with the bowlines we'd been practicing, and all of it was then pulled to the top of the walls and dropped over bollards. The lines led from *Windigo's* bow and stern to each side, holding us in the chamber's center. The huge double-door gates began to close behind us even before our lines were secure. Each door is sixty-five feet wide and seven feet thick, and they rose more than forty feet above our heads. The chambers are a thousand feet by one-hundred-ten feet and can accommodate vessels with a forty-foot draft. The lock was certainly large enough for *Windigo,* even with *Leo* in there too.

Louie told us about the time he had stood all alone on the bottom of a

The huge steel doors, seven feet thick, of the Gatun locks close out the Caribbean at Windigo's *stern.*

chamber emptied for repairs. Craning his neck back, he had wandered with his eyes up the sheer wall of solid concrete, and finally found blue sky directly overhead. There had been nothing to give him a sense of scale, which had made him feel like a speck in a bathtub.

Louie now pointed to the water's surface ahead. It was beginning to boil. This he explained was because of the tremendous force under which the water was entering our chamber. It was coming from the next higher chamber and rushed up through a hundred separate openings in the chamber floor, twenty-six million gallons in less than fifteen minutes, to raise us twenty-eight feet. The turbulence buffeted *Windigo* around. Often she leaned sharply until brought up abruptly on the docking lines, which we were not allowed to take in as the water rose. Had a line broken or come loose she would surely have slammed against the concrete walls and received considerable damage.

When *Leo* left the third lock to enter Gatun Lake she was allowed to proceed under her own power. *Windigo* was still tied directly behind her as she started up and swung around violently in her wash. I had climbed to the spreaders for a view back down the three locks and had quite a time holding on. It was mind-boggling to contemplate all that which had been involved to raise us eighty-five feet above sea level.

A well-buoyed channel crosses Gatun Lake, the huge body of water that supplies the locks. Louie, who had grown up sailing on San Francisco Bay, allowed us to supplement the engine by raising genoa and mizzen. But our speed surpassed my scheduled speed for locking down, so we killed the engine. We

From Windigo's *lower spreader, the crew could look into the lock that had raised them.*

enjoyed the quiet sail, sliding along comfortably at seven knots. Louie was content behind the wheel.

It was August 3, 1914, we had read, that the sea-going tug *Cristobal* had made the first ocean-to-ocean transit—the same day a storm broke over Europe that began World War I. Spectacular opening celebrations were dropped and news of the Canal's official opening was buried in the newspapers. Traffic through the Canal was less than 2,000 ships a year at first and 5,000 within ten years, 7,000 by 1939. By 1966 ships were going through at a rate of one an hour, twenty-four hours a day, every day of the year, and four years later the traffic exceeded 15,000 ships a year. By the time we went through in the mid 1970s, though, traffic was at less than half capacity.

Almost unbelievably, the Canal's tolls for all this remained unchanged from 1915 to 1974, when they increased merely from $0.90 per cargo ton to $1.08. The largest toll paid exceeded $42,000, when the *Queen Elizabeth II* transited in 1975. The average ship pays about $10,000, and *Windigo's* toll was $34.46.

Electric mules handle big ships, but little Windigo *was held by four 100-foot lines.*

That's an incredible bargain, particularly when you realize Louie earned more than that per hour.

Gatun Lake narrows to a channel after ten miles of open water, bending around islands that once were hills before the land was flooded for the Lake. Tucked behind one of these small islands that afternoon we lay drifting for a short time for a fresh water swim, the first most of us had had in some time.

When time came to head on, the high land on both sides blocked the trade winds, so we had to exchange the peaceful quiet of sailpower for the diesel engine. It was the smothering heat, the rains, and the sucking mud of this trench, the Calebra Cut through the Continental Divide, that had caused the horrendous toll in building the Canal almost seventy years before. *Windigo* was travelling along the Cut in the coolness of the setting sun, but the temperature at midday was often 120–130 degrees. It was impossible to picture fifty mammoth steam shovels working here in the early 1900s, loading a continuous stream of dirt trains to haul the muck to special dumps. The more they dug, the more digging there was to be done, as mudslide after mudslide buried their work.

Now *Windigo* was nearing the upper lock on the Pacific side, which is separated from the lower two by Lake Miraflores. In the upper lock we tied alongside a Canal tug that was in turn tied to the chamber walls. Louie instructed us to use nine docking lines, and once they were in place and secured he checked each one, suggesting that several be winched in tighter. Our fenders were compressed against the tug's fenders—big, black tractor tires. *Windigo* and the tug descended easily, with the tug's crew easing their lines as the water level dropped. Her captain leaned out of his pilothouse window and suggested we stay tied alongside through the Lake to Miraflores Locks. Louie declined, telling me under his breath that tug captains sometimes gun their engines when maneuvering, and that the turmoil from the huge propellers can place a tremendous strain on a yacht tied alongside. We proceeded under our own power, refastening our lines to the tug for the next two descents. Looking over the lights being turned on in Panama City we had our first glance of the Pacific Ocean as dusk turned to darkness.

I slowly relaxed, as we motored past the busy docks of Balboa toward our anchorage off Flamenco Island. The launch came for Louie, who wished he could join us for more. So did I. I was also relieved that the transit had been without mishap and surprised it had been so easy. In my last waking moments I began to grasp that in less than twelve hours we had crossed the continent by boat, a distance of only about fifty miles.

16

North to Acapulco

Windigo departed Taboga Island at midday, two days after we had come through the Panama Canal. We ran before a light wind under full sail, heading still further south to round Punta Mala, a point jutting into the southwest corner of the Gulf of Panama. The Humboldt Current's substantial counterclockwise movement in the Gulf helped us along nicely. The northerly wind filled in as the afternoon progressed and blew strongly throughout the night, then dropped to a calm by dawn. Its strength changed constantly, leaving us with never quite the right combination of sails.

At anchor in a cove off Panama that afternoon we were visited by a dugout canoe from shore. It held six young girls, the oldest paddling in the bow, and a man paddling in the stern who also held his two-year-old son. They gave us a stalk of bananas in a gesture of welcome. Rae found some candy for the children and canned food for the family. Two other dugouts came out with more bananas, which we hung from the mizzen boom. For them we exchanged cigarettes and bread.

Our conversation labored on in Spanish, and the outcome was that Rae and two others went ashore in the morning to visit the first family that we had met. They visited, talked, and took a picture of the whole family in front of their bamboo house. Three years later on the trip home I stopped in the cove again. The father and his son, the son now wielding his own small paddle, came out to greet us. I gave them the photograph and the family was immensely pleased. *Windigo* was sent off with more bananas.

It was in this same cove on the trip north that we had overtaken two couples paddling a dugout along shore. I slowed and offered them a tow, figuring they were headed along the shore to fish, but instead they pointed south across five miles of open water to Isla Canal de Alvera. We took them in tow anyway and headed for their island. Course changes were needed several times during the hour's trip, so strongly were we being set by the easterly current. We speculated as to how long it would have taken the couple to paddle there. All day? Much longer? They had palm fronds in the canoe to shade themselves from the blistering sun, and oranges against thirst.

Isla Canal de Alvera turned out to be their home. Their bamboo house was neatly hidden by coconut trees and thick green brush. We cast them loose right in front of it. Family and friends stood on the beach waving a greeting, surely surprised at their arrival behind a big yacht. The four of them expressed their thanks for the tow by handing us a burlap sack of oranges, but they wanted the bag back. Rae let the oranges roll out on deck accompanied by two big scurrying cockroaches. She screeched and jumped to the top of the doghouse, and we caught the two varmints before they could disappear below. The Panamanians nearly swamped their dugout laughing at this reaction to two harmless creatures.

The afternoon held still another surprise. The islands around us looked so nice we decided to anchor for a swim and lunch. Two of the crew went snorkeling toward one small island while the rest of us swam around *Windigo*. The two who had gone off were nearly at the island, slowly kicking along surveying the surroundings below them, when suddenly they both turned and made a rapid retreat to *Windigo*, panting as one pushed the other up the ladder. They had seen six big barracuda hanging motionless in the water, watching them, mouths slightly open, showing rows of razor-sharp teeth.

With retrieved courage they went out again after lunch, this time in the whaler. . . . Thinking they would be safe from further scares they donned face mask and snorkel in order to lean over the drifting dinghy's side, faces in the water. In this peculiar manner they watched the small multi-colored fish and sand bottom slowly pass. Suddenly a huge sting ray rose from the sand directly beneath the dinghy. That was enough. It was time to move on anyway, and in doing so we passed a turtle sunning himself on the surface.

Shifting headwinds that day caused a delay and a confusing night entry into Golfito, a well-protected but stiflingly hot harbor on the Costa Rican coast. The customs official there was purposefully unhelpful the next morning, letting me struggle along with my poor Spanish intermixed with English, only to find him speaking excellent English in the bar that evening. In the six years of cruising in *Windigo*, this was one of the very few times I had unpleasantness with officialdom.

More light and capricious headwinds made progress slow along the coast the next day, but we finally reached Golfo de Nicoya's Hacienda Nicoya, across from Puntarenas. Hacienda Nicoya is a tropical hideaway commonly known to sailors as "Joe Hill's Place." Joe himself rowed out to greet us, with, of all wonderful things, mail. Barbarlee, a new member of the crew, had been enchanted with this place during a previous stay and it was she who had convinced me to stop here for several days.

Joe suggested we come ashore around five for a beer and to meet the people off the other ten boats anchored nearby. Before he left Barbarlee asked about the shower, a subject foremost in our minds. Joe laughed. Pointing to a clump of trees and flowering bushes at the edge of the beach he said, "It's right where you remember, Barbarlee, and we are still blessed with sufficient water, so enjoy it!" The girls grabbed their towels and soap and went ashore, making a beeline for the shower. The rest of us weren't far behind.

A semi-circular bamboo fence covered with flowering vines led into the shower—a rectangular opening under two palm trees. Two pegs in one tree served for clothes and towel and the other tree held up the shower head. When my turn came I quickly lathered up in the soft water. Weeks of accumulated salt began to wash away, a prolonged, gratifying process. Feeling squeaky clean again I put the soap in the soap shell tied to a branch and just stood there with the spray of tepid water falling on my head and shoulders and running down my body. Bird songs in the trees mixed with the sounds of rustling fronds overhead. Monkeys chattered not far away. Looking over the fence and through the thorny bushes beside it I could see *Windigo* and the other boats lying anchored in the narrow thoroughfare, protected so well by an uninhabited brown barren island not far away. I could have stayed far longer, but there were others waiting.

Soon we met the crew from the other boats, all of us sitting in chairs made from branches and on benches around a rough log table. One couple was headed north, others were going south; two boats to the Canal and Caribbean, another to the South Pacific. Those on one boat weren't sure where they were going and another couple wasn't going anywhere; they were going to build right here in Golfito. Without exception, everyone had remained here longer than he had meant to.

The congeniality at Joe Hill's Place was certainly addictive. Mornings were usually spent doing your own thing, for me it was often working on the boat. Lunch was a sandwich on the Hacienda's shaded porch, gazing through palm trees at the boats. Other days it was a quiet time out under an awning in the cockpit, looking at the palm trees ashore. Then there might be an afternoon siesta and a game of volleyball or a stroll in the hills before returning to the Hacienda for Happy Hour and dinner. Payment for all this was simple. Along a wall was a row of coconut shells marked with your name or your boat's name. Bottle caps and sandwich chits went into these shells, for reconciliation later.

For almost everyone on a voyage like ours, there is always something else to see or do ashore, or some repair needed on board. Departure is tomorrow or next week. I'm convinced that this voyaging procrastination exists because the "dream of sailing the seven seas and seeing the world" is so much better in one's kaleidoscopic conception than in reality. It is so much easier to deal with the known in a "safe" harbor than the unknown in a strange anchorage or at sea. Voyagers are almost always interesting people, I have found, each with his own reason for cutting his ties completely with home, work, school, routine, normalcy, security, and society.

Reluctantly but on schedule, *Windigo* departed this peaceful place. The sun had just risen over the Costa Rican mountains as we began the thousand-mile passage to Acapulco. We responded to the three salutes from shore with three blasts on our fog horn, and powered out with the tide on a windless morning. Our destination was Acapulco, on the coast of Mexico, then on to Baja California, British Columbia, and Alaska.

A northerly breeze filled in during the afternoon and gave us an enjoyable sail on a smooth sea. The wind was inconsistent in the following days, constantly changing in strength and direction. In one three-hour stretch we logged twenty-six miles, yet two hours later our speed was down to two knots and we reverted to the engine. In three days of these on-again off-again conditions we covered four hundred miles. The sea was always calm, main cabin and foredeck hatches were never closed. Needlepoint, reading, and small boat chores took up the day.

No one minded the good weather, for we all knew the Gulf of Tehuantepec was just ahead and had heard about this infamous bay's big winds and seas. Northerlies blowing over Mexico funnel through a high mountain pass at the head of the Gulf. Sixty-knot winds and huge ungainly seas are not unusual. We headed for the Gulf's southeast corner, at the Mexican/Guatemalan border, my mind not yet made up about which theory to follow when crossing it—close to shore but out of the big seas, or offshore across the mouth for the shortest passage.

Another sail was short lived, the wind sinking with the sun. A sloppy swell rolled directly at us and reduced our speed under power by at least two knots, all night long. Wind and sun rose as the morning progressed, however, and by noon we had to begin reducing sail, genoa to working jib, then a reef in the main. Before evening we added the second reef and the decision on cross-Gulf theories was made for me. The Gulf's near corner was dead to windward about fifty miles away. No sense wasting the time or energy to beat in to the coast, when from here we could sail across on a close reach, right on course for Acapulco.

The perverse conditions continued. The seas seemed bigger at night, rolling at us out of the dark, looming above *Windigo's* deck and then roaring under us after all. Every now and then a wave broke as we met, sluicing across the foredeck. No one got much rest and some were confined to their bunks seasick. Dawn brought no relief, just stronger wind and the relentless action of giant waves. By mid-afternoon, with only myself and one other crew member able to steer, I dropped all sails and ran off before the wind and seas under bare poles. We dragged the anchor rode and heavy docking lines astern to slow our progress away from our destination. At least there were no worries about running into land; on this course the closest was Antarctica.

Charles Robie at the helm, sailing north to Acapulco.

When dawn finally came wind and waves seemed to be down, although the anemometer didn't substantiate this. It must be that rest and daylight can improve your outlook. It was time to get back on course.

We set the storm trysail, the only time I've used it, with the small jib. On course again, the wind just forward of abeam, we took off. But as *Windigo* angled into the seas she rose over them and then crashed down their other sides, again and again. We were going too fast. If we kept it up we'd strain her hull and rigging. The small jib was replaced by the even smaller storm jib. Our speed dropped immediately from eight or nine knots to less than four. We rolled along comfortably but got nowhere. A little more sail was needed. We hoisted "Bullet," a staysail which kept the sail area very low and spread out. This sail combination worked. We rode over the seas gently, on course for Acapulco, at about six knots.

My dead-reckoning position for this place a thousand miles beyond our last anchorage was only a wild guess, indicated by a fifty-mile-wide pencil mark on the chart. The Loran fixes were varied and unreliable and the midday sun-sight position changed each time it was calculated. But I wasn't concerned; our course would eventually cross the ship traffic that paralleled the coast and close with Mexico's shore. There were no hazards ahead.

On the fourth morning of this "Tehuantepecer" the wind began to abate. By midday we were back to full sail and by evening under power for lack of wind. Sailing south along this coast nearly three years later I told another crew about our trip northward across this Gulf. I fully expected the same treatment this second time, but to my surprise and their disappointment we powered across the whole Gulf with no wind.

Off Nicaragua, the conditions changed gradually two days later. The seas were awesome to that crew three years later. It was a crystal-clear cold night with no moon to show us the seas. The wind was over fifty knots. The staysail had blown out and we were under bare poles running before the wind. Sitting at the wheel with my back to the approaching seas, I could hear the noise of tumbling water grow as breaking waves neared, each one lifting *Windigo's* stern so that I looked nearly straight down at the bow. Wave tops lapped over the rail beside me and ran forward down the deck. Occasionally a breaking wave smacked the counter with considerable force, and because I hadn't shut the valve to the engine's exhaust system soon enough, the seas hitting the counter during the night forced sea water back through the system and into the engine.

I turned *Windigo* back for Costa Rica as soon as the wind lessened, and went to start the engine. No response—not a sound. I pondered the engine problem and its potential disastrous delaying effects. Puntarenas wasn't far off and it's a big city—for Costa Rica—but the likelihood of finding a competent marine diesel mechanic there was slim and there certainly wouldn't be any spare parts available. So, three hundred miles at sea, we removed the engine floorboards and got to work.

With engine manual in hand we drained the exhaust system, then removed, dried, and cleaned the injectors (the equivalent to spark plugs in a gasoline engine). Each cylinder was full of salt water. We sponged each one dry and then sprayed it liberally with WD-40. (In addition to being a lubricant, WD-40 is an excellent moisture absorbant.)

Having done all we could, we put the engine back together and bled the fuel line to get the air out of it and get fuel flowing through again; diesel engines will not function at all if there is the smallest air bubble in the line. Crossed fingers pushed the starting button, and held it. The engine turned over and over without the slightest indication of starting. The last of a can of starting ether was sprayed into the air intake with no effect. The engine turned more slowly now; the batteries were beginning to show the drain.

As a last resort we borrowed liquid antiseptic from the medical chest, transferred it to an emptied cleansing spray bottle, and sprayed a dose of it into the air intake as the engine was turned over again. With the last of the batteries' power the engine caught, sputtered, then ran. It sounded smoother as the hours of use mounted. I felt relieved, and we headed on across the Gulf and on to the Canal.

The Tehuantepecer we had encountered on the trip north to Acapulco blew us further off Mexico than I'd anticipated. The wind died after four days, and the unhelpful light and variable conditions returned. *Windigo* was beyond where my rough dead reckoning position indicated Acapulco should be, and still we had seen no coast. We changed course sharply to starboard to close with it at right angles. Early morning haze along on the horizon caused some false sightings; still no coast. Breakfast was on Rae's mind as a freighter passed at right angles to us. She suggested I contact them on the radiotelephone to find out what they were having, then work the conversation around to "Where is Acapulco?" I didn't think that such a good idea.

At last the coastal mountains did appear. We tried matching them to the Coastal Pilot description of Acapulco's mountains. None fit. Soon we turned to head directly for a promising range. We came alongside an open boat with four fishermen standing in it, each rhythmically pulling his line in hand over hand with a fish on it. In response to our "Which way to Acapulco?" one man stopped long enough to point in the opposite direction from which we had come: "About fifty kilometers." The tossed pack of cigarettes was caught one-handed, which stopped the line pulling long enough for him to light up. We still hadn't gone far enough along the coast.

Our long faces gradually relaxed as we headed in under power. The city's mountains finally appeared as the sun set, and its lights guided us in the last few miles. Picking up a mooring off the Acapulco Yacht Club we tumbled into bed for a long sound sleep.

In the morning Customs, Immigrations, Health, and Port Captain officials visited *Windigo* one after another, each with his multi-copy forms to be signed, dated, and stamped. The only problem arose with the Assistant Port Captain, who insisted that I couldn't come to Mexico because I didn't have a "Zapa" showing *Windigo's* points of debarkation and destination. Customs and Immigration had processed us already without interest in this matter; the Assistant Port Captain finally said it could be taken care of—for a price. We went back and forth for hours. In the end, the Assistant Port Captain got neither his Zapa nor his bribe.

Sitting in the shade of palm trees around the yacht club pool and bar we relaxed with margaritas and swapped stories with other crews. The motor vessel *Vixen,* which had left Joe Hill's Place the day before we did, had chosen to cross the Gulf of Tehuantepec the long way, by following close to shore all the way around the head of the bay. They had been forced to anchor one night within seventy-five yards of the beach because of hurricane force winds and one hundred-knot gusts. Waves broke over *Vixen's* bow, and blown beach sand chipped the paint, removed varnish, and turned one plexiglass window opaque. That was the same night we had run under bare poles for Antarctica.

Ahead for *Windigo* now lay miles of Mexico's coast to wander along before reaching La Paz and the Sea of Cortez, which separates Baja California from the mainland of Mexico. I had no idea what to expect, but the chart showed a coast with interesting-looking harbors and off-lying islands. Margaritas beside the yacht club pool are great for a day. After that it was time to restock the galley lockers and get going.

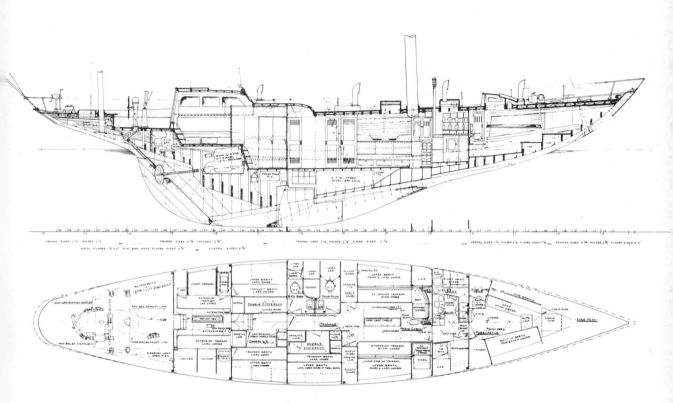

Windigo, *originally* Venturer, *was built to Sparkman & Stephens design in 1956 by one of the finest boatyards in America—the Henry Hinckley Yard in Southwest Harbor, Maine. She was one of their largest wooden vessels, and certainly one of their finest. She is double-planked, with mahogany over cedar, with frames of oak, and expansive teak decks. She was built for offshore racing, and to carry a crew of twelve in safety and comfort anywhere in the world. In these drawings of the boat when launched, she carried a large "coffee-grinder" winch on the afterdeck, and had a small, low cabin forward of the main doghouse. Subsequently, this low cabin was removed to make more deck-space for a pair of coffee-grinders amidships, to improve her sail-handling efficiency. Windigo's hull is powerful and seaworthy and beautiful from every angle.*

Windigo is a yawl, which means she carries a mizzen mast in addition to the mainmast. Many times when the wind piped up, owner Sandy Weld would drop the big mainsail completely, and proceed under the reduced sail of just the jib and mizzen. As always, Windigo would handle well in rough conditions with this balanced sail plan.

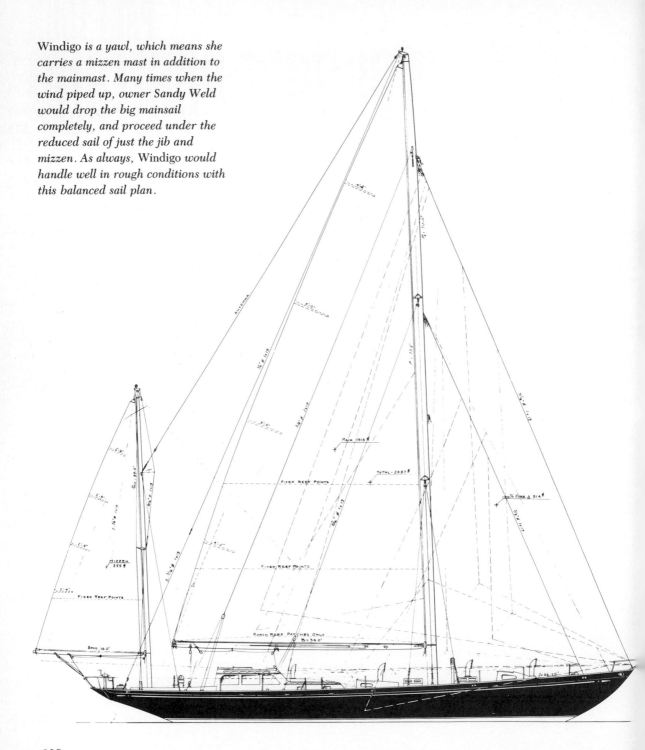

ABOVE: *Bird Rock, in Quebec's Magdalen Islands, attracted naturalist John James Audubon on the Ripley in 1833, as well as* Windigo, *for the spectacle of gannets, kittiwakes, murres, razor-billed auks, and puffins, nesting and feeding. Audubon was driven away by storms, but Windigo's crew got ashore to visit the lighthouse keepers and the birds.*

LEFT: *Four residents of Bird Rock, Atlantic (Common) Puffins, which are the author's favorite birds.*

ABOVE: *In Round Harbor, Newfoundland,* Windigo *served as the observation platform for bird-watchers, who have just spotted a huge gyrfalcon on a cliff.*

LEFT: Windigo, *the ocean-going yawl, at anchor after gunkholing in Cap Cove on Trinity Bay, Newfoundland. Sometimes the best part of sailing is arriving, safe and sound.*

LEFT: *In Guadaloupe, Windigo's crew shopped for fresh fruit and vegetables in the colorful open-air market of Pointe-à-Pitre.*

BELOW: *Under the Piton Mountains on St. Lucia, Windward Islands, the author and crew discuss the evening's anchorage while approaching under sail.*

OPPOSITE: Windigo *under sail in the eastern Caribbean. Note the distinctive curlycue on the cove strip on her bow, which marks her as a vessel built by the Hinckley Yard in Maine.*

OPPOSITE: *The anchor can be seen set on the beach, but Windigo is in deep water, so sharply does the land drop off from shore in the San Blas Islands, just north of Panama.*

RIGHT: *This "mola," a decorative panel made in the San Blas Islands, depicts an island bird. Others show island scenes— even sports events and political scenes around the world.*

BELOW: *The islands' Cuna Indian women and children welcomed picture-taking. Windigo's crew were all sad to leave these friendly people.*

OPPOSITE TOP: *This San Blas Island dugout is in sharp contrast in every way to* Windigo, *except that both are beautiful.*

OPPOSITE BOTTOM: *The author in his preferred vantage point, close to the helm, with a view of the compass, the sails, and the whole vessel. Note the powerful coffee-grinder winches forward of the doghouse on deck. They permit two people working the handles to bring in 1,000 square feet of genoa even in a stiff breeze.*

ABOVE: *In the Panama Canal locks,* Windigo *follows a ship into the Pacific. It took her only 12 hours to travel the 50 miles between oceans. The sloping tracks are for "electric mules"—trains that follow the locks and pull ships through them.*

OVERLEAF: *Anchored bow and stern in a moonscape-like cove in the Sea of Cortez. The barren desert land of Baja California was in full contrast to the aqua-blue water of this cove, teeming with life, from whales and sea lions to tiny brilliantly colored fish.*

ABOVE: *Isla Raza in the Sea of Cortez, a sanctuary for migratory sea birds. Thousands of them return here year after year to breed.*

LEFT: *The chief techniques for navigation aboard* Windigo *were traditional dead reckoning and noon sights, plus a little help from the Loran.*

OPPOSITE: *Prideaux Haven—Desolation Sound—British Columbia.* Windigo *entered many tiny inlets where there would be no sign of humans ever having been there. Eagles or bears along the shore were undisturbed by the crew's presence.*

OVERLEAF: *Reid Glacier. The grand scale of the Pacific Northwest is evident in this photograph of the glacier's terminus, a rapidly receding river of ice.* Windigo's *crew stood on soil that had been exposed to air only 40 years earlier, and under ice for thousands of years until then.*

ABOVE: *Two humpback whales have just completed a lunge close to shore, where they are presumably feeding in their little-known "bubble net" technique.*

BELOW: *The whaler lies in a mirror calm off* Windigo's *stern in Cascade Inlet, Alaska. The tender came near to being lost several times during the voyage, but was a valuable companion throughout.*

PART FIVE

BAJA CALIFORNIA

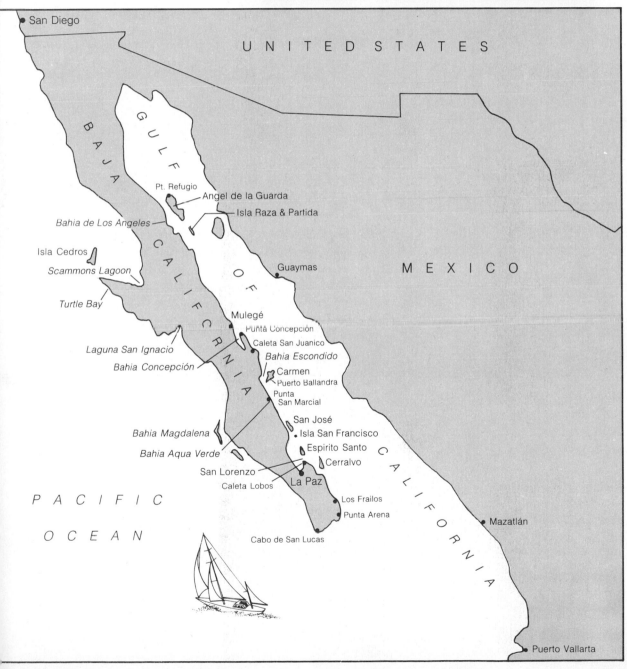

San Diego

U N I T E D   S T A T E S

B A J A

G U L F

Pt. Refugio

Angel de la Guarda

Isla Raza & Partida

Bahia de Los Angeles

Isla Cedros

Scammons Lagoon

O F

Guaymas

M E X I C O

Turtle Bay

C A L I F O R N I A

Mulegé

Punta Concepción

Caleta San Juanico

Laguna San Ignacio

Bahia Escondido

Bahia Concepción

Carmen

Puerto Ballandra

Punta
San Marcial

San José

Bahia Magdalena

Isla San Francisco

Bahia Aqua Verde

Espirito Santo

C A L I F O R N I A

San Lorenzo

Cerralvo

Caleta Lobos

La Paz

P A C I F I C

Los Frailos

Punta Arena

Mazatlán

O C E A N

Cabo de San Lucas

Puerto Vallarta

17 *La Paz*

Ten to fifteen million years ago the San Andreas fault lifted a large section of Mexico's west coast high into the air and flung it westward, ripping the earth wide open. Then the Pacific Ocean rushed into the five-hundred-mile-long void, creating the peninsula now called "Baja California." Some of the nearby volcanic mountains shifted westward when the massive movement occurred, and eventually they slipped from their new heights into the chasm. Their tops now project just above the water to form five major islands, twice as many small islands, and numerous rock sentinels that rise picturesquely from the depths. During the centuries since this new gulf was created, sand and silt have washed from the shore's soft and barren slopes, slowly filling the vast chasm, and huge cliffs have fallen into the sea.

Today, despite the constant filling action, navigation is not hindered, and depths in the Gulf of California's southern half are still in excess of a thousand fathoms. One spot was recently discovered to be nearly twice as deep. These great depths are east of the good cruising area, which is primarily between the off-lying islands and Baja's west shore. The earth's erosion has covered the bottom here with ample sand, providing good holding in the harbors and delightful sandy beaches around them.

My first view of Baja California had been at dawn, the third morning out of Puerto Vallarta. The tops of the six-thousand-foot mountains were just visible on the horizon. The coast, however, was still well over sixty miles off. As the sun rose that morning so did the wind's strength, from the north. It increased to more than thirty knots, requiring a headsail change down to the small working jib. By midday the wind had eased, so we changed back to the genoa, in a routine followed two or three times during each of the last three days. The headwinds that kept changing strength had left *Windigo's* shorthanded crew tired and discouraged with our slow progress toward La Paz.

With Baja in sight our spirits had risen. Speculation ran high as to exactly where our landfall would be. No one predicted Los Frailes, the easternmost point of the peninsula and well south of the most pessimistic estimate. But the distinctive grey bluff, isolated by lowlands on each side, could be no other. We took all day to close with the coast, tacking off Los Frailes late that afternoon. When the sun sank behind the mountains the sky around it was left ablaze.

Windigo *approaches the coast of Baja California.*

Tired as we were, we all sat on deck mesmerized by the glory of the evening. Mainsail and genoa were pulled in tight. Our speed stayed around six knots in the steady breeze. The red sky darkened. A single star appeared, then another and another as the darkening ceiling became a heaven full of twinkling lights. In turn the stars faded as the nearly full moon rose behind us. Its path danced across the water, stopping at the shore. The vast desert, rising from the beach and reaching back to the mountains, had turned white in the light. Constantly changing shadows crossed the landscape before us, created by the irregular terrain and clouds passing in front of the moon.

Nice as the sail was, there was no sense in our pushing on through the night; La Paz was still fifty miles to windward and we were all tired. We anchored close in behind a point of land and the wind died completely, leaving us to roll gently for the rest of the night.

In the morning I discovered we were not in Ensenada de los Muertos as I had thought, but fifteen miles to the south off Punta Pascadero. We got underway before breakfast, disappointed with the extra miles to sail. Short tacking along the beach was a welcome change as it gave us something to watch go by, even though the shore was unexciting. By sailing close to the beach we could also stay out of as much current as possible; wind figures strongly in the current's speed and direction in this part of the Gulf, and after so many days of northerly winds the currents were sure to be flowing rapidly southward—against us. It can

147

flow at a reported two and a half knots in the narrows that we neared.

Darkness was descending as we approached the San Lorenzo Channel, one of the few places along Baja California's coast with navigation lights that work. The reason for their reliability became clear when the cruise-ship-sized Mazatlan/La Paz ferry rounded the northern end of Isla Cerralvo and sped past, ablaze with lights.

Studying the chart I decided to stop in Caleta Lobos, a suitable-looking anchorage just inside Roca Lobos. The light on the rock allowed positive identification along this unfamiliar shore now hidden in darkness. Only the twinkling stars illuminated the area during this short time between twilight and the rising of the waning moon. Slowly passing Roca Lobos, we strained our eyes to detect the break in the shore that indicated the harbor entrance. We found it, and followed the southern shore, a high cliff, watching the depth sounder decrease to fifteen feet.

Shortly after 10:00 the anchor splashed in the water, breaking the silence. The sound bounced off the high cliff wall close beside us. Half an hour later Rae served supper, light and quick. Conversation lagged. The dishes were set aside to be dealt with in the morning.

We stayed the night. La Paz was only six miles from there, but even in daylight it is nearly impossible to differentiate between the rusted red and black buoys of the La Paz channel, and at night it is truly impossible, for they are not lighted.

Awakening to the sun streaming through the open forehatch I had no desire to be up and underway. La Paz, after all, was right around the corner. This was the first really relaxing morning since leaving Joe Hill's in Costa Rica three weeks before. I lay contently looking up, watching a thousand frigate birds wheel back and forth overhead, outlined on a cloudless sky. This magnificent and fearless black bird has a wing span that can reach eight feet, and a prominent, long and slender forked tail. It is strictly a sea bird, but, interestingly, cannot swim. It primarily scavenges from gulls and terns, diving on them while in flight, and forcing them to drop their catch, then swooping down to steal it in mid-air.

Watching the birds soar overhead I reflected on the last eighteen days since leaving Acapulco. We'd been pushing northward for nearly eight hundred miles, and there hadn't been time for all that we'd wanted to see. We stopped as often as possible, even sailing at night so we could spend extra time ashore.

I smiled to myself thinking of the night Barbara Lee and I managed by ourselves to drop the sails, then furl them and anchor in Zihuantanejo while the others slept. Zihuantanejo is a delightful small city, alive with a mixture of old arch-windowed stone buildings and newer open-fronted stores bursting with

Mexican goods. Our next stop, Manzanillo, was larger, its sheltered harbor very commercialized; we had stayed there only long enough to clear with the Port Captain and Immigration Department before crossing the bay to anchor under the Los Gatos, an ornate white hotel-condominium that we dubbed the Taj Mahal. We enjoyed sitting under palm trees beside the Los Gatos pool, drinking margaritas and rum punches out of hollowed-out pineapples, and feeling luxurious.

Zihuantanejo and Manzanillo, with sheltered harbors, were the only real cities along the six-hundred-mile coast from Acapulco to Puerto Vallarta. Normally we had found merely an open bay with protection from the prevailing wind and sea, and often a small settlement nestled behind the beach somewhere along the shore, identified by the fishing boats pulled up on the beach. These are fiberglass replicas of the wooden canoes so suitable for beaching in surf. Men in cut-off trousers several sizes too large mended their nets in the shade while their children played on the beach. Scrawny dogs scavenged for food.

Still lying on my back I kicked off the sheet and light blanket needed during the cool night. A breeze, already warmed by the sun, wafted through the forehatch. I could still see the frigate birds. Occasionally the cliff's sharp top came into view as *Windigo* swung aimlessly on her anchor.

The sight of the cliff brought it home to me that we had already reached the Sea of Cortez, an area I knew very little about. The few charts and guides available indicated an intriguing cruising area, but the description of dry, hot Baja deserts gave me some trepidation. The others on board were obviously enjoying the slow morning too, for I was still the first to rise, anxious now to reach La Paz and learn about the Sea of Cortez, also called the Gulf of California.

We were underway by mid-morning and anchored among a dozen yachts in the roadstead off La Paz shortly after noon. During siesta, when all government offices and stores close, we read of La Paz's colorful history. It includes pearls and pirates that go back to the 1530s. Tales of beautiful women and treasure lured Spanish explorers to the "Vermillion Sea." Hernando Cortez sent a vessel to explore "the island paradise of 'California'" in 1533. It met with disaster; the captain was killed by his crew, most of whom were in turn slaughtered by Indians ashore at what is now La Paz. The few who escaped told of huge quantities of pearls, which brought Cortez himself there in 1535.

Today La Paz is the largest and most important town on Baja's east side, at the southern end of the six-hundred-fifty-mile-long peninsula. Its coast is scalloped with lovely coves, bays, harbors, and off-lying islands. It is a natural port of call for all who cruise the Sea of Cortez.

After lunch I went ashore to locate an agent to handle the validation of the ship's papers, by presenting them to the Port Captain and Immigration Department. I chose to use an agent in La Paz because of *Windigo's* frequent crew changes here, which require a new crew list each time, often over the weekend when government offices are closed. The agent expedited this all far better than I could have.

La Paz's several supermarkets carry a wide variety of food, much of it imported from the United States. The town's own fresh fruits and vegetables are delicious, and grown mostly on neighboring valley farms recently irrigated for this purpose. The stores have probably the best supply of yachting hardware anywhere in Mexico, but only basic marine equipment. Anything else must be shipped in from the States, a hopeless prospect. One advantage of my frequent crew changes was that the new crew could bring needed parts—from burners for the galley stove to water pumps and head parts, and always the eagerly awaited accumulation of mail.

A topic of utmost concern among yachts cruising in Central America is where one can get "safe" drinking water and clean fuel. I had been surprised that at Puerto Vallarta's fairly new Terminal Maritima fuel still had to be brought from the city in one enterprising individual's 300-odd-gallon tank, which had no meter and was rather uncertainly secured to four wheels and towed by an old pickup truck without doors. Drinking water wasn't available at the facility either; it was brought from the processing plant in five-gallon glass bottles and emptied into the boat's tanks one by one. The thought of filling *Windigo's* five-hundred-gallon water tanks this way horrified me, but once I learned to rotate the bottom of the inverted bottle it wasn't so bad. Rotating the bottle caused the water to flow smoothly in a circular motion, creating a vortex in the bottle's neck and allowing air to rush in replacing the water.

La Paz now has a modern drinking water treatment and pumping plant that provides good drinking water throughout the town. It is available to boats, along with gasoline and diesel fuel, at a boatyard about a mile from the municipal wharf. Other boats complained of fifteen to twenty percent overages, but with diesel costing twenty-three cents per gallon, there was only the principle to complain about.

The standard procedure for those too deep to lie alongside the wharf is to drop a bow anchor offshore, then to back in as close to the pier as the boat's draft will allow. With lines to the wharf holding the stern in place, water and fuel hoses can be passed across the intervening water to fill the boat's tanks.

I was told about the procedure, then inspected the area myself in the outboard. Having seen the layout we headed upstream the next morning. *Windigo's* anchor was hanging from the bow, and long lines were laid out aft. I calculated the incoming current's effects and dropped the anchor. Fortunately, no wind was blowing to further complicate our maneuvering; coping with the current was

One especially arduous task during the voyage was to fill Windigo's *500-gallon water tanks from five-gallon jars, in Puerto Vallerta.*

going to be enough as it was much stronger than I'd anticipated.

Windigo lay on the anchor parallel with shore, some two hundred feet off the fuel dock. Her stern swung very near the tired old black-hulled tug tied alongside the outer end of the concrete wharf. Bruce took one end of the line in to the dock, and the other end led through the stern chocks and forward to the coffee grinders.

Four of us worked the winches in their lowest gear, and quickly discovered how strong the current actually was. Pulling *Windigo* broadside to the current was a slow, tiring job. The sun beat down on us. Drops of sweat fell on the deck but evaporated almost instantly. Finally *Windigo* lay nearly 45 degrees to shore, about half the distance we had to go. There was unanimous agreement to rest. Leaning on the winch handles while Rae fetched some lemonade, we watched astonished as *Windigo* continued to swing, coming perpendicular to shore. It took only seconds to realize the bow was swinging, not the stern anymore. The anchor was dragging. *Windigo's* bow was gathering speed as we watched, and heading for the tug's black side.

I jumped for the engine controls and called to cast off the stern line. I opened the throttle wide. The water under *Windigo's* counter churned into a white turmoil, yet it was hidden from our view by a cloud of black exhaust from the engine. The few seconds *Windigo* took to gather headway seemed an eternity. Visions of her white hull being pinned against the black-hulled tug flashed through my mind. We cleared the tug. *Windigo's* mizzen boom just ticked her bow.

Hauling up the anchor, we checked to see that it wasn't fouled, then reset it. The stern line was retrieved and the long process of pulling *Windigo* around began again. By lunchtime two extra sections of garden hose had lengthened the yard's hose just enough to start filling our water tanks, a time-consuming process anyway. We ate our lunch slowly, listening to the cool sound of rushing water and stretched out in the cool saloon, out of the sun's heat. Rested and fortified— and by now with a nearly slack current—we quickly pulled *Windigo's* stern close enough for a fuel line to reach our tanks.

The current was slack when we were ready to leave, with the tanks full, the water and fuel paid for. A gentle breeze was now blowing onshore, ideal conditions to have arrived in, but also good for departing. Except that the anchor refused to come free from the bottom.

Our problems multiplied rapidly because of our unique method for raising *Windigo's* anchor. We use a twenty-five-foot length of chain between the anchor and nylon anchor line. A large cringle and shackle connect the line and chain. They are too big to fit through the bow chock, and in any case the foredeck winch isn't suitable for handling chain, so another method of hoisting the anchor and chain on board has evolved. The spinnaker halyard is led forward and attached to the anchor chain, tension is taken on the halyard, the anchor line is

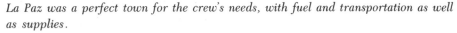

La Paz was a perfect town for the crew's needs, with fuel and transportation as well as supplies.

slackened, and the halyard is carefully winched up, raising chain and anchor out of the water for stowing on deck. This method works very well in more than twenty feet of water so the anchor is free before strain is taken on the halyard, and *Windigo* does not have a chance to get pulled over on top of it, with the halyard dragging chain against the hull, marring paint and gouging wood.

We didn't realize we had trouble until far greater strain had been taken on the spinnaker halyard than usual. *Windigo* had also drifted forward, leaving the anchor well under her and the halyard pushing hard against the spreaders.

We remedied that and tried again. The anchor was coming up ever so slowly. Finally we could just see it—with its fluke caught under a huge chain. Overboard I went, and tied a line around the free fluke. When this line was tightened and our lifting line loosened, the anchor could tip, and the heavy chain could slide free.

The consensus was unanimous. We'd rather load a hundred five-gallon glass water bottles and filter fuel through cloth in Puerto Vallarta, than experience this again. . . .

Anchoring off La Paz was interesting and often risky. The bottom is sand, too soft for *Windigo's* small-surfaced heavy Yachtsman's anchor to hold well in. We dragged several times—once when I was at the airport, and came back to see *Windigo* riding quietly at anchor in a different place. I looked at Rae quizzically, wondering how she had managed to pull the anchor up and move *Windigo* all alone. Having done this myself several weeks before, I knew the difficulties. She confessed that three guys on a neighboring boat had seen the trouble and, in that willing way that sailors have, had come to her rescue.

We took time to enjoy La Paz. Palm trees mushroom above its waterfront street, their fronds rustle in the midday breeze, and their shade protects people sitting at small tables talking, sipping coffee, beer, or a coke. The town is small enough to cover on foot. It is quiet, with a sense of prosperity. Bustling businesses occupy century-old buildings next to modern stores, their proprietors helpful with our often unusual needs. During each stop here we had no difficulty with laundry, international telephone calls and—the most cherished undertaking—a hot shower.

For our needs, La Paz was perfect. The anchoring problems and fuel/water difficulties simply made us especially appreciative of other things. None of us had journeyed to Baja to see its cities, so our stays in La Paz eventually became shorter and shorter. We'd enter from Calete Lobos or Pichilinque on the morning of a crew member's departure, and return to either of those two quiet harbors after arrival of the new crew, and our reprovisioning. We all wanted to taste as much of this bold, desolate coast as possible.

18

To Bahia Concepcion

The two hundred twenty-five miles from La Paz to Bahia Concepcion is characterized by groups of coves and bays, separated by stretches of open coast. The hot, sandy landscape is rugged, rising rapidly in long ridges and gullies to a massive jagged mountain range that runs the length of Baja, very similar to an inverted mold of the Grand Canyon.

The first islands north of La Paz are Islas Espiritu Santo and Partida, with many good anchorages on their western shore. Although it is only eighteen miles from La Paz, an easy trip, it is a significant break with civilization. There is no fresh water on the islands and only a special breed of black jackrabbit lives there. When Cortez was here he found several hundred Indians on Isla Espiritu Santo, sustaining life somehow from the sea. He named the island "Isla des Perlas" for the pearl-bearing oyster beds there. In the early 1900s a Frenchman living in La Paz built narrow stone corrals on the edge of the bay. Here baby oysters were protected until they were large enough to be placed in oyster beds within the Gulf. The project was ruined during the Mexican Revolution, before its value could be proved. We walked along the smooth concrete of the remaining walls trying to picture the oyster farms in operation. We thought more of eating the oysters than of the pearls they might contain.

The best protected harbor on Espiritu Santo is Caleta Partida, actually a strait between two islands. Anchored near the head of this cove was a forty-five-foot ketch from southern California. It was dwarfed by the harbor, an extinct volcano cone. An expedition from *Windigo* landed on the sand spit because we had heard a fishing camp was located here, but the only sign of its existence was a partially filled-in latrine. Numerous bird and fish skeletons lay everywhere.

Back on board, we sat in the cockpit watching the sun's shadows creep up the colored lava walls of the old volcano. The neighboring ketch sat bathed by the sun, her white hull sparkling in the light, and her two varnished spars looking like Star Trek swords glistening against the dark background. The air began to cool. Flames from two small campfires danced at the base of the headland, where fishermen were camped, with their dories pulled up on the beach. Baja's mountain range, thirty miles away, sparkled in the sun. Its detail disappeared as the shadow chased the sun across the earth's surface.

Departing Caleta Partida we turned northward, looking into the deep coves formed between lava bluffs. At the head of most coves is a small estuary, beach, mangroves, and a dry arroyo. The water is clear and the bottom is reflective sand with a variety of small fish, unperturbed by our presence. Seeing a picture of *Windigo* anchored in any one of these inlets brings back a flood of memories.

Isla San Jose's two-thousand-foot peaks were barely visible in the haze, as we headed toward Canal de San José, and even though thin clouds covered the sky, the sun's strength penetrated the teak decks, making them too hot to walk on. Isla San Francisco, where we wanted to spend the night, was also lost in the haze. We were in no hurry, for it was only twenty miles away. We could enjoy the light breeze, with only the genoa, mizzen staysail, and mizzen set. To hoist

Windigo sails wing and wing in light breezes in the Sea of Cortez.

and later furl the mainsail was too much for this laid-back crew. Most wanted only to sprawl on deck to absorb the sun's rays. Soon even the helmsman, protected from the sun by an awning over the wheel, was comatose. The rest of the crew were in their own mental cocoons.

A cannon shot was heard in the distance. Scanning the horizon nothing was seen that might have caused such a noise. Another loud report, and again we searched the sea—still nothing to be seen. Charlie, who was steering, kept looking to starboard when something erupted from the glassy surface about one mile away. It fell back with a tremendous splash, the sound taking several seconds to each us: a manta ray. Nothing happened for about ten minutes. I'd heard that manta rays jump three times in succession. We waited expectantly. The fish was surely too distant for even the most powerful telephoto lens to show anything but a speck. Still the cameras waited. Then it happened—what a sight—even at this distance. Nearly two tons of fish hurdled fifteen feet into the air, then landed flat in a tremendous bellyflop. The performance occurred five times in ten minutes.

Awake now, I wondered about getting moving. No ripple disturbed the water's surface. Scanning the area I looked for the tell-tale sign of wind—patches of darker water caused by miniature waves. In the distance I saw hope, a breeze on the water. It appeared to be approaching and strengthening. As it neared, the breeze turned into a huge herd of porpoises. They swung parallel to our course, soon engulfing us.

For a mile the water's surface was alive with porpoises. There were perhaps several thousand. For twenty minutes an amazing show encircled us. Ten to fifteen animals would be airborne within forty feet of *Windigo*, on both sides.

Many rose nearly to the surface, then dived under *Windigo* or darted off in the other direction. They were forever criss-crossing above and below or in front of each other, never colliding. The distinctive black back and white bellies merging into an hour-glass pattern on their sides were clearly visible. Some porpoises leaped clear out of the water. These were the ones that thrilled us: their grace and ease was incredible. Usually they re-entered the water smoothly head first, occasionally with a "lob tail," an extra flick of the tail. Several even turned on their side in midair to land with quite a splash.

Sometimes four porpoises swam together, turning and diving, in the same formation. These teams even jumped clear of the water, droplets of water dripping from their sleek bodies as they soared ten to fifteen feet through the air. Somehow they knew where to land, with hardly a splash, without landing on others, to dart off together—lost again in the dark blue depths. Watching them one had to believe they live in perpetual happiness.

At some signal the herd that had entertained us so well wheeled away and

In Bahia Concepcion, porpoises surrounded Windigo *for many splendid minutes, leaping clear of the water.*

headed toward La Paz. Standing open-mouthed, stunned by the spectacle, we gazed after "our" herd, longing to remain part of them.

The sails were dropped and the engine turned on. We moved off in the opposite direction, recovering slowly.

The only other time I have seen sea creatures playing so beautifully and with so much abandon was in Desolation Sound, in British Columbia. We were powering over a flat sea when a dozen grampus whales approached. These small whales are about twelve feet long and have a blunt head and creased forehead. They stayed with us for forty-five minutes, frolicking under *Windigo's* bow. On looking into the clear water we could see them appear eight to ten feet down, as they swam in and out, back and forth, playing tag with themselves and *Windigo*. Often they turned on their side, exposing their white belly under mottled bluish grey-green back with dark flippers and tail. The bulbous head comes to a slight point. When the small mouth is closed, the puckered jaw curves upward toward the animal's eye in a perpetual smile. The whales were criss-crossed with scars, apparently from contact with dolphins and squid, which they eat. Several whales sidled up to *Windigo*, gently rubbing along her hull as they swam past.

As air breathing animals they needed to have their heads and blow holes break the surface often, their pronounced dorsal fin cutting sharply through the water. Each of us used several rolls of film before they departed. Exhausted from following their lively playing we were almost ready for them to go. Grampus whales, I learned later, are seldom seen within sixty miles of the coast and usually south of central California. Our encounter with this group was unusual, but so rewarding for us.

Isla San Francisco has three open bights suitable for anchoring. I felt comfortable using only one of them, the large bay on the island's southeast corner. The main part of the island is a pile of lava rising to six hundred ninety feet. Its western side slopes gradually; its loose, rocky eastern side is steep and drops directly into the sea. It was up this side that we scrambled one gorgeous afternoon, dressed in bathing suits, sneakers and hats. My camera banged against my side. We had already walked the huge crescent beach of white sand at the head of the bay. The beach ended at the foot of a rock cliff. Drawn on by the quest to reach the top we were soon moving straight up the rocky hillside. Extreme care had to be taken not to kick loose rocks onto those below. The razor-sharp rocks sliced our sneakers, and would quickly slice us if we slipped or tripped.

The early afternoon sun beat down intensely. I wondered how badly burned we would be. Dust clung to our bodies. My throat was dry. I longed for a cold beer, or iced tea in *Windigo's* refrigerator. But our discomforts were forgotten on reaching the island's summit. Sitting on a table top rock we had a panoramic view. To the north lay Isla San José, its backbone gradually tapered toward us. To the left of Canal de San José was the bold coast, rising quickly to the mountain range, lost in haze.

We looked down over the dry rock ridge across a dry valley to another ridge, then to the water six hundred feet below. The water's deep blue turned a light green near shore. *Windigo* looked minuscule on the still water, her mizzen still set. Her anchor line was barely distinguishable as it curved to the water, disappearing in the pale green.

On Isla San José we swam and explored.

A forty-five-foot local fishing boat anchored off the entrance to the lagoon; seven young men were setting their net near shore. One end of the net was held by a man who stood on a sand flat while the others, spread evenly along the net's length, waded into waist-deep water. The far end was pulled around in as large a circle as possible, returning to the sand. While four men pulled the net in, flanking it as it came, the other two slapped the water with their hands to drive the bait fish ahead of them.

Their catch was small, but the men didn't seem to care. They enjoyed this work, splashing in the water. One was stripped to his undershorts. The others wore long pants; one had rolled his pants legs up to the knees yet was wet to the waist. Their unkempt dark hair matched their eyes and weathered faces. They chattered continuously as they worked. The copy of Fielding's *Guide to Birds of North America*, which my birding friends Phips and Jane had given to *Windigo* in the Caribbean, was put to good use in Isla San José, where we saw myriad long-legged and exotic birds. The inscription Phips wrote on its now-tattered cover perhaps best describes my own birding interest: "Sandy, you have to look to see the birds." In spite of this, I have learned to identify many species, enjoying in particular the pelicans, frigate birds, brown boobies, and puffins. To simplify, I classify the thousands of different birds into two types—the chickadee type and the eagle type. This system works well for me.

Their method of catching bait fish was similar to the four tuna boats we saw one morning in Caleta San Everisto. They didn't even anchor, just steamed into the cove and stopped. While drifting, they launched their powerful workboats to set the nets, two boats per net. One man stood on the boat's bow to see where a school of fish was. One boat stopped, holding one end of the net. The other boat moved swiftly in a wide circle, the net flaking off its stern. When the circle was complete, the bottom of the net was pulled together, like a purse. Then the two workboats, their big propellers churning the water, slowly dragged the net to

Fishermen work their nets near Isla San Jose.

the mother ship. Pelicans arrived, diving into the water encircled by the nets, which was alive with small fish trying to escape. Once the net was alongside the mother ship a large winch tightened it further. Then men with long-handled nets, standing in doors opened in the boat's side, scooped the fish into the ship's hold. Within an hour the boats were gone.

We had seen several families living on islets near Isla San José, where nothing grows and drinking water has to be brought in. The families keep busy fishing and drying their catch in the sun, spreading it out on the rocks.

The government charts aren't much use along this coast for cruising because they lack detail. The Sailing Directions are even less helpful. The best guide was the *Baja Sea Guide*.

The *Guide* says to stay "well outside San Marcial Rock and reef," which extends northward of Punta San Marcial. "Navigators familiar with the dangers of the inside passage may save a good bit of time in calm weather by passing close along the shore and thus into" Bahia Agua Verde. The U.S. chart published in 1942 and revised in 1966 has scanty soundings throughout the Gulf. Its detail increases around Punta San Marcial, showing a minimum depth of thirty-three feet through the middle of the reef. Yet the *Sea Guide* indicates twelve feet in the same area. The first time I ventured around this point we were under power. It was another windless day; the sea was flat. I wondered about the *Guide's* and chart's discrepancy in regard to the water's depth through the inside passage and decided to become "familiar" with the route.

Cautiously we headed for the low San Marcial rock islets. When Roca Solitaria bore 275 degrees we turned for it. This large white needle-shaped rock off Agua Verde provides an unmistakable landmark. The rocks became visible as we passed over them, but the depth sounder never registered less than fifteen feet. At other times we sailed through here in light winds, always with caution.

The nicest anchorage in Bahia Agua Verde is in the cove on the northwest corner of the bay. We stopped here except when it was too crowded, which was any time we weren't the first boat there. A large rock, with ten feet of water over it and twenty feet around it, is located nearly in the middle of the cove, right where I'd choose to anchor. Instead we anchored well away from the easily identifiable brown patch in otherwise greenish water.

Half a mile south of our anchorage trees were kept green by springs that seep down from the five-thousand-foot peaks. Brightly colored boats were pulled up on the shore by the Mexican fishermen who camp on the beach. They had pulled their long dugout canoes with flared bows up on the beach. On one stern hung a large outboard. Nearby, fish nets were folded neatly on the sand. Several men squatted at the water's edge, cleaning fish. The entrails floated out to where dozens of gulls and pelicans waited to pounce on them. The cleaned fish were tossed into a bucket for drying later. Two turtles lay on their backs on the beach, their legs tied back so they couldn't flip over and escape. Sea water was poured over their bellies occasionally, and in this way they were kept alive for days until they reached the market, or were eaten. Turtle meat is delicious, I'm told, and is the only red meat many coastal fishing families ever see. But I had a hard time seeing these harmless creatures lying helplessly on their backs for so long.

The Mexicans sat on the sand talking in low voices. Most wore large-brimmed, light-colored straw hats, cotton shirts, with the sleeves rolled to the elbow, and pant legs rolled up to the knees. Under the rock cliff was their camp, a small pile of gear around a camp fire. They were quiet that evening, and when we went ashore the next morning, there was no indication they had camped there.

Seeing a path up from the beach, Rae and I climbed a rock-covered slope. Cactus spotted the gulch. In only a short distance the temperature rose quickly. There was not a breath of air to cool us. On the ridge top we looked down at *Windigo* and her near-perfect reflection. The brown and red hills surrounding the cove were also sharply defined and beautifully reflected. Nothing moved, except for *Windigo's* crew searching the beach for shells.

Descending the back side of the barrier ridge, we followed a goat path past a tiny cemetery that was tucked in a cul-de-sac. Shells and stones outlined the graves, and weathered scraps of wood were formed into a cross. We came upon a twenty-five-foot-wide dry river bed with towering palm trees lining its sides. An incredible transformation must occur after a severe rainstorm.

We walked back following the river bed to the ocean, where it ended at a cliff. Crystal-clear water dropped ten feet to white sand. Small colorful fish darted in and out along the rock wall, a thriving habitat so close to such barren desert.

Our view of the sunset was something special: a spectacular sight of slowly changing light along a wide vista of water, long ridges that rise like steps to form the mountain range that runs the length of Baja, with twin peaks towering over Puerto Escondito.

We continued northward, heading for Puerto Escondito, a popular place for cruising boats and sports fishermen. It is landlocked and provides secure anchorage in the worst of blows. It is not, however, a port in the commercial sense. A large concrete wharf has been built for a ferry terminal, and a newly paved intercoastal road now crosses from there to the west coast's deep-water port of San Carlos. The idea was to make a fast means of transporting people and goods from Baja's west coast and the Pacific to Mexico's mainland without going all the way around the peninsula. The ferry operation has yet to become operational. There are plans for luxury motels and an expanded airstrip for Escondito, but little seems to be happening. The only activity on the wharf was kids fishing. No fuel, provisions, or services were available. "Fresh meat, still on the hoof" is obtainable at a ranch nearby. Many people were camped along the south shore of the inner harbor. The campers were mostly Americans who had driven down the infamous Baja highway. Their living arrangements ranged from pup tents to large mobile homes. Many had trailered their boats as well. Their stories of flat tires, hijackings, and breakdowns were numerous.

The channel into the inner harbor is about seventy-five feet wide, from shore to shore. The navigable part is about thirty feet wide, with a depth of nine feet and maximum current of four knots. I was tempted to take *Windigo* in, but high tide was at an inconvenient hour. Instead we anchored in the "waiting room," a deep indented cove where most boats wait for slack before entering.

I investigated the channel and inner harbor on the windsurfer and was nearly caught by a fisherman casting from the shore. Inside is a perfect bay with five or six small coves suitable for anchoring. You could select your surroundings,

Hiking across Isla Carmen.

The only marina in the Gulf, north of Guayamas, under the landmark "Tetas de Cabra."

choosing between a long open beach fronting on a river plain, or a small rocky hill spotted with cactus and low brush, or a stretch of white sand beach or mangrove thickets. We enjoyed a beautiful sunset over the mountains.

In the morning we watched several pelicans feeding nearby. They circled about fifty feet above the water; the markings on the top of their wings were visible as they banked away from the hill near us. In this position we could see how the long neck bends back against the body making the head appear to be attached near the junction of the wings, with the long grey bill extending straight forward.

It still amazes me why they don't break every bone in their bodies when they dive into the water. They hit it with tremendous force, yet one never loses sight of them, and by the time the splash settles the bird is floating quietly, its neck extended straight up, its bill raised with the large throat sack swelling, and a bulge slides down its neck.

One pelican seemed sore having hit the water so often. It drifted near us, induced with pieces of pancake left over from breakfast. We couldn't decide whether it was the maple syrup, butter, blueberries or dough, but our tosses

Puerto Ballandra, where the author did some of his finest fishing.

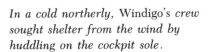

In a cold northerly, Windigo's crew sought shelter from the wind by huddling on the cockpit sole.

grew progressively shorter as we coaxed it to within ten feet of *Windigo*, its large brown eyes alert to every move.

Our departure that day was delayed; the weather had changed. The brilliant blue sky and cold wind was a sure sign of a strong northerly blowing outside our anchorage. A reef was tied in the mainsail and the small working jib replaced the genoa. On clearing Punta Coyote, thirty-five knots of wind hit us. It was good sailing, but cold. The wind had only recently blown across the snow-covered mountains. Every piece of clothing was worn under foul weather gear. Several people huddled in the lee of the doghouse, while others sat on the cockpit floor, using the windward seat as a backrest and windbreak.

We had little heart to push into this cold gale. The twenty-five-mile beat to Puerto Ballandra was long enough. This harbor is well protected, an ideal place to ride out a strong wind. After a late lunch of hot soup liberally flavored with rum we ventured ashore. One group explored the sweeping crescent beach and two mangrove lagoons. Two old wooden ships' ribs protruded from the sand of one lagoon.

When rowing back to *Windigo* after a day of climbing a strange noise was heard. We determined it was a whale blowing just outside the harbor. A second whale was seen swimming inside the harbor; apparently this place had good reason to be called Whale Bay.

As evening approached two of the crew decided to fish. They had brought fishing tackle all the way from Boston, for the Sea of Cortez is renowned as a sport fishing area. Having assembled their equipment and selected a choice lure, one fisherman stood amidships on the port side, the other on the starboard side. There was ample evidence of fish being around. I even wondered whether to proceed with the planned supper or to wait for the expected fish. No strikes. The planned meal was prepared. Before long one of the men tired of this inaction. He put his rod down to go below for a drink.

I'm no fisherman, but wanted to give it a try so asked if I could use his rod while he was below. After a ten-minute lecture on how to use this old fishing rod, I was allowed to hold it. My instructor was left handed, so naturally held the thing upside down and worked it backwards. We stood amidships, opposite the gate in the life lines, which was still open after the expeditions ashore. I listened—pretending to pay attention. But I understood how it worked for I'd used a rod and reel before, although was somewhat pressed to recall exactly when.

When finally left alone, a ripple appeared on the water's surface about sixty-five feet away. Wondering whether I could land the lure anywhere near the spreading circle I eased the rod's tip back over my shoulder. Then with a smooth forward movement of my shoulder and arms, then a snap of the wrists, I sent the lure flying. Seconds after the lure hit the water, I did likewise. I sailed cleanly through the open gate in the life line and landed in the water. Being no hero, I let go of the fishing rod, which promptly disappeared. I swam to the whaler and climbed back on board. Everyone had heard the splash, and I guess my startled cry, for they gathered instantly and asked what had happened.

No one else had seen the fish, which I really think was the whale we had seen swimming inside the harbor. The other whale was still outside, swimming back and forth. No one believed me that night, but in the morning the wooden lure was found floating some distance away with a badly bent hook. By following the line, I dived and retrieved the rod from the bottom of the bay. It was washed, carefully dried, and returned to its case by the owner, who wanted me to have nothing more to do with it. Nor did it emerge from its case again during the trip.

Eighty miles of open coast lies between Puerto Ballandra and Bahia Concepcion, a distance we sailed non-stop several times. I preferred stopping, however, in the large and beautiful Caleta San Juanico, tucked between two points. Many rocks, some projecting above the water, make this an interesting anchorage with good protection in most winds. The shore has reddish-brown bluffs, barren hills where an occasional cactus survives, and broad beaches. A climb up any of the low hills opens up unbelievable views: the ocean to the east and the mountain range to the west. Closer at hand one looks down small valleys, a barren, dusty land with the contrast of the clear water gradually turning from greenish to dark blue. Light blue sky usually holds some puffy clouds around the peaks. A breeze blowing off the water keeps the air comfortable.

Bahia Concepcion is one of the most popular areas in the Gulf. Activity is centered around Bahia Coyote. The main highway passes Bahia Concepcion, bringing campers by the drove. Commercial campgrounds have been built along the bay's shores. One caters to the large mobile home trade, with thatched umbrellas shading tables set along the beach. Another was packed with tent people. The many colored tents were set one on top of the other in a patched quilt effect. People sat in folding chairs around folding tables, drinking beer. The inevitable cooler was close by, a portable propane stove lay near the tent flap. Kids played on the beach or swam. Other campsites bridged these two extremes. What a contrast to the coves we had been in.

It was a pleasant change, particularly for those interested in visiting Mulege, a "major" town on Baja's east shore. It is located about two miles from the Gulf on the bank of a river, giving the town a tropical atmosphere. Palms cover the area with neat gardens of fruits and vegetables underneath. Nearby is the mission church first built in 1766. By the shore are luxury hotels. Overlooking the town is a large white washed prison, but none of my crew ventured that far.

One evening, when arranging for a taxi to take the crew into town the next morning, I met Harold. He and his wife were traveling with another couple in two large converted buses. Harold had been an electrician in the U.S. Navy. He was in Baja for the winter, and I think he was glad of a diversion from his quiet mobile home routine, when I asked if he would check out the alternator. It is supposed to charge the batteries whenever the engine is running but was no longer functioning. The auxiliary generator was able to keep the batteries from running down, but this was inconvenient and noisy, disturbing the quietness that we cherished so much.

In the morning, I picked up Harold and his friend. He brought a complete tool chest with all kinds of test equipment. The alternator was installed underneath the refrigeration unit, and was very difficult to work on. Harold tagged the wires and removed the unit. Spreading the parts out on the doghouse floor he pulled it apart, testing various functions as he went. Other than some minor

Fishermen haul in their nets off Guaymas, with the advantage of an outboard motor on their dory.

cleaning, there seemed to be nothing wrong with the alternator, so he reassembled and then reinstalled it. It still didn't register any current. Puzzled, Harold began tracing wires; the last one led to a blown fuse. When it was replaced, the system worked nicely. Harold, his friend, and their wives joined us on board for dinner that evening.

We had just covered the area many consider to be the best in the Sea of Cortez, from La Paz to Bahia Concepcion. I would have spent more time in this area and continued farther into the Gulf. But there wasn't time. My primary purpose in sailing to the west coast was to cruise British Columbia and southeast Alaska. Summer was rapidly approaching, it was time to head north.

As it turned out, I did return to Baja, delaying my trip to the Northwest, to explore as far up the Bay as Puerto Refugio and its sea lion colony.

Windigo *lies peacefully at anchor in Bahia Coyote.*

19 *Turtle Bay*

I delayed our departure and placed phone calls to all corners of the U.S. trying to locate at least one more crew member to sail with Rae, Nancy, and myself from La Paz to San Diego. No one was able to go sailing for two weeks. I could find no one in La Paz interested in making the thousand-mile trip. I could have obtained bodies with questionable qualifications for exhorbitant fees who "didn't much like sailing with the owner on board." I wanted no part of that under any circumstance. Besides, law enforcement officials have repeatedly warned against signing on strangers; "it is the best way to run into serious trouble, like losing your boat or being killed."

I felt that the three of us could safely make the trip as long as we took our time, even though sailing north along Baja's west coast is not an easy trip, even with a full crew. On leaving the peninsula's southern tip there are only three harbors along the coast suitable for shelter from the strong prevailing winds. There are few navigational hazards along the coast, so we could always head west—out to sea—if the weather deteriorated. *Windigo* would take care of us unless we did something stupid.

Before leaving La Paz we tied a reef in the mainsail. I assured Nancy and Rae that it wouldn't be taken out before San Diego. We would use the small genoa or working jib, while the larger sails were all stowed below. When our speed dropped, we could always turn on the engine to help us along, motorsailer style. We had enough fuel to power over half the way if we had to.

The engine had been acting up during the last six weeks, revving up momentarily at normal cruising speeds. Reducing speed seemed to correct the problem. I didn't anticipate powering much anyway, for the prevailing northwest winds are reliable.

We motored from La Paz to Cabo San Lucas, where the northwest wind met us. Heading offshore we set watches, four hours on, four hours off. The two girls stood one watch together, while I had the other one alone. The midnight to 0400 watch is a killer when you're by yourself. The last three hours seem like an eternity. Time simply stands still. Your eyelids grow heavy, your head nods, and you wonder how to stay awake another five minutes. Occasionally the boat wanders off course, until the shaking sails bring you back. When relieved by the new watch I couldn't sleep well, and kept hearing the girls discuss sail changes, "should we" or "shouldn't we." A few minutes of this, and then, "let's wait ten minutes." Ten minutes later the conversation was repeated.

The fourth afternoon out of La Paz, we anchored just inside the entrance of Bahia Magdalena. The three of us looked forward to a full night's sleep. I rechecked the *Sea Guide* about using the inside route from Magdalena Bay northward along the series of lagoons that stretch for seventy-five miles. This waterway is separated from the ocean by extensive bars of constantly shifting sand, broken by openings and curling breakers. Oh, what a reprieve from beating if only it were possible to exit safely at the northern end. There was no use dreaming about it, only a fool would try.

In the morning, we departed under power. The wind had died, leaving behind a lumpy sea. During the afternoon the engine began speeding up often, even when running at very low RPMs. On top of that I felt a cold coming on. Around midnight the engine stopped, faded as though it had run out of fuel. We hadn't run the engine that long, and the tanks had been full when we left. Pondering the problem during my pre-dawn watch, I concluded that, because of the engine's sporadic speeding up, it had consumed more fuel than was normal and that we had in fact run out of fuel.

Without the use of the engine, and with gentle head winds blowing, I reluctantly pulled the big genoa out of its locker. Turtle Bay, one of the three protected harbors along this coast, was one hundred fifty miles away. There I hoped we could find shelter, rest, and fuel.

We passed Laguna San Ignacio, one of the lagoons in which California gray whales mate and bear young. I had hoped to enter the lagoon, but these hopes died when we ran out of fuel. There was still Scammons Lagoon, north of Turtle Bay, but it was to the east of our course and closed to boats. Captain Scammon, aboard the brig *Boston*, discovered this lagoon in 1856, and found a grey whale breeding area larger than anything he had ever seen before. An era of slaughter began that nearly decimated these whales. By the 1890s whaling along this coast had ceased, for it had become unprofitable. The disappearing species hung on until the international agreement of 1938, which banned killing most whales, including the California grey whale. Now large herds make seven-thousand-mile journeys from their summer feeding grounds in the Arctic, traveling along the North American coastline, to the shallow breeding lagoons of Baja. We hoped to see them beginning their northward migration, if not in the lagoons, at least along the coast.

It seemed forever that we fought light headwinds, a strong southerly current, and my cold. Finally, we hove to off Turtle Bay and waited for daylight before entering. It was our eighth morning out of La Paz.

After sleeping all morning, I knew I should arrange for fuel, but couldn't make the effort. My cold had settled in. The girls helped me launch the whaler and I was about to head for shore when a man rowed over. We had seen the thirty-two-foot boat he was on the previous day, sailing along the coast. They had arrived an hour ago, having lost one blade off their propeller. Tom asked if we had a SSB radio on board, and could he make a call to the boat's owner. Since the owner couldn't be reached until after 6:00, I suggested he and his crew have supper with us. Misery, I figured, loves company.

When I reached the long pier in town, a young Mexican asked if I wanted diesel fuel. "There will not be enough water at the pier later, the tide will be high in about one hour." We could get fuel this afternoon, or not at all. I returned to *Windigo* while he went for three barrels of diesel. The wind was blowing directly away from the pier at about fifteen knots. The whaler was lashed alongside like a tugboat, and it moved *Windigo* against the strong wind surprisingly well. At the pier we tied stern to so the fuel could be siphoned from the barrels into *Windigo's* two tanks. They only took seventy gallons, although their total capacity is one hundred fifty gallons. Disheartened, I realized we hadn't run out of fuel, so the engine's problem was still there. Gloom settled over us as we drifted back to anchor.

That evening Tom was unable to contact anyone on the radio. During supper we swapped tales of woe. Tom and two friends were sailing the boat back to California for the owner. They hadn't been happy with the boat's condition when they boarded it in La Paz. Now, fed up, they were ready to leave it in Turtle Bay for the owner to bring back himself. While in La Paz Tom had experienced similar problems with this boat's engine, but after changing the fuel filters the problem was corrected. I decided to give it a try. But no, the filter was clean as a whistle. Tom arrived while I was still reconnecting the fuel lines. On hearing how clean the filter was he asked about the two external filters. I hadn't looked at them, not knowing what they were, and not really wanting to pull them apart, too. Tom wouldn't let it go at that. He disassembled them himself, with me watching. The first was clogged with fuel-saturated muck, and the other was almost as bad. He installed the spare filters. The engine started and ran beautifully.

Tom had solved my problem. I wished I could help with his, but *Windigo's* spare propeller was too large for a thirty-two-foot boat. We did transfer forty gallons of fresh water into his nearly empty tanks, but that was minor compared with the relief of having the engine work again.

That alone nearly drove my cold away. One more day of rest and we'd be off.

On the north shore of the bay is a town whose main activity is canning abalone. The fish is canned and shipped by truck or small freighter. Some is frozen or flown out fresh from the sand air strip. All fresh water and almost all food and

In Puerto Refugio, sea lions sunned themselves on the rocks or swam nearby.

materials are brought in the company's small freighter. The huddle of dusty dwellings was enchanting. The streets were sand, laid out in straight lines leading away from shore. Many of the tiny houses were fenced in, with sand yards, neat and tidy. A few dusty broken-down cars were parked at the edge of town, used only as a link over the rough coastal road. Great excitement prevailed in the town: the circus was here. Elephants were harnessed, ready to pull the huge tent to the tops of the three tent poles. Excited children were helping erect the stands and setting up folding chairs, a reenactment of yesteryear.

We had an early supper of fresh bread from a bakery in town, and lobsters, caught and sold to us by a small boy in a canoe, who had dived for them all afternoon. We returned to the circus, which was in full swing. Novelty acts and concessions were set up around the big tent. Inside, we found seats and watched the high wire and balancing acts, the animal tricks, and clowns. It held the audience captive, including ourselves.

We stayed to the end, then headed back with the audience. Most were teen-agers heading for the Community Center, where rock music rang forth, the walls vibrating from the noise and crowd on the dance floor. The heat inside must have been unbelievable; people moving toward the doors glistened with perspiration. Outside, groups of boys talked quietly, beer and cigarettes in hand. Kids darted in and out. The noise outside was too loud for me, but the volume was just about right back on board *Windigo*.

We departed early, motoring along the coast over a windless sea. The engine ran smoothly. Ahead a small sailboat raised her sails as she approached Isla de Cedros. While I watched, the small boat was knocked down by a blast of wind. She righted, and immediately dropped all the sails. *Windigo's* main was still reefed, so when the thirty-knot wind hits us we were just right. When we were clear of the island, the wind settled down to a steady twenty knots. We set the small genoa and had a good night's sail, but in the morning light headwinds returned, with fog. It had taken us fifteen days to bring *Windigo* the thousand miles from La Paz to San Diego. My sister and family were waiting to join us for the next leg, with fifteen interested crew members. Where were they when we needed them two weeks ago?

20 *Disasters*

The masthead rested on deck three feet from where I sat in the cockpit. The top third of the eighty-seven-foot aluminum mainmast had just broken off.

Early that morning we had passed Point Conception on our way north to San Francisco. The prevailing northwest wind was gusting above forty knots by the afternoon. As the wind increased, the sail area was gradually reduced, and finally we dropped the mainsail completely. Under number three genoa and mizzen, *Windigo* handled the conditions easily, footing well, although not sailing as close to the wind as she would have with a second reef in the mainsail and the working jib. Most of us spent the afternoon on deck watching the California coast materialize. During a watch change, we tacked off shore, within five miles of the rocky beach. The twelve-foot seas were short and steep, a terrible length for *Windigo*. These rough conditions were normal, caused by the ocean floor rising from great depths, and the waves bending along the coast.

A few waves were perpendicular to our course, like the one we had just slammed into. Watching *Windigo's* bow rise over the receding wave, I leaned forward to be in the shelter of the doghouse, sure that spray would soak the cockpit when the bow buried itself in the next wave. It did. At the same time something that felt like a rope slapped me across the back. When I looked around, I saw the masthead resting on deck three feet away. The genoa was over the side along with an untold number of ropes and wires. What took perhaps two seconds to occur took nearly three months to replace—plenty of time to reflect on the sequence of events.

When *Windigo's* bow stopped abruptly on that wave, it hit the side of a wall of water. The mast's forward inertia broke the windward running backstay. Now released, the middle of the mast continued forward until it broke. In coming down, the masthead fell outboard of the windward rail, then sprang back up and over the life lines as the rigging recoiled. It came to rest on deck, without scratching it at all. Had the mast landed directly on deck or on the doghouse, the consequences would have been drastically different.

I didn't like our position: being blown onto a lee shore by thirty- to forty-knot winds, with night approaching. The smart thing was to call for assistance now, before the situation became desperate. The Monterey Coast Guard Station answered my call immediately, and assured me help was on its way.

Windigo's *lofty aluminum spar, which later crumpled when a backstay parted.*

A year earlier, when installing the VHF antenna, I had sacrificed some of the radio's range by placing the antenna on top of the mizzen mast, instead of on the mainmast as many people recommended. I thought that if I lost the mainmast I'd want to use the radiotelephone. On the other hand, if the mizzen mast broke, I felt we could cope without calling for assistance. I felt no smugness as I gave the Coast Guard our exact position, the intersection of three Loran lines.

There was plenty to do before the Coast Guard arrived, securing the broken section as best we could, and retrieving the sail and gear trailing over the side. I had no idea how much could be accomplished or how to assign tasks to everyone. Consequently, the three teenage girls sat on the main cabin floor singing songs, the four grownup females, willing but tentative about helping on deck, stayed in the doghouse handing up tools and listening for any call on the radiotelephone. Hugh, a friend from Colorado, took over at the wheel and kept *Windigo* heading into the seas while my brother-in-law Paul and I began picking up the mess.

Before anything could be done with the broken spar the rod headstay had to be detached from the masthead. The stay hadn't broken, and now led from the masthead across the doghouse, over the rail, and bumped alongside under water, then rose to the bow and stem fitting. The stay had crushed the bow pulpit, twisting it like a pretzel. As *Windigo* rose to each wave, the weight of the genoa jerked the stay wildly. To remove the stay, two fittings had to be aligned and the stay held steady long enough to remove the clevis pin. To do this we used more lines than the little people of Lilliput used to hold Gulliver down. We spent close to an hour removing the headstay. When finally detached, it was secured to the rail, extending beyond the stern.

The mast's broken end hung twenty-five feet above the deck, held there by stays and internal halyards. Paul and I lifted the masthead over the doghouse, and put it down on deck. We discussed lowering the whole section onto the deck. The spinnaker pole topping lift supported the mast, while stays and halyards were removed. Once freed from entanglement, the entire upper spar was lowered and twisted so one spreader extended over the port rail and aligned with the life line's gate on the port side. The gate was opened to allow the spreader under the life lines, then refastened.

With the broken section secured on deck and lines attached to the remaining section for support, we took a short break to bolt down a bowl of hot chili. For the first time since the demasting, I noticed automobile lights zooming along the Coastal Highway. They seemed awfully close now that it was dark. How fast were we drifting? How near were those rock cliffs anyway? A ship was passing offshore. Perhaps they would stand by if the Coast Guard had been delayed. Calling the Monterey Coast Guard Station to find out, the cutter *Cape Hedge* answered instead. They were approaching from the south, inshore of us, and had us "in sight" on radar. It would take them less than an hour to reach us. What cheering news.

The time had come to retrieve the genoa dragging alongside. Paul and I began tying lines around the genoa and headstay, cinching them as tight as possible, then pulling the bundle close to the rail before tying the lines off. The weight of the sail full of water was tremendous, and our efforts were very unproductive. I couldn't think of what else to do, we had to get it back onboard or be towed in with it dragging alongside. We couldn't cast the sail adrift, because the genoa hanks wouldn't slide over the headstay fitting. To cut it with the hack saw would take all night. We simply had to bundle it as best we could. Occasionally Hugh called, "hang on" when he saw an unusually large wave approach. At his call, Paul and I hung on as *Windigo's* bow rose into the black night. As she plunged down, sheets of spray shot out from both sides. The wave's crest usually broke over us, and foam surged down the deck to cascade over the stern. As *Windigo* rose to yet another wave the three-quarter inch rod headstay snapped like a toothpick. Paul, who was securing a line around the sail when the stay broke, felt the vibrations run through his body. There was now a way to rid ourselves of the sail. Carefully untying the headstay secured alongside, I let it go. It slid through the genoa hanks and plummeted to the ocean's floor, a thousand feet below. I wondered if the sixty-five-foot rod would penetrate the ocean's soft bottom like a spear and what portion of its shaft would remain exposed, quivering in the murky water. The genoa's three corners were released and the sail floated clear. Quickly the short remaining portion of headstay was secured and all lines were tidied up.

The *Cape Hedge* was now approaching. I was surprised when the cutter approached our port bow as far away as she did. No one could possibly throw a line that distance. Instead of making another circle as I anticipated, the *Cape Hedge* slowly backed straight down on us, her bow heading into the seas. When her stern was a mere wave's crest away, the monkey's fist flew across *Windigo's* foredeck. Paul quickly pulled the tow line on board, leading it through the hawser in *Windigo's* bow. But the line's end wouldn't even reach the mast. A large knot, tying two lines together, wouldn't pass through the hawser. When the monkey's fist was thrown, the *Cape Hedge* had begun moving forward so as not to be swung broadside to the seas. With our delay over the knot, they quickly ran out of line, and, unable to hang on, we had to cast our end loose. While they circled for another try, I dug out two strong nylon docking lines. A line was attached to a coffee grinder winch and led forward to the foredeck. The *Cape Hedge* approached again, and I marveled at how well she handled, backing down on us in those huge seas. This time a bowline was tied in the hawser and we were in tow.

We got underway shortly after eleven heading for Morro Bay. I was disappointed to be heading south, but knew that it was far easier to run down the waves in the cutter's wake than to punch into them for forty miles. The ladies took over steering while Paul and Hugh turned in, and I catnapped in the dog house. The wind didn't let up all night.

Windigo spent nearly three months at Lido Shipyard while the broken mast was being replaced. I was disappointed at having to backtrack to Newport Beach, but I had high hopes of a short delay. The mast had broken cleanly, right where the spar had originally been welded together. These hopes were soon dashed—the bottom section had a permanent bend. A completely new mast had to be built.

The Special Project Division of MacDonald Douglas was called upon. They bent six thirty-foot long sheets of aluminum on a huge press into half circles. Those were welded together to form three tubes, then welded again to form one ninety-foot-long tube. *Windigo's* crew then spent hundreds of hours attaching the hundreds of fittings that made the tube into a mast.

Intimately familiar with every fitting on the shiny new spar towering above us, we departed Newport Beach in mid-August; headed for San Francisco, where I'd leave *Windigo* through the winter. I was still determined to see the Northwest, but was not anxious to sail the thousand miles from San Francisco to

The tender was a great boat when the outboard motor worked, but it lacked dignity when the crew had to use paddles. They were happy indeed to receive a tow from a local boat in Los Angeles, Mexico.

Seattle along that unfriendly coast. Besides, I'd been enchanted with the Sea of Cortez and decided to return there for March and April, then to head for Seattle again, this time via Hawaii.

On another stormy night during the voyage another type of disaster occurred. Off Isla Partida, I lay on deck watching *Windigo* swing violently at anchor in the winds and current. In the morning we found that the trusty tender, the whaler, had overturned, losing oars and oarlocks, and submerging the outboard engine. We tried in vain to revive the engine, but I was continually reminded of a wonderful description of all outboard motors written by John Steinbeck when he visited this area and wrote about it in 1942. In his *Log of the Sea of Cortez* Steinbeck wrote:

> We come now to a piece of equipment which still brings anger to our hearts and, we hope, some venom to our pen. Perhaps in self-defense against suit, we should say the outboard motor mentioned in this book is purely fictitious and any resemblance to outboard motors living or dead is coincidental. We shall call this contraption, for the sake of secrecy, a Hanson Sea-Cow—a dazzling little piece of machinery, all aluminum paint, and touched here and there with spots of red. The Sea-Cow was built to sell, to dazzle the eyes, to splutter its way into the unwary heart. We took it along for the skiff. It was intended that it should push us ashore and back, should drive our boat into estuaries and along the borders of little coves. But we had not reckoned with one thing. Recently, industrial civilization has reached its peak of reality and has lunged forward into something that approaches mysticism. In the Sea-Cow factory where steel fingers tighten screws, bend and mold, measure and divide, some curious mathematic has occurred. And that secret so long sought has accidentally been found. Life has been created. The machine is at last stirred. A soul and a malignant mind have been born. Our Hanson Sea-Cow was not only a living thing but a mean, irritable, contemptible, vengeful, mischievous, hateful living thing. In the six weeks of our association we observed it, at first mechanically and then, as its living reactions became more and more apparent, psychologically. And we determined one thing to our satisfaction. When and if these ghoulish little motors learn to reproduce themselves the human species is doomed. For their hatred of us is so great that they will wait and plan and organize and one night, in a roar of little exhausts, they will wipe us out. We do not think that Mr. Hanson, inventor of the Sea-Cow, father of the outboard motor, knew what he was doing. We think the monster he created was as accidental and arbitrary as the beginning of any other life. Only one thing differentiates the Sea-Cow from the life that we know. Whereas the forms that are familiar to us are the results of billions of years of mutation and complication, life and intelligence emerged simultaneously in the Sea-Cow. It is more than a species. It is a whole new redefinition of life. We observed the following traits in it and we were able to check them again and again:

1—Incredibly lazy, the Sea-Cow loved to ride on the back of the boat, trailing its propeller daintily in the water while we rowed.

2—It required the same amount of gasoline whether it ran or not, apparently being able to absorb this fluid through its body walls without recourse to explosion.

3—It had apparently some clairvoyant powers, and was able to read our minds, particularly when they were inflamed with emotion. Thus, on every occasion when we were driven to the point of destroying it, it started and ran with a great noise and excitement. This served the double purpose of saving its life and of resurrecting in our minds a false confidence in it.

4—It had many cleavage points, and when attacked with a screwdriver, fell apart in simulated death, a trait it had in common with opossums, armadillos, and several members of the sloth family, which also fall apart in simulated death when attacked with a screwdriver.

5—It hated Tex, sensing perhaps that his knowledge of mechanics was capable of diagnosing its shortcomings.

6—It completely refused to run: (a) when the waves were high, (b) when the wind blew, (c) at night, early morning, and evening, (d) in rain, dew, or fog, (e) when the distance to be covered was more than two hundred yards. But on warm, sunny days when the weather was calm and the white beach close by—in a word, on days when it would have been a pleasure to row—the Sea-Cow started at a touch and would not stop.

7—It loved no one, trusted no one. It had no friends.

Perhaps toward the end, our observations were a little warped by emotion. Time and again as it sat on the stern with its pretty little propeller lying idly in the water, it was very close to death. And in the end, even we were infatuated with its malignancy and its dishonesty. We should have destroyed it, but we did not. Arriving home, we gave it a paint, spotted it at points with a new red enamel, and sold it. And we might have rid the world of this mechanical cancer!

My outboard fit Steinbeck's description in every detail. It rode on *Windigo's* stern pulpit for the remainder of the trip, while we paddled the whaler around.

I have often been asked whether I have experienced any disasters. I take that to mean a major disabling incident—one you can't recover from. My answer is no, but certainly my reaction to that question would have been different on the morning we entered Morro Bay, and on another morning a year earlier, while still in Massachusetts.

I had been sleeping soundly at home outside Boston when the phone woke me shortly after 6:00 A.M. The Coast Guard asked if I owned a boat named *Windigo,* for she had sunk at her mooring. We'd been racing Saturday and I'd been on board yesterday afternoon. Everything was all right then. Driving to the boat I tried to convince myself that it was some other boat; even so I traveled those sixty-five miles in record time.

Sliding to a stop in the sand opposite *Windigo's* mooring, I felt my heart sink. Her high sides had sunk until only ten inches of freeboard showed. Alongside was the familiar old workboat *Turmoil* from Parker's Boat Yard and the flashing blue light of a Coast Guard boat.

On board *Windigo*, both portable gasoline pumps from the yard were working. No one knew where the source of water was. Descending into the cabin I was chest deep in bright yellow water; the dye markers attached to the life jackets had burst. A film of oil from the engine floated on the surface. I worked my way forward, looking for an upwelling that would indicate the source of this disaster. I found none.

The water level in the cabin was dropping; the two pumps were gaining. When only two feet of water remained above the cabin sole I went below again. This time water bubbled to the surface in the after head and over the refrigeration compressor. Closing the through-hull fittings to these two units stopped the bubbling. There were no other sources of water. When these areas were exposed, it was obvious that both hoses had been deliberately cut. The doghouse hatch had definitely been forced open. The sextant, two wall speakers, and a small portable radio were missing. This was vandalism at its worst.

As the receding water exposed the engine, the mechanic stripped it, and dried whatever he could. The engine was back together and turned over by late that afternoon. The mechanic was optimistic that it would start in the morning, and advised running it for many hours. The longer the better, he said, as it was important to dry the engine out before the salt water began to eat it up.

Everything was loaded into *Turmoil's* big cockpit. The pile of soggy sails, rope, cushions, bedding, books, and charts grew steadily. The gear ranged from ruined toilet paper to spare light bulbs, from canned foods to mushy oatmeal. It was appalling. This was all taken ashore to be dealt with later.

The engine did start the next morning, so we motored the three hours to Fairhaven where the clean-up program started. Another pile accumulated from a boat that I thought was already stripped. The yard washed above, below, and behind every partition to remove the salt, yellow dye, and oil film. Four electric heaters were placed below, and run day and night to dry her out. All the electronics had to be replaced, as well as all electrical connections—a monumental job done by one man, who scrunched into unbelievable places in tortuous positions to accomplish the task. The sails, cushions, mattresses, and bedding were all cleaned and dried, although some had to be replaced. Everything had to be sorted, and if not thrown out, washed and dried. The engine was run daily, and never did show any ill effects from its dunking.

My scheduled departure for the Caribbean, and eventually the Northwest, was for the middle of October. Somehow we departed on schedule, six weeks after the sinking.

*Porpoises leaping alongside always
seem to be joyous creatures.*

On our way down to Baja for the second visit some months later, another disaster occurred. We were headed for Newport Beach to have the bottom painted and a whole list of things done before leaving for Mexico. Departing San Francisco, we saw what few see—the sun rising under the Golden Gate Bridge. On board were six other good sailors. I wasn't used to such a large able crew for such passages. This was luxurious. There were two watches of three people each, with me standing out, as navigator and general helper.

We were traveling over a moonlit sea, as smooth and shiny as a mirror. The sails were dropped and furled. The decks were soaked from dew and we wore foul weather gear on deck to stay dry. After midnight, the lights on shore gradually went out—a sea fog had closed in. Overhead the stars twinkled, then suddenly even they were snuffed out. The masthead light reflected moisture particles and cast a five-foot ball of light. Occasionally, a lonely fog horn wailed from ships in the channel, several miles to the south.

Daylight fought its way slowly on board. The fog was thick. The blue sky reappeared overhead, but land, which we knew to be close to port, remained hidden. Slowly, a light westerly breeze developed. What a delight, after twenty hours of continuous motoring, to glide quietly over the sea, mainsail and genoa set wing and wing.

As evening approached, our speed dropped to below two knots. At this rate it would take a long time to cover the remaining twelve miles to Newport Beach. No one wanted to disturb the peaceful evening with the engine again, but I, for one, wanted to get in for dinner. Four large steaks were on board for the occasion which I hoped to barbecue on an electric grill, plugged into shore power.

As the engine sprang to life, the genoa was dropped on deck. Engaging the gear, my eyes watched the tachometer as I advanced the throttle. The meter's needle moved to fifteen thousand RPM, the normal cruising speed. Everything seemed normal, yet the water wasn't moving past us any faster than it had been. Jumping to the stern, I peered into the water wondering what was wrong now. The engine's cooling system was pumping water properly, exhaust smoke floated close to the water from under the stern as usual, but the water was not being churned by a turning propeller.

Everything seemed normal and the engine sounded fine. Looking in the engine compartment, I asked Ken to engage the engine, and I could see the shaft wasn't turning. It was disconnected from the engine—about two inches separated the two fittings. I squeezed into the limited space to reach the shaft. My leverage was terrible; there was no way I could pull it into position.

The genoa was reset, while replacing the floor boards, and I contemplated sailing into Newport Beach Harbor with no power at all. I called the yard on the radiotelephone to advise them that we would be in that evening. They were expecting us and had a slip for us, and were planning to haul *Windigo* first thing in the morning. We could anchor off Lido Island and wait for assistance in the morning, but that was not an appealing alternative.

A quick supper was consumed before watches were resumed. It was dark

Riding up in the bow, away from it all.

now. It could be a very long night—our speed was less than one knot. My brother and Ken began trimming the sails to catch every puff, and to untangle the maze of lights that had appeared along Huntington Beach and Newport Beach. I turned in for some rest.

An hour after falling asleep, I was awakened. We were reaching along at three knots, and the green flashing light off the breakwaters at Newport Beach had been identified. The wind was freshening. I was concerned. At what speed would the drag on the propeller force the shaft farther aft? Should this happen, the propeller would jam the rudder so it wouldn't move, and we'd be unable to steer. A fog bank was now approaching from the south, and it was about the same distance from the harbor's entrance as we were, moving at about the same speed.

I ordered the genoa eased, our speed slowed little, then the sail was dropped. We lost our race with the fog. It swallowed the bell buoy's green light, then the red light on the breakwater, while we were still a half mile away. Continuing for the breakwater I thought of alternatives: we could circle the bell buoy, anchor off the beach, or head offshore until the fog lifted. None of these ideas was appealing.

Passing the breakwater's outer end, we turned in. A large fishing boat was steaming out, with her trawling arms already extended. Wanting the channel to ourselves we circled around, when suddenly the fog lifted slightly.

As we crept along the breakwater the visibility improved. Diffused lights appeared to our left, on the end of Balboa Peninsula, then along the Corona Del Mar shore. The wind was light, from astern. One crew member stayed by the mainsheet, adjusting it to keep our speed around two knots. The harbor chart was on hand. Compass courses were laid out on it, all the way to the yard, and were used the whole way in. Moving slowly along the channel, which is bordered by rows of boats moored bow and stern, I wondered about the ferries plying back and forth across the narrowest part of the harbor. I'd seen three ferries working two slips without interruption, threading their way across a weekend flow of boats ranging in size from sailing prams and windsurfers, to huge yachts, larger than *Windigo*. Our timing was just right. We crossed behind one ferry and ahead of the next.

I tried to anticipate all the contingencies. I tied the whaler securely fore and aft beside the cockpit, ready for use. The big anchor was readied forward, a folding anchor was set up on the stern. Docking lines were laid out on both sides and the fenders piled amidships for use wherever they were needed. We discussed what I expected to happen and I assigned people specific tasks. I couldn't think of any other preparations.

Ghosting along parallel to shore we fell silent, caught up in our own

"A disaster is some event you can't recover from." There were no disasters on Windigo's voyage.

thoughts. The sterns of a continous row of docked boats, their noses toward shore, were barely visible only a few feet away. The stillness was heavy, eerie, and beautiful. Breaking it, a woman's voice carried across the water, saying "What a pretty sight. Is someone on board?" One of us replied "Oh yes, we're just out for an evening sail."

Then the shipyard appeared. Just before the big railway was an open dock, the one we would head for. As we passed it, Dave dropped into the whaler and on his second try the outboard sprang to life. When sure it was running I put the helm hard over. Dave climbed back on board to help lower the mainsail, which came sliding down with eager hands clawing it. The outboard spluttered and died. I called "David, get that thing going!" and I turned *Windigo* toward the dock. There were no encouraging sounds, and I had no helpful suggestions. I saw that if we didn't reach the dock, we would be carried against the heavily greased vertical lift, painful on the topsides. The stern anchor was dropped and its line paid out.

We weren't going to make it. I had Roger cleat the stern anchor line; we could swing on that and reorganize. But the anchor didn't hold! (On retrieving it, we found one fluke hadn't been locked into the open position; it had folded shut and slid easily along the bottom.) *Windigo's* bow nudged the outer piling. Thinking quickly, Ken jumped off and ran around to the other side of the slip where a line was thrown to him. This line was led to the coffee grinder amidships, and slowly we pulled ourselves into the slip.

Dave looked up at me, shaking one end of the whaler's gas hose, and asked in a frustrated, disgusted voice, "Do you think it would help if this were attached to the engine?" Nodding, I groaned; I was the guilty one.

Before the docking lines were properly secured, the steaks were sizzling on the barbecue. We sat down to a midnight dinner, a fitting one for a good trip with a memorable ending.

There is one disaster with lasting effects that occurred in my travels on *Windigo*. It was the loss of nearly a thousand slides of Baja and the Northwest. I was in Newport Beach, preparing for the passage to Panama and return to the East Coast. My car was loaded with equipment not needed for southern cruising, ready to be driven east.

During my absence one afternoon, two cartons were taken out of the back seat. One contained a spinnaker, which is of course replaceable. But what could someone do with a huge spinnaker, or slides of Baja and British Columbia? They were useful only to me! It took a long time to recover my spirits after that senseless incident.

21

Ocean Passages to the Northwest

At dawn, Sunday, May 1, we left La Paz a second time for the Northwest. Having experienced disaster earlier on this leg along the coast, I was anxious to avoid the twenty-four hundred miles upwind to Seattle. One alternative required sailing nearly five thousand miles—via Hawaii, the favorable aspect being that the route theoretically required only one jibe and provided favorable winds all the way. I estimated both routes would take about the same length of time. Going via Hawaii would be considerably easier on both crew and vessel. It seemed crazy to sail all that way and plan only seven days in Hawaii, but my sole purpose in going there was to use Honolulu as a stepping stone to reach Seattle. My highest priority was to spend the full summer cruising in British Columbia and Southeast Alaska.

The rhumb line to Hawaii is 265 degrees True, or nearly due west, but because of the wind's direction, and to ease sheets for better speed, we sailed on a course of 245 degrees True. There was a long way to go, nearly twenty-seven hundred miles, with northeast and east winds prevailing most of the way. Sailing south of the rhumb line at the beginning would make little difference on the long passage.

Romping along at eight and a half knots under a bright blue sky, the crew watched with mixed feelings as the mountainous tip of Baja receded below the horizon. I, on the other hand, was up to my elbows, repairing the head, which had broken late the night before.

To say this is a messy job is an understatement. The details I will not describe. Once the head was apart the problem was obvious: the piston lever was broken beyond repair. This bronze sandcast part is vital to the toilet's functioning, and no spare part was carried on board.

I began wondering if the part could be located in Honolulu. With little hope of raising anyone on the SSB radiotelephone, I turned the set on. The high seas operator answered immediately, and she patched me through regular telephone lines to the manufacturer's office. My luck held, my friend David was in, and he assured me that a piston lever would be awaiting our arrival in Honolulu, in fact, he would hand-deliver it, since he was going to the islands next week anyway. The magnitude and significance of being able to arrange with someone twelve hundred miles to the north for a tiny part to meet us twenty-five hundred miles to the west, while we sailed slowly over an empty sea, gave me a strange feeling. (Unfortunately, the second head packed up soon thereafter, and we had to use a tiny unit in the forepeak, even though it leaked badly.)

The wind gradually weakened the next day, our speed slowed and the seas subsided. For a week the wind ranged between five and ten knots. We enjoyed some good sailing, close reaching under full sail, but always over a sea of mixed ocean swells, and much of the time we powered, supplementing the light wind, trying to get westward into the northeast trades.

With nine persons on board, good watch systems could be used. With only Roger and myself knowledgeable about *Windigo* and offshore sailing, one of us had to be on deck at all times, so we had two watches, each with four persons. Jill, the ninth on board, was cook. She didn't stand a regular watch but joined the day watches when possible. Each day one person had a "day off," helped Jill cook, serve, and clean up in the galley, caught up on sleep with a full night off, and, in general, did whatever he or she wanted.

The watch system I use on passages is three four-hour night watches and two six-hour watches (1900 to 2300, 2300 to 0300, 0300 to 0700, 0700 to 1300, 1300 to 1900). This system rotates watches daily, an aspect most people like even on short trips, and important on longer passages. With no automatic pilot or steering vane, someone had to steer at all times. This means someone is on deck all the time, which I think is important. The night watches, with four people and little to do, could become long, and the stories and revelations told were astounding. During the day, household chores were performed, salt water bucket baths were taken on deck, laundry was washed, and books were read. These activities were interspersed with hourly tricks at the wheel, and sail changes.

I enjoyed few of the spectacular sunsets that everyone else relished. They occurred as I agonized over what the weather would do throughout the night. I wanted to get the sail combination set before dark so that no sail change would be needed in darkness. Huge ominous clouds often materialized at dusk, and sometimes they remained overhead all night, occasionally producing strong shifting winds. Where were those steady trade winds?

Some days we ran the engine for hours. We crept along on a vast mirror. I hadn't planned on powering much during this trip, but we were almost at the point of limiting the motoring to two hours each day for the purpose of recharging the batteries. The *Pilot Chart* shows the northeast winds to blow in this area over eighty percent of the time, and indicated no calms. In the twenty-four hours after leaving Cabo San Lucas, we had covered just over two hundred miles, but expectations for a fast trip were dashed quickly after that. During the next six days we averaged only one hundred fifty-five miles per day, which would have been even less had we not powered much of the time.

As the second week started, the northeast trade winds began. During the day we sailed below our desired course, running wing and wing, with the genoa held out to starboard on the spinnaker pole. The pole was lowered for the night and we sailed higher than the rhumb line to keep the sails full, on an easier and safer angle of sailing. One night we lowered the mainsail completely as thirty-knot winds swept the deck. Running before wind and waves under working jib and staysail, the angry black seas melded with the dark sky, and it was a strange sensation to be flying along with nothing but blackness surrounding us.

When first planning this trip, I had had no chart available to measure the distance from La Paz to Honolulu. I knew the Transpac Race is considered more than twenty-two hundred miles long, and that boats the size of *Windigo* take ten to eleven days to cover that distance. The record time was nine days thirteen hours set by *Big Ti* in 1965. Under a different name and ownership, *Windigo* had raced to Hawaii. I had no intention of racing now, but reasoned that by starting well to the south of the Transpac's start, I'd have more than adequate time if I allowed fourteen days for the passage.

Shortly before leaving Baja I finally measured the distance and found it to be about twenty-seven hundred miles, considerably farther than anticipated. Honolulu is 22 degrees north of the equator, La Paz 24 degrees north, and Los Angeles 34 degrees north. Yet Los Angeles is closer to Honolulu than La Paz, and San Francisco, farther north still, is even closer. This made it graphically clear how the west coast lies in a northwest-southeast line. The map showed La Paz to be east of Phoenix, Arizona; Salt Lake City, Utah; and Helena, Montana, none of which is anywhere near the ocean. As we started out from La Paz, I wasn't really concerned about the extra distance because the trade winds are predictably strong and steady. It seemed likely that we would best the one hundred seventy-five mile average I use in determining off-the-wind passage times. (I use an average of a hundred miles per day when beating.) Little did I know that we would have two days under one hundred forty miles and only three days over one hundred eighty-five miles.

Some ocean passages are better than others, but I have yet to enjoy one. I make them to get *Windigo* from one cruising area to another, to see new places and meet new people. As far as I am concerned, one sea is too much like all the others. Seldom is the ocean smooth, except during calms, which aren't good for sailing. The boat is constantly in motion; heeling, rolling, and pitching. Things are constantly sliding, usually away from you, ending up in the scuppers, or overboard, against a bulkhead, or on the floor. You need to hang on any time you stand up, which makes everything much harder. One side effect of this constant balancing act is how fit you stay. Muscles are forever flexing, even when you're asleep.

Most of *Windigo's* crew signed on for an "ocean passage experience." They had varying backgrounds in smaller boats along the coast, but wanted to see what it was like to sail out of sight of land. It surprised me to find that the ocean passages were the easiest to fill. I finally appreciate that it is the romantic sailing experience that people are seeking. One morning I overheard two crew members comparing notes. One vowed not to be on a boat for more than two successive nights ever again, the other wouldn't sail out of sight of land again. The consensus was that sailing was hours upon hours of boredom mixed with misery and moments of sheer terror, interspersed with periods of contentment and being in tune with nature.

A few ocean passage crews are like Randy and Sara. He wanted to chuck the tread-mill life he thought he led to go world cruising with his family. His wife, Sara, didn't share the same ambition. She had been delighted about a vacation to Hawaii, until she learned they'd be sailing there. Early in the trip she expressed amazement that she was actally standing night watches "What kind of vacation is this?" At first she gingerly took her hour's trick at the wheel, hesitant when the wind blew and waves built, but she hung in there. Randy, unlike many, loved all aspects of the sailing. He was the only person on board who remained unconcerned about taking longer than expected to reach Hawaii. By noon on May 17th, our position was one hundred seventy miles east of Honolulu. Bets were made on the exact time Diamond Head would bear 50 degrees. Everyone was anxious to get in, but Sara was now talking about staying on for the next leg.

We searched in vain for the island's mountain tops as the sun sank behind a low cloud bank. The east wind moderated, then swung into the southeast, necessitating a jibe. It was the first time the main boom had been on the starboard side. We maintained six and a half knots for another hour, then our speed gradually dropped. By midnight it was under three knots. The prospects of more wind seemed slim. By 0400 the moon's light shimmered across a mirror-like surface. Where was the wind that made for those fantastic photos of the Transpac yachts finishing off Diamond Head, surfing down waves under shortened sail?

We passed Diamond Head just before noon. All sails were down, furled and stowed. No ripples marred the sea's surface. I missed my ETA at Diamond Head by six minutes, the closest guess by far. Only a few mild complaints were heard about my being solely responsible for the engine controls and therefore our speed. No one wanted to stay out any longer for a few bucks.

The scheduled seven day layover in Honolulu was shortened to four. A second piston lever for the second broken head was shipped to us the next day.

Five of the crew took off for home the same night we arrived—some vacation in Hawaii. Those who remained did laundry, reprovisioning, and a few odd jobs on board between relaxing and wandering around Honolulu.

The gimballed table in the main salon kept food reasonably level, no matter how rough the weather got.

Silliness in Hawaii.

A Japanese glass fishing buoy is hoisted aboard in mid-ocean, with a trail of barnacles and other sea creatures attached.

The new crew arrived and settled on board. All preparations were completed by Saturday afternoon so we decided to spend the night in Pearl Harbor instead of remaining in the small crowded Alawai Harbor. This happened to be the only weekend of the year that Pearl Harbor is open to private boats.

In the morning, after a leisurely breakfast, we got underway. Drifting past the *Arizona* Memorial I tried to imagine what this harbor had been like in December of 1941. We glided out the narrow entrance under sail, passing two Navy ships on their way in.

On rounding the island's southwest corner the sails were hauled in for an exhilarating sail in smooth water, along the lee of the island. A border of white sand separated the deep blue ocean from the green plantations sloping up the mountain side. We approached the island's northwest corner with little wind while tying in a double reef and setting the small working jib, incongruous as this seemed. We could see the water ahead in a turmoil. On clearing the island, thirty-five-knot winds hit us. Thankful to have shortened sail prematurely, we headed out into the high, steep seas, sailing hard on the wind, our next stop Seattle.

Those who had not anticipated the worst hurried below for their complete foul weather gear. Everything that was not well secured flew to leeward. Nothing was spared. No one stayed below for long, because sea legs had to be developed, and sea stomachs acquired. Most people were affected by *mal-de-mer,* an inner ear leveling problem that affects people in varying degrees, but after three days at sea, even the sickest recovered and functioned again normally.

Waves washed the foredeck, racing aft along the scuppers back into the sea. Spray whipped over the windward rail, soaked the forward half of the boat, occasionally drenching the doghouse windows, but hardly ever reaching those huddled in the cockpit. Everyone was there, determined to stay on deck, bundled up against the rapid drop in temperature. Some had growing apprehensions about this trip they had gotten involved with.

The conditions didn't bother *Windigo;* we weren't over-canvassed. She rode the seas easily. She wasn't straining or pounding as we headed north. steering a compass course of 345 degrees, or 2 degrees west of True North. The wind's direction kept us from sailing straight for Seattle, about 45 degrees True. The practical route back to the States from Hawaii is to sail north first, around the Pacific High that generally sits off the U.S. coast. The winds blow in a clockwise direction around the High's center. We had sailed to Hawaii on the northeast and east winds along the High's southern sectors. The northwest winds that prevail along California's coast are from this same High, its north and eastern sides. Sailing north from Hawaii we wanted to sail along the High's western side until the winds come from the west and eventually northwest for the reach into Seattle. When the wind shifts from south to west is when the one jibe theoretically takes place. Theoretically it is fair winds, Force 3 and 4, all the way, with calms less than 3 percent of the time. The major unknown was the exact position of the High and how intense it was. This would determine how far off the direct route we should sail to insure favorable winds.

The first two days after clearing Oahu were cold, wet, and rough. Few people ate anything, which suited Jill fine for she wasn't able to stay in the galley for long. The heat from hot mugs of soup was appreciated by all, even by those unable to consume it. As miserable as most of the crew was, all stood their watches. Perhaps they considered it better to be cold and wet on deck than horizontal and miserable below.

On the third day the wind eased and the seas subsided. The sky, which had been cloudless, now brought a new light and warmth. The crew began to smile and joke again, appetites returned. The fourth and fifth days were ideal; twelve-knot easterlies, flat seas, warm bright days, clear nights with heavenly constellations, and good food which made for wonderful sailing. These were the most enjoyable days in the whole thirty-day passage from Baja to Seattle. We averaged seven and a half knots for two days. It was delightful sailing under cruising sails, the wind just forward of the beam.

People often ask me about the fish we catch from *Windigo*. I certainly enjoy eating good fresh fish, but don't have the patience to catch it. Seldom do I trail a line on passages. One fish that was caught from *Windigo* was a dorado, or dolphinfish, caught along Mexico's west coast. They are good game fish, and can tear tackle apart as they make unbelievable leaps in the air. Once hooked, these fish start changing colors, and on each jump it seemed to be a different fish. And, they are good eating. The one we caught fed fourteen for dinner, the most ever squeezed around *Windigo's* saloon table for a meal.

Another fish was caught from *Windigo* well offshore. One afternoon I was awakened by a loud commotion on deck. A large fish was jumping clear of the water astern. There was no way to play it, taking in slack and playing out line when the fish dived. It was far too large to pull in. The line remained tied to a cleat. Three of us pulled the fish in—a huge sailfish. When it was close, we stared in amazement at the hook. It trailed in the water, behind the fish. There was a perfect clove hitch wrapped around its bill, and the line was caught behind one gill. Expecting the line to slip off the bill any second, we hauled the fish to the transom. A stout line was looped around its tail, led through a block on the mizzen boom, then to a winch. The thin tail was pulled up against the boom, but the fish's bill still dragged in the water. It was more than twelve feet long and weighed over two hundred pounds. I was not anxious for the fish to be cleaned on board (blood, guts, and teak aren't a happy combination), but we laid the fish on plastic garbage bags, and it was cleaned and filleted. One side went into the freezer for a barbecue ashore. The other side was eaten, cooked in several ways. I was sorry to have caught such a magnificent creature; there had been no "sport" in it, it's not good eating, and we were unable to preserve the fish, with its large royal blue dorsal fin, for mounting.

On passages, I like to have two people directly involved in the navigation. I usually advance the dead reckoning position (DR) from an hourly log kept by each watch, showing the course actually steered, and average speed. I also take noon Loran readings. The mate, in this case Roger, took noon sun sights to determine our latitude and longitude. On board was one good sextant (expensive) and two plastic ones (inexpensive). The plastic ones were used by any of the crew who wanted to practice taking sights and learn the process. Many people took advantage of this opportunity, which caused Jill some trouble. She was as interested as everyone else in where the small circle was placed each day, representing our progress across the chart. But she had to plan the midday meal around "local noon" (the exact moment the sun reaches its zenith at any point is that latitude's local noon; from then on the sun is going down). The local noon changed relative to our clocks. Then when shipboard time was adjusted for time zone changes, it further complicated her lunch planning so she wouldn't serve it when three or four people were deeply involved with taking sights. The sun sights and Loran readings consistently gave us fixes within twenty miles of each other, often less than ten miles, all the way from Baja to Seattle.

On the trip to Hawaii we saw no sea life until we were within a hundred miles of the islands. Then several small birds and three humpback whales came over to investigate. We saw no ships either, just jet trails high in the sky. Heading north from Hawaii, we saw numerous black-footed albatross that followed us for days at a time. These big birds glide inches from the water, their drooping wing tips occasionally flicking a wave top. At night they slide in and out of the sternlight's beam, keeping the night watches entertained. We also saw two ships in three days; the ocean was getting crowded.

One day I called a freighter on the VHF radio for a weather forecast and learned that a depression was located some two hundred miles north of us. It was moving slowly to the northeast. This low had undoubtedly caused the unsettled weather of the last few days. During the evening, the wind continued back-

In mid-ocean, tireless albatross followed Windigo *for days.*

ing and steadily increased in strength. By midnight the wind was from the northeast, blowing a steady thirty-five knots, gusting to forty. Sailing under the working jib and mizzen we headed north, making little headway and considerable leeway. Cold rain fell in sheets. The visibility was zero.

Windigo lurched over the seas, which built quickly, but she wasn't straining under so little sail. Her crew had gained their sea legs and stomachs. A simple hot meal was eaten below, served quickly before the food could spill. People had learned how to lean against bulkheads, balancing precariously on one leg, while stuffing the other leg into foul weather pants and sea boots as *Windigo* rolled unpredictably in every direction. Donning foul weather top over layers of heavy sweaters was only slightly easier. Then came scarfs, hats, hoods, and gloves.

Each time I think of that night my mind conjures up a picture of Sven sitting behind the wheel, his right shoulder squared to the wind, hunched up to protect his face from the driving rain and spray. Two fluorescent orange fishermen's gloves protruded from the sleeves of his dark green slicker, which was drawn tightly around his neck. A broad-brimmed, black fishing hat was pulled low on his head, and was cocked to windward to keep the rain from his neck. Sven's face glistened, and a droplet of water hung from his nose. His eyes sparkled and a smile spread across his broad face, his jaws working a wad of tobacco. He enjoyed this foray with nature.

The wind blew for eighteen hours. It was the first and only time since leaving Baja that a noon sight was unobtainable. In the middle of the afternoon, the wind simply stopped, leaving us to roll unmercifully in lumpy seas. The slatting sails and jarring gear were hard on *Windigo,* and even harder on my nerves. For three and a half days we flopped around. We simply had to wait for the prevailing northwest wind—for the Pacific High—to reestablish itself, for we had used almost all the fuel.

Before dawn on June 7th the wind at last moved into the north northwest. My spirits rose, as we eased sheets for Cape Flattery, the entrance to the Straits of Juan de Fuca. Blue sky could be seen on the western horizon. The cloud cover of the last few days was breaking up. We were moving rapidly again, and began to realize that our landfall was imminent.

Our landfall was perfect. Cape Flattery emerged from the clouds, and four hours later, without altering course, with the sun setting behind us, we passed the lighthouse on the Cape. All night we sailed up the Straits of Juan de Fuca, staying well away from the busy shipping lanes. Sunrise brought a clear morning and a spectacular sight of the snow-capped Olympic mountains rising behind Port Angeles. We had to power down Puget Sound to Seattle, then tied up at the huge, city-operated marina. Everyone was happy to be ashore. Long hot showers were the first order of business, then dinner and a full night's sleep. The best part of ocean sailing is arriving, safe and sound.

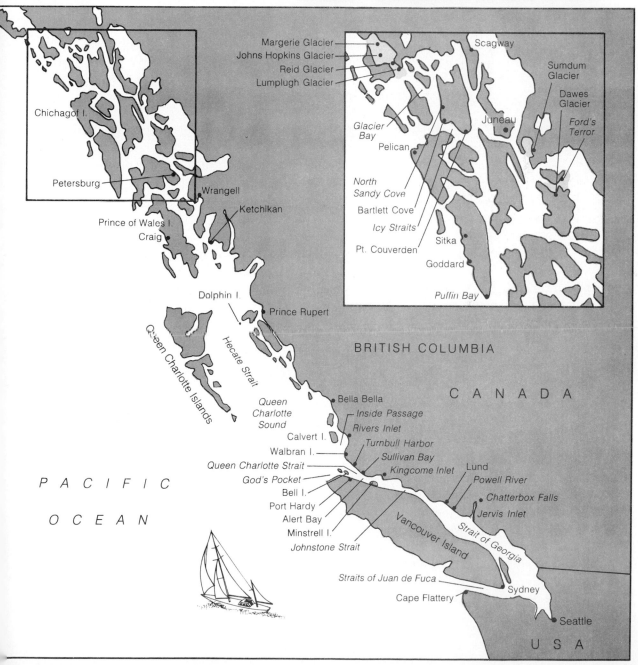

Margerie Glacier

Johns Hopkins Glacier

Reid Glacier

Lumplugh Glacier

Scagway

Sumdum Glacier

Dawes Glacier

Glacier Bay

Juneau

Ford's Terror

Pelican

Chichagof I.

North Sandy Cove

Bartlett Cove

Icy Straits

Pt. Couverden

Sitka

Goddard

Petersburg

Wrangell

Puffin Bay

Ketchikan

Prince of Wales I.

Craig

Dolphin I.

Prince Rupert

Queen Charlotte Islands

Hecate Strait

BRITISH COLUMBIA

CANADA

Bella Bella

Inside Passage

Rivers Inlet

Queen Charlotte Sound

Calvert I.

Walbran I.

Queen Charlotte Strait

God's Pocket

Bell I.

Port Hardy

Alert Bay

Minstrell I.

Johnstone Strait

Turnbull Harbor

Sullivan Bay

Kingcome Inlet

Lund

Powell River

Chatterbox Falls

Jervis Inlet

Vancouver Island

Strait of Georgia

P A C I F I C

O C E A N

Straits of Juan de Fuca

Cape Flattery

Sydney

Seattle

U S A

22 *Heading North*

Windigo lay alongside the venerable *Diamond Head* and other Seattle boats during a club gam in Mystery Bay, thirty miles north of Seattle. When we left, we stopped in the winding channel to watch the other boats depart. They headed south, back to Seattle. We turned *Windigo's* bow northward.

The northwest coast of North America is a vast cruising ground of protected waters. The Inside Passage from Seattle to Skagway, Alaska, spans over a thousand miles, but the coast itself provides 100,000 miles of islands, fjords, bays, and rivers. Mountain ranges block civilization's advance, with peaks that are snow-capped even in summer, and the coastal road stops only a hundred miles north of the United States/Canada border. This is the area that I had transited the Panama Canal to see.

Crossing into Canadian waters, we entered in Sydney, and one of my most vivid memories is of *Windigo* lying at anchor off this town as the sun was setting. The colors were vibrant, with Mount Baker in the distance, its snow-covered top nearly pink. We traveled slowly through the Canadian Gulf islands, enjoying this stretch of forested islands and rocks scattered to form a sheltered group with sparkling waterways in between. It is a good area to explore, to savor, before setting a course for more remote areas. One day was spent running before a light southerly up Trincomali Channel, chasing a twenty-five-foot yellow catboat named *Sylvester*. *Sylvester* left the cove before us in the morning. She continued for Dodd Narrows while we went through Gabriloa Passage and into Strait of Georgia. Months later we would see her again, sailing up Icy Strait near Glacier Bay.

We passed many good harbors on our way up Jervis Inlet, but we were headed for Chatterbox Falls, which is, rightfully, the most photographed waterfall in British Columbia. From nearly overhead a ribbon of water falls from a height of one mile. Its cascading froth of foam falls into the inlet just a few yards from where we tied up alongside a float.

A ranger lives at the base of Chatterbox Falls during the summer months, supervising boats that visit each year. We were ahead of the crowds, tying to the float with only one other boat. We made the three-hour climb to a small log cabin at the base of a hidden falls. The view from there is beautiful, down the

Tied up near Chatterbox Falls, British Columbia, Windigo's first destination in the Northwest.

full length of the inlet. Later, we sat in *Windigo's* cockpit and marveled at the shadows forming different characters in the rock face above us.

As we passed the northern end of Savory Island, the depth sounder read over one hundred fifty feet, much too deep for anchoring. A dozen small boats were moored close to the beach, however, and a forty-foot ketch lay on her side on the sand beach. Anchoring near some small boats, we rowed ashore for some exercise.

I headed over to the grounded ketch and learned that this was not a planned grounding. They had arrived the previous evening at high tide, and anchored in deep water. As the tide fell, the boat grounded and settled over on her side. They expected to refloat around noon. In the meantime, the two men were taking advantage of a bad situation and were cleaning the bottom. Oh, how fortunate, for almost anywhere else in the Northwest they would have laid over onto rocks, compounding their problems immensely.

They took a break to show us where to find oysters on the rocks nearby. Using screwdrivers to pry the oysters loose, it took us only a short time to fill two buckets. Farther along the beach was a huge bed of butter clams (hard shell), and, a little deeper in the sand, some soft-shell clams. Mussels were added to the harvest for a good three-course meal of shellfish.

A gentle southerly carried us slowly into Desolation Sound, an area far from desolate. It is the Northwest's mecca of enjoyment, of leisurely cruising in warm, gentle air, delightful swimming, and marvelous anchorages, surrounded by spectacular scenery and good salmon fishing. In the summer months the harbors are crowded, but we moved on before all the boats arrived. At Lund we left the road behind. The only access to this area is by boat or plane.

Off Bassett Point we passed within fifty feet of the shore for our first show of bald eagles, thirty in flight at one time. Many more birds sat in tree tops near us.

Trying to leave the protection of Big Bay, we hit the turmoil of Yaculta Rapids flowing against us. Even though we were going through the water at

Steps being taken for a delectable meal of oysters near Savoy Island.

seven knots, eddies and whirlpools swung *Windigo* from side to side. Everyone on board stayed low, and hung on. This was no time to fall overboard. I increased the speed to eight knots and still we did not gain on the shore. I tried to find less current close to both shores, but without success. After forty-five minutes with no progress, we retreated back into Big Bay to wait for the current to subside. It was like a mill pond.

At slack, two small sailboats joined us for the beat up Nodales Channel. They were so pretty in the late afternoon sun, with their sails sparkling at the base of the green-forested mountains at the water's edge. Those two boats helped put this whole country into perspective. The boats, thirty-five-footers, were mere dots against their background.

Tying to the government wharf in Shallow Bay, we enjoyed an unbelievable sunset across Cordero Channel. The Thurlow Lodge, nestled in a clearing at the head of the wharf, enjoys this fantastic scene whenever the weather is clear. The lodge staff asked if we were the boat that had had difficulty leaving Big Bay that morning. Word travels fast in this country even without roads or telephones. Communication is by two-way radio, open to anyone. It is a good means of tying people together in the wilderness, particularly when there is trouble.

The attrition rate of cruising boats after Desolation Sound is very rapid as you move west and north. The quiet, carefree cruising is gone, replaced by rapids and narrow passages, strong winds and foul weather. Johnstone Strait is to be avoided whenever possible, by all but commercial vessels and fishermen in a hurry. Those with time choose the numerous waterways to the north, where you can lose yourself in the never-ending labyrinth of channels. To reach this area you must pass through Chatham Channel, where you must time slack current, and avoid meeting a tug towing a long log-boom. You can relax, as we did, at Minstrel Island, a popular place for both fishermen and yachts. A new general store had been built on the old wharf and an old three-story wooden building was once a hotel, now badly in need of paint. In front of the hotel, the grass was lush and well cropped by one pony, two calves, and three rabbits. These animals all ate at the same wash tub; the rabbits' little front feet rested on the edge of the container, their long ears wiggling in the larger animals' eyes. The only nonconformist, a cat, purred loudly. During salmon season, the cats are fussy, and will eat only salmon cheeks and tongues.

Across from Minstrel Island, in Cutter Cove, we dropped the crab trap. From *Windigo*, we watched as two black bears ambled across the tidal flats in search of supper. We hastily dispensed with our search for clams, and stayed safely aboard.

A listing log-carrying ship is nearly ready to off-load her cargo in Johnstone Strait.

The rough waters of Johnstone Strait have caused the lumber companies considerable losses. A tug can lose its whole tow if caught in rough seas, leaving the logs to drift in all directions. We had watched these booms, half a mile in length, being made at the logging camp at the head of Narrows Inlet. Three small steel dodge'm boats had made orderly log-booms out of a hodge-podge of floating logs. They maneuver the logs with their saw-toothed bows which give them an amazing grip on the logs. One small but important part of lumbering is the little boats that scour the shores for a company's stray logs, pulling them off the rocks, and collecting them to be towed once again.

In Johnstone Strait we saw the lumber companies' answer to this problem: a log-carrying ship. Empty, it is a strange looking craft, perhaps three hundred feet long. The top of the flat barge is only about five feet above water; its bow, however, rises some forty feet, as does the stern, where the bridge and living quarters are. Built on the starboard rail, and rising high above the open deck, are two cranes. These cranes hoist logs onto the open deck, piling them high.

A log-boom protects Windigo *from a hodge-podge of floating timber.*

We saw one of these ships about to unload. It was already listing to port, stopped parallel to a wooded shore. A little tug busily positioned a string of logs from the shore to the bow and to the stern of the log carrier. Thirty minutes went by, then forty-five minutes, with no one doing anything. The ship's list continued to increase, first one level of windows in the ship's side disappeared under water, then a second. We could now see the flat bottom above water on the starboard side. After an hour the third floor windows were disappearing. We had been poised expectantly for some time; nearly the whole side of the load of logs was underwater.

Suddenly the logs shifted, sliding to the left into the water. The ship moved to the right, literally jumping out from under its load. In a matter of seconds this big ship moved sideways for about fifty feet. The congestion of logs spread on the water. Casting off, the ship headed for another load, still listing sharply but now with pumps clearing out the port ballast tanks. It was all a complex, ingenious procedure!

In the waterways along Queen Charlotte Strait, I wanted a glimpse of King-come Inlet, which is so delightfully described in Margaret Craven's novel *I Heard the Owl Call My Name*. In the story, a young minister with only a short time to live joins an Indian village for his final months. He witnesses their rituals, learns their beliefs, and through this experience he learns the meaning of life well enough so as not to fear death himself.

From Sullivan Bay we timed our passage through Stuart Narrows, but then headed inland again. Drifting over the dark green water, we were surrounded by forest-covered islands of all sizes and shapes, with bays and passages every-

Fresh salmon for dinner.

where. It was difficult to decide which way to head. I wanted to circle Watson Island, but names like "Roaring Hole Rapids" made me timid. Instead we turned into Turnbull Harbor. There, to our surprise, we saw buildings on the far shore, and a large motorboat tied up in front. It was some sort of lumber operation, but we could see no cleared land on the surrounding hillsides. The camp's owner invited us to tie up behind the big motor vessel. He and his wife, who is confined to a wheelchair, live in the two-story house built on a barge. He claimed to be the only independent lumberman within a hundred miles; all the other cutting operations are owned, one way or another, by the big lumber companies.

Beside the farthest float was a massive pole, three feet in diameter, which stood vertically on the edge of the shore. It was stayed by huge wires, and heavy cable led up the steep hill to a similar pole on the ridge top. We climbed up under the cable, to look out over a huge lake, where we heard the buzz of chain saws.

Bundles of logs were there, ready to be lifted out of the lake and pulled down to the harbor below. One end of the bundle would be supported by the overhead cable, the other end dragged down the well-worn hillside. In the harbor, the logs would be made into rafts to be towed out in the fall.

As we picked our way among the tiny islands one clear morning, a breeze gave a vibrant feeling to the sparkling air. We were ready for a good sail, having motored through most of this congested area. Even though only three people were on board, we set the big genoa and the main and mizzen for a beat through the islands. It was a sail to make up for all the motoring.

Grabbing three cameras I left *Windigo* to Sarah and Jeff. From the whaler I began photographing her under full sail on a close reach, with a white bone in her teeth. I admired *Windigo* from various angles; this was only the second time I'd seen her under sail.

Off Donegal Head the wind lessened, and we watched a pod of killer whales approach, their tall dorsal fins slicing the water. This group performed nicely, jumping clear of the water for ten minutes before moving on. We motored on, into Alert Bay, the second largest community between Prince Rupert and Campbell River. We took full advantage of supplies available there, the last we would see for quite some time.

23 *July Fourth*

At the northern tip of Vancouver Island sailors must brace for crossing Queen Charlotte Sound, the most exposed part of the Inside Passage. It's a distance of about forty miles to the protected waters in the lee of Calvert Island. The passage can be rough, particularly if a northwest wind is blowing off the Gulf of Alaska, which is really the North Pacific Ocean. It can be very rough, the seas extremely unkind, if the strong current flows against the wind. The passage can also become a navigator's nightmare when fog covers the area like a blanket.

Boats often spend a day or two among the islands that lie off Vancouver Island's northern coast, waiting for good weather and preparing for the passage across.

Farther west from God's Pocket, a tiny cove popular with fishermen, is Bull Harbor, a long narrow arm which nearly splits Hope Island. The harbor offers fine protection from all weather, and a government weather station is situated at the head of the harbor. We didn't see a soul on shore until two young children called to us from an open second-floor window of one of the half dozen houses. Walking along the shore at Roller Bay was an experience; the rocks rose fifty feet above the high-tide line. Huge sea-worn logs lay helter-skelter. The sea was smooth that day, yet swells crashed onto the stone beach with a thundering noise. I tried to imagine what the place would be like during the winter storms, and was thankful that I'd never see it.

We stopped in one cove that is unmentioned in any book I have read, and is unnamed on the chart, so we labeled it *"Windigo* Cove." Surely we weren't the first to use it, but it had to have a name. It is located on Bell Island, not the good open anchorage between Bell Island and Heard Island, but the narrow passage between Bell Island and the two small islands south of it. As we entered through the narrow western passage, branches reached out for *Windigo*, but I was more concerned with the rock ledges on both sides, wondering how far they reached out. This well-protected cove, with its trees hovering protectively over us, was just wide enough to swing in and had a special effect on us.

Returning in the whaler in the growing dusk after a look at the sunset, several of the crew circled the two small islands, stopping to visit a fish-buying boat anchored there. Lying near by, on a single anchor, were four fishing boats that had just sold them their catches. The fish-buyer and his two young hands were busily cleaning fish and icing them down. With a full load, they would take the fresh salmon to market in Vancouver. One of the helpers worked quietly, his hands flashing back and forth efficiently. But it was probably the first season out for his younger companion, and because it was early in the season he was still green at the job, and appeared nervous. He kept tossing cleaned fish overboard, instead of below; and the head and tail were swept below instead of overboard. Each time this happened, the captain's eyebrows twitched, causing a momentary pause in the continuous stream of stories of his fifty years of salmon-fishing experience.

The next morning, July Fourth, the weather was clear and still. We departed early, twisting through the rock passage west of Bell Island. Soon our sails were set, in a light west wind. Exposed as this area is, it was one of the few good sails we had north of the Strait of Georgia. During the two summers I cruised the Northwest, we motored probably ninety percent of the time. Some of this was in

Crossing Queen Charlotte Sound early in the morning, Windigo *passed this salmon seiner, headed out for the day's work.*

the interest of seeing what we could, choosing to motor at around seven knots, rather than to sail at three. Basically the summer winds (July and August) are light and variable. From September to May the opposite is true: one gale closely follows another.

For our crossing of Queen Charlotte Sound we had one of those rare days when not only the weather was perfect, but the current also cooperated. The morning's ebb assisted us out, then the afternoon's flood helped us up Rivers Inlet. Off the inlet's entrance the wind died, leaving us to proceed under power as we approached over a hundred fishing boats, each with its net out, stretched across the inlet. Close attention was required to keep from getting tangled in them.

I pondered which of the hundreds of possible harbors to stop in for the night. To decide on one meant missing the others, so I wanted to select a good one. I chose Hemasila Inlet, an arm nearly two miles long and no more than one hundred twenty feet wide, with water depths from one hundred to one hundred seventy feet except at the very head of the inlet, where I hoped to anchor in thirty feet. We crept along the inlet, amazed at its beauty, and the tree-covered, rock cliffs that rose as high as eight hundred feet. An eagle's nest was perched in a tall spruce tree. We heard the birds singing, or were they warning cries? A sea otter scurried into the water as we approached, and a puppy-faced seal eyed us curiously from a safe distance astern.

The chart shows a large rock in the center of the narrowest section just before the shallow basin, with water enough for us to pass. I eased *Windigo* forward, toward the left bank. Her rail was no more than ten feet from the shore, and branches brushed against the stays. To starboard, the rock in the middle of the passage was less than ten feet from scraping *Windigo's* belly.

We made it through, into the small basin, dropping the anchor in twenty-five feet of water. We had a momentary swim, but it was too cold. All evening we sat on deck listening and watching the birds and small animals on shore. I drifted off to sleep listening to rushing water from several small streams close by. It was a good day, a day full of new experiences for us, a day that our forefathers would have enjoyed.

The following year I left Seattle earlier, arriving in Ketchikan, Alaska, on July First. We explored Prince of Wales Island, with its thousands of surrounding islands, coves and bays. We decided to stop at Craig, a town of about two hundred. The docking lines had to be wrapped around the oil-covered pilings on the pier high above our heads. I wondered if stopping here had been such a good idea, because everything was going to get grease covered.

New job for the skipper: untangling the branches in the mizzen rigging as Windigo *heads up-channel to Hemasila Inlet, north of Queen Charlotte Sound.*

A holiday spirit prevailed. People were clustered along the government wharf and on shore. At noon, a cannon was fired, and a band played the National Anthem. It was the beginning of the Fourth of July festivities.

Main street was crowded with people. Tables were set up selling homemade pies, ice cream, candy, balloons, flags, and hot dogs—the items seemed to go on and on. I think we were the only tourists there, all the other people worked in the many lumber camps on Prince of Wales Island, or were from the nearby canneries.

Both sides of the street were lined with spectators as the events commenced. A three-legged race was followed by an egg toss. Two lines of people faced each other, starting out three feet apart. On signal, each person tossed one raw egg to his or her partner in the other line, then stepped backward one pace. The egg continued to be tossed until it broke, usually in the catcher's hands, egg yolk oozing between the fingers to drip into the dirt road. Some eggs were thrown too softly, to splatter on the street. Others were thrown too high, caught at head level, to splatter in the victim's face. A typical reaction was to cover your face with your hands, or quickly wipe your hands on your pants. Cheers and heckles boomed from the sidelines. Two couples remained, toss after toss, until one egg finally broke at forty-five feet.

To one side the tug-of-war matches had begun. Men, used to man-handling huge logs, teamed up on both ends of a heavy manila rope with a knot tied in its center. The battle of strength see-sawed back and forth, muscles strained, supporters shouted.

Most of the contestants in the pie-eating contest were teenagers. Some of the pies were eaten, but most were spread over the kids' faces. One bearded face was covered with dripping blueberry pie, all except for his two shining eyes. Oh, what a waste! Other contests of skill and strength continued on the main street, and on the outskirts of town where there was more room.

At four o'clock, the main street cleared. The next event was walking a greased pole, which had been secured to a float in the harbor, extending about twenty-five feet horizontally over the water. The object was to walk its length and pick a red flag off its outer end. Youngsters sat at the edge, their legs dangling over the side, adults crowded two and three deep to get a view, and small tots perched on many a shoulder. The small float was crowded with contestants. We had a front row seat, as *Windigo's* stern was only thirty feet from the pole. The first boy inched along about five feet before tumbling into the cold water. The pole was about a foot in diameter at the float, tapering to less than six inches at its end. The heavier the contestant the more the pole moved under his weight. The first to succeed was a youngster, who steadily and methodically side-stepped his way to the end, grabbed the flag, then fell into the water. One lad lost his balance, but had the presence of mind to fall forward, grabbing the flag as he passed. All kids received rousing support from the spectators while they were still on the log. Then they heard hoots of laughter as they swam back to the float in defeat.

24 *Harbors in Alaska*

We threaded our way among numerous small islands toward Goddard, about five miles south of Sitka. I didn't know what size community to expect there, nor did I care. We only wanted to visit the hot springs. Two small new buildings appeared on the hillside, and green grass speckled with tiny yellow flowers spread upward to them from the shore, with a forest beyond. No other structures were in sight. The place was deserted except for ourselves. We climbed to the two buildings, each about fifteen feet square and containing a fifteen-foot cedar barrel with a bench in it. Water, much too hot to get into, feeds the tubs from a cistern up the hill. Another line feeds cold pond water from farther away. Both lines flow continuously. The overflow runs down the hill into a soggy, green field. We lay back in the tubs, soaking in the warmth, gazing at an exceptionally serene setting.

The next day, the wind blew at thirty-five knots and gave *Windigo's* crew a thrashing, as we worked up the fog-shrouded coast. With relief, we turned into the tiny Puffin Bay, which looks like a hitchhiker's thumb on the chart. I wondered what effect the surrounding two thousand-foot hills would have on the strong wind. I knew they were two thousand feet high because the chart said so, but we couldn't see up the sides of these steep rocks as we entered under mainsail. The anchor was dropped in the center of the cove, which was just large enough for *Windigo* to swing in. The wind, thirty-five to forty knots, blew right down the valley at the cove's head, where a brown river gushed into the cove. When all was secured on deck, the cook made her special skiers' delight, Yukon Jack mixed with hot apple juice and spices, which warmed us to our toes.

The rain and wind continued all night and into the next day. In the morning I decided not to push on; we would wait for the wind to subside. Dominoes dominated our day. At one point I looked out into the blackness to see hailstones covering the deck. By daybreak the clouds were half way up the hillsides, and torrents of water poured down them, making streams where none had been before.

Studying the charts, I tried to find a cove that would leave us well positioned to cross Hecate Strait to the Queen Charlotte Islands. I selected Totem Inlet, on Dolphin Island. The chart indicates ample water in the narrow channel, which opens into a perfect sized cove. The whole place looked intriguing.

Two kayakers paddle away from Hot Springs Island, on the Queen Charlotte Islands shore.

212

An ancestor of one of Windigo's *crew worked in a mine, now abandoned, south of Ketchican, Alaska.*

As we approached Totem Inlet the current was ebbing, carrying us down Schooner Passage. The narrow channel suddenly opened to our view, too quickly for me to change my mind about entering. Had I had more time to think about it, now that I'd seen it, I doubt that we would have proceeded. *Windigo's* bow was already splitting the shores; we were committed. It was dark in the shadows of the tall trees that grew on the banks beside us. As it was nearly low tide, we had fifteen feet of wet rock wall rising above us, much of it covered with seaweed. The temperature dropped noticeably.

Halfway in, with the rocks squeezing out toward us, I realized this was folly. Should we ground on a edge, the bow would be swung by the ebb current and pinned against the rocks. Chipmunks scurried away from the shore, birds chattered in the trees, and I held my breath; there was no way to go but forward.

It got no shallower than eleven feet, and we dropped the anchor in the cove, surrounded by the thick underbrush, weathered trees, and silver-grey stumps. Later, sitting in the cockpit enjoying cocktails, I concluded this was my favorite place so far, but entering it had been the dumbest thing I'd done all year.

When I selected Bella Bella as a place to change crews, I knew only two things about it: commercial airlines have scheduled flights to it, and fuel and supplies were available to restock *Windigo*. It was the only town between Port Hardy and Prince Rupert with commercial flights.

Bella Bella's waterfront consisted of a string of floats parallel to shore, a large wharf, and several buildings. Nothing more was in sight. The main part of town must be over the hill, I thought.

We tied up along the floats next to a dozen gill-netters, their nets piled high or spread on the wooden racks to dry or await repairs. In one corner of the general store at the head of the wharf was the Post Office, which also served as the airline ticket office. Beyond the wharf was the town dump, two oil drums

The incongruously paired pier/airport in Bella Bella, where Sandy made many of his crew changes.

whose contents were burned and then dumped on the shore to be picked at by ravens and sea gulls, and eventually to wash away. This was all there was to Bella Bella.

While we were tying up, the butcher and his son, age thirteen, carried scraps of meat to the end of the wharf, and began tossing the pieces into the air. This brought sea gulls. By their shrill cries they alerted the ravens, big, jet-black birds that drove the gulls away. The commotion lured a pair of bald eagles, who watched from the trees. Finally one swooped down, grabbing a piece in mid air, and returned to a tree before swooping in again. What a sight, the butcher feeding eagles in his white blood-splattered apron by the corner of the wharf, its vertical pilings so old and rotted that grass and flowers were growing in the ends.

The airport, I came to realize, was the same float to which we were tied. Pilots use the waterways as paths to follow to find harbors. They carry charts identical to *Windigo's*. Our float was reserved for West Coast Air. This was the terminal which my crew was departing from, and at which the replacement crew was arriving. At least we didn't have far to carry the bags.

We surmised that Canada has a law requiring toilet facilities at all commercial airports, for on the end of the "Air Craft Only" float was a one-holer, built out over the water. A nice new slanting shingled roof was supported by four weatherbeaten sides, and a neat crescent moon was carved in the door.

The plane was heard flying low over the water, appearing from behind a hill. It settled on the water, spray flying out behind. The gas attendant and the butcher and his son had all arrived to manhandle the wing onto the float. The postmistress had closed the Post Office and was on hand to collect tickets. Packages and passengers were offloaded, and the ongoing passengers climbed on board, somewhat skeptical about this mode of transportation—the aircraft's cabin windows were nearly submerged in the water.

Pelican, a town with a winter-time population of around a hundred, had ten times that many people when we arrived in early August. It was hidden between towering hills, on Chichagof Island in a major salmon area. The town floats were crowded with fishing boats, with a forest of trolling poles secured vertically. We tied to a float just vacated by a seiner. A plane nosed up behind us, its propeller nearly ticking *Windigo's* mizzen boom.

"Going ashore" here was said with a smile, for the whole town was built on stilts. The road was a boardwalk raised off the ground about fifteen feet and just wide enough for the one small truck. There were no other vehicles. In addition there is Rose's Bar and Grill, famous all along the coast. It was packed, much too crowded for me. Two barges were tied beside the walkway, a house on one, and a garden with flowers and vegetables on the other. Years ago, so the story goes,

a tug towed these two barges out to the fishing fleet as a floating house of ill repute. Statehood, in 1964, for some reason put an end to that business.

Late in the afternoon the Alaskan Ferry made its one monthly stop in Pelican. The whole town turned out for supper—on board. The Ferry offered the least expensive food and drink in town, and by far the best. At Rose's a hamburger cost $4.00, a thin tough steak $15.00. For the fishermen, Rose's is a change from salmon, and much better than preparing their own food, and far from quiet.

The west coast of the United States has only seven natural harbors, but from the Canada/Washington border the situation is reversed. The number of islands, bays, and rivers of all sizes is incredible. To select our next anchorage from all the possibilities was almost troublesome.

Sorting shellfish for the evening meal.

We would round an island and find a perfect natural harbor, unnamed, and seemingly undiscovered. We could have been the only humans on earth. We would anchor in the center with just enough swinging room. What we couldn't reach in *Windigo*, because of her depth, we explored in the whaler. Often we would come upon a gravel spit, alive with squirting clams, and fill our buckets quickly with one-inch butter clams or quohogs for dinner. The tender morsels would be picked from the hot shells by tweezers made from empty mussel shells. Sharp eyes spotted the white tails of bald eagles in the tree tops, and signs of bear were occasionally noted. This was real wilderness. This was why I had come.

25 *Maddens Terror*

Jim Madden, his wife, his daughter, and five friends joined *Windigo* in Wrangell, Alaska. Within five minutes of boarding, Jim asked if I'd heard of Fords Terror. His bag of gear lay unimportant on the deck, absorbing the atmosphere of the small crowded harbor, as he reached for papers in his inner coat pocket. He handed me a hand-drawn sketch of the fjord's entrance—the terror part—and a used envelope with pertinent comments and suggestions. The gist of the comments quickly became apparent; Fords Terror is an extremely scenic area where the tidal flow at the narrow entrance exceeds sixteen knots, with rapids, and whirlpools shooting "rooster tails" off the rock walls.

It is called Fords Terror in recognition of the man who in 1889 innocently rowed into the fjord at slack current. When ready to leave, he found the current had changed, the fjord's entrance had turned exceedingly turbulent; rapids and whirlpools slewed huge icebergs around wildly. Ford was trapped in the fjord for six terrifying hours.

I'd never heard of Fords Terror, and, with this information, had little interest in knowing more. It is located off Endicott Arm, which joins Stephens Passage between Petersburg and Juneau. Our general plan had been to head in that direction, but I was noncommittal about seeking Fords Terror. Perhaps the idea would gradually be forgotten, for it was at least three days away. The information, I noticed, was left prominently positioned in the navigation area.

As we left the muddy, rain-soaked street of Wrangell, the sky cleared for the trip through the largest concentration of government markers in the Northwest—Wrangell Narrows. The maze of markers and buoys supposedly looks like a Christmas tree at night.

At the narrows' northern end is the town of Petersburg, settled by Norwegians. The town is the fourth or fifth largest in southeast Alaska, depending on when the ferry and airplanes arrive and depart relative to Wrangell. The inhabitants had a special quality of friendliness and trust: I cashed checks on a Massachusetts bank without question, and was nearly persuaded to referee a softball game when the regular referee had to replace a player.

Departing early, I hoped to reach the headwaters of Endicott Arm, see the Dawes Glacier, and return to the inlets entrance for the night, a distance of about eighty miles. The bold, deep shores of Endicott Arm provided no possibility of anchoring. No one had mentioned Fords Terror since leaving Wrangell, but I noticed the sketch and description had reappeared from under the charts, where I thought they had been adequately buried.

The morning's low ceiling was a disappointment, but we had to see what we could, regardless of the drizzle. Breakfast, eaten while underway, was interrupted while we slowed by Sunset Island, where seals and sea lions looked as though they were having fun, unconcerned with the wet weather.

On rounding Port Astley, two hours later, no one was ready for the sight we saw. The Sumdum Glacier, its surface bathed in sunshine, swept down the mountain side, stopping just behind the beach. It was breathtaking. Its name means "one that makes a lot of noise."

The clouds continued to dissipate, revealing the tops of the five-thousand-foot-high sides of the inlet. High snow fields merged with low clouds, and spray from waterfalls filled the surrounding air. A continuous roar from distant falls broke an otherwise complete silence. Three huge icebergs were grounded near Sanford Cove.

To placate the chief organizer of this crew, I decided to locate Fords Terror, to poke into its outer section briefly. Then we would continue to the Dawes Glacier as planned.

We identified the high waterfall on the rock wall on the sketch. This we were to line up with, but, when aligned, we still couldn't make out the treacherous entrance. There was no visible route through that solid rock wall. Perplexed, yet relieved, I turned *Windigo* around and headed for Dawes Glacier.

The rounding of a second headland revealed a breathtaking view of the Dawes Glacier. It was in sun, while the surrounding hillsides were darkened by shadows. A black ribbon of rock curved down its surface, a moraine, rocks ground from valley sides as two separate glaciers combined the rubble from their sides into one ribbon of rock and dirt.

The helmsman had to pay close attention to the "bergie bits" that were large enough to damage *Windigo* if hit hard. A lookout went forward and our speed slowed as we began twisting around the drifting ice. We proceeded along the sheer rock cliffs to within one mile of the glacier's terminus, a huge wide ice face. What a feeling to be surrounded by ice. I was somewhat apprehensive about getting free from it all, but was intrigued with our surroundings and the glacier.

Roger went off in the whaler to get pictures: pictures of icebergs, the glacier, and *Windigo* close by. Nick decided to step off onto one. Jim advised against it, having sailed among icebergs in Greenland. The berg's surface was melting, and was exceedingly slippery. I was unable to hold *Windigo* against the berg due to a slight current, leaving Nick standing precariously on the iceberg. A pool of ice

Windigo *enters the narrows of Fords Terror.*

water was just behind him in the middle of the berg. The inlet's ice-chilled water was four feet below him, inches in front of his toes. He didn't move a muscle until Roger got there with the whaler.

Heading back down Endicott Arm, *Windigo's* crew took a deep breath. What an experience, what an incredible day. Little did we know that the best part of the day was still to come.

On impulse, I turned toward Fords Terror again. There had been no talk about it, but my curiosity had been stirred. Why hadn't we located the narrows? Perhaps nosing among the icebergs had built my confidence. Anyway, I wanted to give it one more quick try.

This time we proceeded within a hundred yards of the inlet's high curved end. We now saw a second waterfall, higher and thinner than the one seen earlier. This one fit perfectly the sketch's description. To port was the narrows, nearly hidden between a low spit by a rock wall and a bold headland that curves out, and nearly blocks this portion of the inlet. The channel didn't look treacherous, there was no white water, whirlpools or even eddies that we could see. The tide appeared to be near low. Wondering what the conditions were around the corner, I asked Roger and Nick to go ahead in the whaler to investigate. They did, returning with word of a one- to two-knot ebbing current, a clear entrance, and an awesome sight beyond.

Looking at Jim, I shrugged. Advancing the throttle I wondered how anything could beat the sights we had already seen that day. Positioning *Windigo* in line with the high waterfall behind us I headed for the narrows, sketch held tightly in my hand. At least the kelp that grows on the bottom wouldn't be floating to the surface as it reportedly does during slack, choking off the entrance and fouling the propeller or clogging the engine's saltwater in-take. One rock, shown on the sketch, was just visible to starboard, an excellent reference point. Kelp floating on the surface identified other rocks. To port was the "sand spit," consisting of the largest sand particles I've ever seen. Near its tip was a huge boulder, apparently deposited there at some time by an iceberg. I gave little attention to any of this, concentrating on the depth sounder and on the kelp in shallower water on each side of us. The water's depth had jumped from a hundred feet down to about twenty in just a boat's length. It continued to grow shallower, rising to fifteen feet, then ten. Finally, the depth slowly dropped off again.

We turned the second 100-degree corner, hugging the rock wall worn smooth by years of rushing water. The depth rose once again, before dropping off the depth sounder. I no longer watched it; my eyes bulged in disbelief at the phenomenal sights. I slowly turned in a complete circle, still standing behind the wheel.

My impulse was to leave immediately, before conditions in the narrows changed. Turning *Windigo* back, I explained my thoughts and sensed agreement from the others.

But I continued to hold the wheel hard over after completing the 180-degree turn. All eyes turned in my direction, surprised and questioning. It had dawned on me, as I began the turn, that we should stay in the fjord. The odds of any of us ever returning here were incredibly small. Since we were safely within its confines, it seemed a mistake to miss the chance to see it all. If that meant delaying our departure, so be it. We could wait for the next slack water, which would be around midnight. With a twenty-foot rise and fall it would be safer to leave at high slack anyway. No one raised any objections.

Roaring waterfalls within Fords Terror.

Waiting for the few minutes of slack water at the entrance to Fords Terror, Windigo's crew saw that an iceberg had just grounded on the other side.

The whole place was out of proportion. Its immensity was impossible to grasp. Beyond the second headland the scenery was bigger and better. We wouldn't have believed it possible.

What appeared like a small fir tree, growing on a ledge just above high water, towered way above *Windigo's* masthead when we got in closer range. The noise of thundering waterfalls ricocheted off the rock cliffs. The inlet's sides were sheer cliffs rising straight out of the water to four thousand feet, then eventually rising to ten-thousand- and fifteen-thousand-foot snow-covered peaks. One wide ribbon of white water captivated our attention as it descended the mountainside, disappearing into forests of green and behind ridges. It appeared time after time, finally fanning out over the beach and rushing into the sea.

I began to consider spending the whole night in Fords Terror, now being openly referred to as "Maddens Terror." The only difficulty was finding a place shallow enough to anchor in without *Windigo* banging against the fjord's sides. I decided to tie *Windigo's* bow to boulders on shore beside a stream. The stream's flow should hold us off the beach. It should also have built up a fan of gravel shallow enough for a stern anchor. I shuddered when thinking about what vicious blasts of wind must tear around these cliffs under other conditions. The anchor lay in eighty-five feet of water, yet *Windigo's* bow swung over only three feet of water.

My alarm woke me at 5:30 A.M. It must have been low tide, for there were only two inches of water under the bow. Overhead the sky was again blue and cloudless, the sun having risen long before. Its rays, however, were still hours from reaching the fjord's waters. The air was crisp, with perhaps even a frost on deck.

A low thin haze hung over the narrows when we arrived. We didn't approach because white water was visibly boiling there. The top of a large iceberg could be seen beyond the sand spit. Only twelve hours before, there hadn't been any ice near Fords Terror, yet here was one apparently grounded off the narrows.

Sailing under spinnaker into Glacier Bay.

What if it grounded in the channel?

Roger went ahead in the whaler for a closer look. He was to wave us on when the current became slack. I cautioned him to be extremely careful and not to get caught in whirlpools or rapids. Seeing the curling four-foot waves, he was convinced to keep a safe distance, sheltered behind a rock, until the water quieted down. We waited. Seven o'clock came and went. Still we waited, still able to feel the current draw us out.

Roger moved into the narrows. We watched as he drifted through, then powered back to drift through again. The current was obviously weakening. I allowed *Windigo* to be drawn closer. Shortly before eight o'clock, kelp rose to the water's surface near us. Later it began to wiggle like a snake, no longer stretched out straight on the surface, a sure sign the current was about to change. Roger reappeared around the corner and waved us on; the current had changed. Sure enough, right behind him came a three-inch-high ridge of water —a small tidal bore. In the narrows, kelp streamed in the same direction we were going and a moment later it was flowing in the opposite direction. There was no such thing as slack water here. At one point my rapidly beating heart stumbled. The depth sounder flickered between nine and ten feet. No one moved, much less spoke. The keel may have touched bottom, no one was sure.

We were soon clear, in deep water again. Everyone released a long-drawn-out sigh of relief. Looking back, we saw the recently grounded iceberg, sand spit, towering rock walls, and Maddens Terror.

26 *Glacier Bay*

northeast gale blew a blanket of fog off the Alaskan coast on May 3, 1778, and enabled Captain James Cook to see a very high mountain. He named the peak Mount Fairweather—a mountain that towers over Glacier Bay. On board with Captain Cook was George Vancouver, who returned to this area sixteen years later as captain of *H.M.S. Discovery*. Vancouver found the entrance to what we now call Glacier Bay, which was then only six miles long. Thunder continuously rolled back and forth across the tiny bay as huge pieces of ice broke off the glacier's face: a "compact solid mountain of ice, rising perpendicularly from the water's edge." Scientists have since estimated the massive ice sheet that covered Glacier Bay was over four thousand feet thick.

Two hundred years later *Windigo*'s crew saw the same mountain while whale-watching in the eastern extremes of Icy Strait—a hundred miles away. The sight, including the extensive Fairweather Range, was like a magnet—drawing us into Glacier Bay.

Incredibly, the land near the entrance around Bartlett Cove is still springing back from the tremendous weight of ice that once covered this area. Today, Bartlett Cove is a thriving rain forest. Hemlock and spruce trees tower above the moss-covered forest floor.

Heading up the Bay from the National Park Service Headquarters in Bartlett Cove, we stopped at the Marble Islands. Each summer the islands are taken over by visiting sea birds. The most plentiful are gulls, pigeon guillemots, and puffins—birds that delighted *Windigo*'s crew. Thousands of birds dotted the sides of the rocks; many were still immature, still in their dark feathers, some merely fluffy balls of feathers.

Wachusett Inlet, off the Muir Inlet, is a strange place of drab browns and greys: gravel deposits left recently by glaciers that once covered the area. It is in complete contrast to the rain forest around Bartlett Cove only forty-five miles away.

Behind the long, narrow inlet lies an irregular plain of gravel and ponds of all sizes. Beyond I could see a waterfall, its sound carrying clearly over the barren terrain. The river had cut deep gullies into the landscape that I followed to the source—a glacier. While I was climbing, it took me some time to realize that I was looking at a glacier. Its surface was no different from the gravel deposits I was walking over. The remains of this glacier was only a sheet of ice a few feet thick, about ready to drop its last stone to the ground.

There was nothing green here, nothing living—or so it seemed. On a closer inspection I could see crusts of lichens clinging to rocks. Farther away tough plants were already taking hold of the land just released from a frozen past. Rapid growth here is insured by long hours of daylight during the summer and plenty of moisture. In time, thickets of willow and alder have become established. These eventually die out for lack of sunlight, blocked by young spruce trees that have found a suitable habitat. Looking toward Muir Inlet, this succession was in evidence. Even at Bartlett Cove this process continues as hemlocks replace the spruce.

Heading for Muir Inlet, we kept a sharp lookout for humpback whales, killer whales, seals, mountain goats, and eagles. And for icebergs.

Our interest for one month was whale-watching in Glacier Bay, organized and sponsored by the Oceanic Society and led by marine scientists Sharon Gwinn and Ronn Storro-Patterson. The goals of that expedition were to supply additional data on humpback whale activities in Glacier Bay. The research was designed to observe and record whales, to document interactions of whales with vessels, and identify individual whales. I acted as bus driver, and *Windigo* provided lodging and transportation.

We caught up with two whales off Point Couverden a hundred miles east of Glacier Bay, keeping about a quarter of a mile from them. They moved slowly, close to shore, making shallow dives and occasionally lunging partially out of water. We followed them under sail and could see, through binoculars, frequent moisture-laden blows.

The morning's breeze died completely, leaving the water's surface mirror-clear, and allowing us to see air bubbles on the water just before the whales surfaced in unison. The strings of bubbles became complete circles, made in a clockwise direction thirty feet in diameter. Seconds after the circle closed, both whales' heads appeared simultaneously through its center. The whales were on their sides, mouths open, throats expanded, with water pouring through the baleen. This is thought to be the whale's method of schooling its prey, called "bubble net feeding." It appeared as though only one whale were making each net, and we watched them make seven in forty-nine minutes. As these rings were being formed, we could see small silvery fish, probably herring or capelin, jumping inside the ring of bubbles. Not many people have witnessed this behavior as clearly as we did that day.

During our first two-week period, we saw eight to ten whales fluking, flippering, and blowing. The most interesting of these was a mother-calf pair. The calf was estimated to be fifteen to sixteen feet long, with the wrinkled skin char-

Looking eastward into Reid Inlet, with a tiny Windigo anchored below.

Less than a hundred years ago Wachusett Inlet's barren, pebbly shores were covered by glaciers.

acteristic of newborns, and probably wasn't over five days old. It was the first record of a newborn humpback whale in Glacier Bay. The two stayed close together, diving simultaneously with shorter than normal periods between blows. They were the only whales that made a concentrated effort to stay away from *Windigo*, which wasn't hard for we lay still in the water as they swam back and forth close to shore.

Continuing up the Muir Inlet we had to twist and turn among the floating icebergs that nearly blocked the inlet. A torrent of water flowed from under the McBride Glacier, discoloring the inlet. Across the inlet is a huge rock wall that was polished smooth by the Muir Glacier. An equally high knoll separates the McBride and Riggs glaciers—our destination.

We were being squeezed by ice, particularly around the rocky points. Our forward progress slowed more, then stopped. We lay drifting in a nearly ice-free area directly in front of the Riggs Glacier, half a mile away. Stopped much closer to this ice wall was the sixty-five-foot tour boat *Thunder Bay*, looking tiny in comparison to the seemingly medium-sized rocks at the base of the glacier. An awesome sight was before us, particularly on such a beautiful day.

Even the specially built *Thunder Bay* hadn't penetrated the tightly jammed ice farther up Muir Inlet that summer. Yet the previous year she had reached the Muir Glacier nearly every day. *Windigo* and another yacht were the only sailboats to reach the Riggs Glacier that year. It was a case of trying on the right day. Only a week before we couldn't squeeze through the ice as far as Wachusett Inlet.

A float plane picked us up one day in North Sandy Cove and flew up the Muir Inlet. Then we turned up the McBride Glacier, the plane laboring as it climbed the wide river of ice. Maintaining altitude, the pilot turned to follow the Riggs Glacier to its terminus. Circling it, we descended slowly. What a sight!

Flying now barely two hundred feet above the icebergs, we continued up the Muir Inlet. Seals sunning themselves on the ice looked at us. The inlet's walls towered overhead. Turning a corner brought the huge Muir Glacier into sight. This glacier, for some quirk of nature, is currently receding at about one mile each year.

I wondered if times weren't returning to the era of rain forests along the Muir Inlet. Radiocarbon tests, taken on stumps we had seen, show that trees growing here were three hundred years old when killed by glacial deposits six thousand years ago. This mind-numbing prospect is another example of what this incredible place is all about.

On one trip into Johns Hopkins Inlet our attention was focused on eight double kayaks right in front of us. The kayakers were students from Juneau who had paddled the sixty miles from Bartlett Cove. They were planning to camp as close to the glacier as they could. I was already concerned about maneuvering *Windigo* in the ice, and considered they had gone too far already. However, after a short conversation and the transfer of a six-pack of Cascade beer to the leader's kayak, all boats advanced slowly. Everyone was very startled when a humpback whale blew about forty yards away, among the kayakers.

On another day we met two men paddling a canoe out of this same ice jam. Giving them a lift back to their base camp we learned of their plans to climb two peaks, neither of which had ever been climbed from the inlet side before.

We were less ambitious. We climbed from boulder to boulder, recrossing streams, and reaching a small knoll overlooking Reid Inlet's mouth with a phenomenal view of the bay. Standing at an elevation of about twenty-five hundred feet, one looked eastward, thirty miles down Glacier Bay; north all the way up Tarr Inlet; west toward Johns Hopkins Inlet; and south at Reid Glacier, five miles away. Looking down at the sand spit we saw *Windigo*, looking like a dust particle on a ballroom floor. She was the only object to which to relate the size of anything, and at this distance she was too small to do any good. It was impossible to grasp the immensity of what spread out before us. It was also difficult to comprehend that only a hundred years ago a thick sheet of ice had covered all of the water we could see from this knoll.

As fantastic as the view was from here, I imagined it would be even better from higher. Slowly, I began the climb, heading toward the snow fields, climbing on loose rocks. The expanse of snow gradually increased, and the exposed rock that I could follow dwindled. I knew I should turn back; being alone I had gone well beyond the border of sensible climbing. But I couldn't stop without first seeing what lay beyond the next rise. I was getting tired, using muscles that are seldom called upon while sailing.

On reaching the summit, at about thirty-eight hundred feet, I found shelter behind a pile of rock where I ate lunch. Descending was hard on the legs, and one thigh muscle had a cramped feeling. It was still a long way down to *Windigo*. Stepping down onto a rock, one thigh muscle knotted agonizingly. Slowly and carefully I walked down a shallow valley, to a bog with numerous pools. I crumpled to the ground thinking how ridiculous this was. Close by, though, was a suitable place to rest.

Getting into a shallow pool of warm water, I lay back, my hands folded under my head. Thoughts about Glacier Bay began running through my mind; an area of ice, massive headlands, towering snow-covered peaks, barren land, glaciers—some advancing, others receding—icebergs, water, space, and light. It was all on a scale so incomprehensibly immense and out of perspective that the ensuing silence was extremely noticeable.

I recalled a five-minute conversation with Brad Washburn, then Director of the Boston Museum of Science, and a world-renowned mountaineer, on the dock at Bartlett Cove only a few weeks before. He wanted to take pictures from the exact location he had taken others twenty years ago in order to compare. Lying in the warm water, I resolved to return here for the same purpose in twenty years. Thinking about it, I decided to find some way to return every ten years. This fantasizing got me no farther down the mountain side, but it did allow my legs the rest they needed, and gave me time to reflect on what we had seen in this incredible area.

One day we approached the Margerie Glacier as a cruise ship touring the bay blew its whistle repeatedly. The skipper was hoping the whistle's sound waves would jar a chunk of ice off the glacier's face, an ice wall that rose over two hundred feet above the water and extended more than a mile in width. The ship leaned visibly with people crowded on its starboard side, waiting expectantly for something to happen. Nothing did happen.

The skipper finally gave up, and they departed. Five minutes later, a huge

Riggs Glacier flows into Muir Inlet (taken from the air).

A cruise ship in front of the Margerie Glacier gives an idea of the scale in Glacier Bay.

section of the ice wall fell. Two people on *Windigo* saw it go. Its resounding report and thundering roar reached us in time for everyone to see the resultant "smoke" subside. Waves, created by the ice landing in the water, spread out, rocking icebergs and dislodging birds from their icy perches. *Windigo* finally rocked gently in its aftermath, half a mile away.

We stopped off the Lamplugh Glacier more than any other, partly because of its convenience and partly because it was calving small bergs, yet we could still get close to it. The currents seemed to disperse the ice rapidly. Seeing the ice front change from day to day and from week to week made it very clear that the massive river of ice really was moving. One day a bear's face was carved in the glacier's face. Two days later he was gone.

I think Johns Hopkins Inlet is the most spectacular of all of them. I never tired of seeing it. Each time we were there it was different, and the weather perfect, which helped. Billowing white clouds hung on twelve-thousand-foot peaks, backed by blue sky. The constantly changing clouds gave the impression that the whole inlet was in motion. The inlet's rock walls rise from the water to snow-covered mountain peaks with glacial tongues snaking down their sides. Along one perpendicular wall, rock slides often broke loose from great heights, to land among the icebergs. At the head of this inlet is the Johns Hopkins Glacier, which sweeps in a broad swath and a series of falls from the saddle between two thirteen-thousand-foot mountains. On my first visit here we were barely able to thread our way through icebergs to reach the inlet's elbow-like turn, where the full splendor of the inlet opened to our view. Other times we picked our way farther, once getting to within two miles of the glacier's terminus.

Everyone visited Joe and Muz Ibach's three tiny cabins at one time or another. In the summer of 1924, a year before Glacier Bay National Monument was established, Joe Ibach discovered three gold-bearing veins high on the hillside facing Reid Glacier. It was the beginning of a thirty-two-year association with this inlet. Joe was a "venturesome, self-reliant, restless" man. A prospector who "was always looking over the next rise with the expectation of finding a fabulously rich strike." He was a dreamer, always searching for a promising fracture, constantly bringing in new rock to be tested. In 1940, the Ibachs built their small cabins at the base of the steep hillside, near a sand spit that had been covered by thick ice in 1930, and behind which *Windigo* was now anchored. Joe and Muz have spent sixteen summers on this tiny plot of land, landscaping it, bringing in soil for a vegetable and flower garden, planting the three spruce trees that still stand, and prospecting.

On one still, moonless night, when anchored in North Sandy Cove, I was awakened from a sound sleep. Lying in my bunk, I wondered why I had awoken; everything was quiet. There was no wind, and I sensed nothing wrong. Then I heard a whale blow, loud and clear. It blew again, very close. Quietly going on deck I saw the whale not more than fifty yards away. Others had been awakened and were on deck also. No one made a sound. We watched fascinated as the whale blew a series of air bubbles underwater.

It then turned toward *Windigo,* its back still visible on the surface, and approached us amidships. When only thirty feet from us the whale blew again, and simultaneously its black back sank beneath the water, leaving behind only a tiny ripple as evidence of this huge creature's presence. A moisture-filled cloud of foul fishy-smelling air drifted over us.

I wondered how the whale would swim past. There wasn't enough space for

Whale dives in Icy Strait, so close to Windigo.

it between the bottom and *Windigo's* keel. My heart stopped momentarily as I thought about it becoming tangled in the anchor line. I was convinced he knew *Windigo* was there, but could he also identify the anchor line? Nothing happened. Moments later two blows were heard beyond the islands.

The others returned below while I moved forward to lie on the bagged genoa in the bow. Thousands of stars twinkled brightly in the heavens overhead. Lying there I realized I'd accomplished what I had set out to do, to see the harbors in the Northeast, Caribbean, and Northwest. Along the way my horizons expanded and two other areas were added—the San Blas Islands and Baja California. Three years had turned into five. I did things that I never would have dreamed of doing, and cherish (some of) them. On the other hand some of my carefully made plans ran afoul, sometimes for the best, but not always.

Windigo turned out to be a fantastic vessel for my purposes, in a way that wouldn't be plausible, feasible, or suitable for others, but it was a way that provided me with immense pleasure and satisfaction. It was an experience in which all the headaches, disappointments, hard work, and disasters were only a small part compared to the whole phenomenon. My ways often frustrated some people and angered others, but on the whole they seemed to work, for those

Windigo framed by a hole in an iceberg.

Muir Inlet icebergs offer a welcome respite or a treacherous hazard, depending on the point of view.

who joined *Windigo* during her travels received a great deal of pleasure and enjoyment from their experiences on board. Many people kept returning and nearly all were extremely supportive of the operation. Many who sailed on *Windigo* saw parts of Central and North America they would never have seen, and they now savor their memories of her, and of the land and people we visited.

Looking at the multitude of stars my thoughts turned to which area I like best, a question I'm often asked and one I have no specific answer for, because each area is unique. There are places I'd rather return to before others, such as this anchorage in North Sandy Cove and Glacier Bay. But there are other coasts, still new to me, to sail and explore.

I was getting chilled and it was time to return to bed. In reality I had to get *Windigo* safely home before I could think about new coasts to sail. New horizons were to dream about and to plan for later.

The Illustrations

Maps: Argenziano Associates
Spot Drawing: Dana Burns

Roger Archibald: 30, 32 left, 32 right, 71, 129 above,
    129 left, 140 above, 140 left, 141, 155, 157, 162, 167, 168,
    172 upper, 172 lower, 178 upper, 178 lower, 191 upper,
    195, 209, 214, 218, 221, 223, 224, 225, 237 lower.
Peter Barlow: 8
Alan Bemis: 111, 117
Nancy Blackett: 138–9
Rick Cowen: 46, 81, 86
Carol Crocker: 229 upper
Gail Dana: 236
Margo Delaney: 77
Dick Dewey: 65 both, 66
Henry English: 109 right, 137 top, 137 bottom, 175, 185
Steve Fisher: 151, 137 above, 232
Sharon Gwinn: 89, 182
Phips Hallowell: 13, 112 right, 131 above
Sarah Hallowell: 237
Mark Matlack: 75
Sherm Morse: 79, 132 below, back jacket
Anne Sheffield: 24, 39
Sparkman & Stephens: 127, 128

All others: Sandy Weld

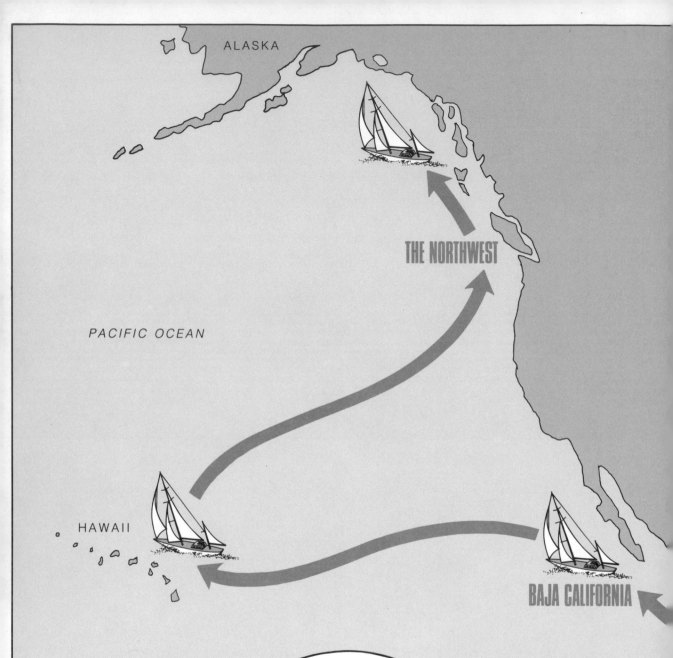

ALASKA

THE NORTHWEST

PACIFIC OCEAN

HAWAII

BAJA CALIFORNIA

Voyage of the Yawl Windigo
1974–79